LISTENING BEHAVIOR

LISTENING BEHAVIOR
Measurement and Application

ROBERT N. BOSTROM
University of Kentucky

With special contributions by

Mary Helen Brown
Margaret Fitch-Hauser
Pamela J. Kalbfleisch
Raymond W. Preiss
Eileen Berlin Ray

Joy Hart Seibert
D. Bruce Searle
Milton Shatzer
Enid S. Waldhart
Lawrence R. Wheeless

THE GUILFORD PRESS
New York   London

© 1990 The Guilford Press
A Division of Guilford Publications, Inc.
72 Spring Street, New York, NY 10012

Printed in the United States of America

This book is printed on acid-free paper.

Last digit is print number: 9 8 7 6 5 4 3 2 1

Library of Congress Cataloging-in-Publication Data

Bostrom, Robert N.
    Listening behavior.

    Includes bibliographical references.
    1. Listening. I. Title. [DNLM: 1. Auditory Percep-
tion. 2. Communication.   BF 323.L5 B747L]
BF323.L5B67   1990   153.6'8   89-23472
ISBN 0-89862-397-9

Preface

It should be obvious to anyone that listening is one of the most important components in interpersonal communication, and that most of us do not listen very well. "Listening" as a communication construct has been badly abused in the last few years, with some persons confusing listening skill with listening attitudes, and as a result, no one seems to know what a "good" listener is. At the same time, there is a dedicated group of professionals who help others listen better in their classes, seminars, and workshops. When I talk to these professionals, they usually mention that their greatest handicap is that we do not know enough about the process, and we need more information about listening so that we can improve it. This book marks the beginning of a specific research enterprise, and is dedicated to the idea that nothing is more important than understanding the way we perceive, process, remember, and understand oral messages. It examines specific functions of listening and explores them in considerable detail.

If one of the most desirable phenomena in social science is "thematic" research, in which specific studies are tied together by common threads of theory or practice, then this book is valuable from another point of view. The reception and retention of information presented orally ("listening") has only recently been made the subject of such thematic research, primarily because of the absence of common approaches to theory and measurement.

Recently, however, a renascence of interest in listening research has followed the introduction of defensible measures of listening abilities. One of these is the focus of this book, the Kentucky Comprehensive Listening Test. This test utilizes memory models as the basic analogue of receiving ability. Specifically it distinguishes among short-term, short-term with rehearsal, and intermediate-term retention of oral materials. Looking at listening in this fashion opens new vistas of research which had not before been possible.

A substantial body of such research is reported here. First, definitional and methodological issues are explored. Following the discussion of definitional issues, the interaction of medium of presentation and gender is studied. Whether face-to-face, audio, or video presentations are most efficacious is an important question, but as it turns out, the medium is confounded with gender. The relationship between listening abilities and other communicative skills is then studied. One of the crucial issues in listening theory is the role of grammatical structure and decoding, and it is explored in a chapter, as is listening and receiver apprehension, followed by a discussion of listening in the organizational environment. Motives and schemas are also treated and listening and the mass media are analyzed as well, followed by listening as a method of detecting deception.

These diverse studies on a common topic illustrate that research in listening is indeed coming of age, and that interest in the topic is as keen as ever. Further, these explorations hold great promise in our thinking about the improvement of listening in the marketplace, in the school, and in the home. Only by understanding the fundamental nature of the process can we hope to improve it.

Each of the contributors to this volume has brought specific skills and interests to the listening process. Most of the studies presented here have used specific measurement of short-term listening, short-term listening with rehearsal, and interpretive listening. Others have taken a thoughtful look at crucial concepts in information processing, such as schemas, receiver apprehension, deception, and television. This diversity of viewpoint enriches our understanding and challenges us to look in new directions when we conduct our research.

Our special thanks are due for the tireless efforts of Linda Kahlich at the University of Kentucky and Rowena Howells at Guilford. Their patient and understand efforts have made this book possible.

I know I speak for all of the researchers represented here when I express the hope that when we understand listening better, we will understand one another better. And when we understand one another better we can build a better society and a better world. It is to these aims that good listening should be addressed.

ROBERT BOSTROM

CONTENTS

Chapter Four

LISTENING, COMMUNICATIVE SKILL,   42
AND ATTITUDES ABOUT COMMUNICATION

Chapter Five

SEMANTIC DECODING, SHORT-TERM STORAGE,   57
SENSATION SEEKING, AND RECALL OF INFORMATION

Chapter Six

Chapter Seven

Chapter Eight

Joy Hart Seibert

Chapter Nine

Eileen Berlin Ray
Robert N. Bostrom

Chapter Ten

Chapter Eleven

Chapter Twelve

LISTENING BEHAVIOR

CHAPTER ONE

Conceptual Approaches to Listening Behavior

All speech, whether written or spoken, is in a dead
language until it finds a willing and prepared hearer.

...Robert Louis Stevenson

Communication, for most of us, involves the exchange of messages, and usually is accomplished by speaking, listening, reading, and writing. When we say that we are studying communication, most of us mean that we are examining ways in which messages are designed, organized, mediated, or evaluated. Of course, these processes are of great theoretical and practical interest. But to assume that messages are received, processed, and retained in approximately the same form as the sender intended may be entirely unwarranted. Even very simple messages are easily distorted. Sometimes this distortion is caused by problems in attitude, in motivation, or in physical settings. But often problems are caused by individual differences in processing ability. When we study such processes, we usually say that we are studying "listening" ability.

Individuals vary widely in their ability to receive information, and the causes of this variation are poorly understood. Clearly messages, contexts, and media all affect the reception of messages. But individual differences in receiving ability still account for large differences in communication effectiveness. Unfortunately, many of those who create messages seldom allow for this basic individual difference in processing ability. Why people differ in this respect, and more importantly, what can be done to improve them, may be of great practical value.

Listening is probably the most common communication activity. In a much-cited study, Paul Rankin (1929) asked persons to report how

1

much time they spent in various types of communication. They reported that they listened 45% of the time, spoke 30% of the time, read 16%, and wrote 9%. In a more recent study, Klemmer and Snyder (1972) studied the communicative activity of technical persons. These persons spent 68% of their day in communication activity, and of that time, 62% was "talking face-to-face." Klemmer and Snyder did not distinguish between speaking and listening, but it seems safe to assume that at least half of the face-to-face activity was listening. Brown (1982) estimates that executives in a modern corporation spend at least 60% of their day listening. Wolvin and Coakley (1988) point out how listening mediates most of the rewarding parts of communicative behavior. In other words, almost everything that gives us pleasure in the communicative interaction is due to the listening process.

To say that listening is an essential communication skill is to risk restating the obvious. Any activity that occupies that much of our attention should be done well.

In spite of the obvious importance of listening, researchers in communication have not paid it as much attention as other aspects of the process. As a consequence, for many years our knowledge concerning listening has not kept pace with our understanding of other aspects of communication. Recently, however, we have seen a resurgence of interest in research in listening, and we are beginning to achieve some better understanding of this vital communication activity.

In this book, we will report on a significant segment of this research. First, we will examine the conceptual foundations of listening, together with a recent model of the process. Then we will describe some recent attempts to measure various aspects of listening. Differences that appear in various media will next be examined, along with gender comparisons. Then we will examine the decoding process, both from the point of view of language and grammar, and then with schemata. A persistent problem, that of receiver apprehension, will be examined as it relates to listening. Following that, listening as it relates to successful adaptation to large organizations will be examined. Lastly, we will concern ourselves with some of the implications of listening for mass communications.

In all of this, we will not only review recent research, but will present new data from ongoing research programs.

Before we do all of this, however, we should have some idea of the basic nature of the process. How do we listen? What is involved in "good" listening? How can we improve it? These and other questions are importantly related to the way that listening is defined and, too often, measured. We need, therefore, to have a clear idea of what we mean when we use the word "listening."

What is Listening?

While Wesley Wiksell (1946) and Ralph Nichols (1947) alerted the readers of the *Quarterly Journal of Speech* to the problems inherent in listening, it was in Nichols' dissertation (Nichols, 1948) that we saw the first significant attempt to study the process and discover what, if anything, determined good listening. In this pioneering study, Nichols assumed the retention of information presented orally was the principal criterion of good listening. He examined this retention and its relationship to many different factors, such as distance from the speaker, previous training in subject matter, size of family, parental occupation, and hearing loss. He concluded that retention was "related to" intelligence, ability to discern organizational elements, size of vocabulary, and very little else. In other words, intelligent persons retained more information than did unintelligent ones, those who understood organization also retained more, and those with a large vocabulary retained more than those with a smaller vocabulary.

Listening as Factual Recall. Nichols' assumption that the essential measure of listening was the recall of factual data from a lecture after an unspecified period of time had passed was a logical one. Since his research, many investigators have used this criterion as a basis for an assessment of listening success. Studies in this kind of framework have been conducted by Thompson (1967), Hsia (1968), Beighley (1952, 1954), McClendon (1958), Goldhaber (1974), Rossiter (1972), Palamatier and McNinch (1972), Klinzing (1972), Buchli and Pearce (1974), and Beatty and Payne (1984).

Not long after Nichols' research was published, the "factors" relating to listening skill were used as the theoretical justification for a commercial test of listening behavior (Brown & Carlsen, 1955). But instead of using the actual findings of the Nichols study, this test made use of subscales which measured vocabulary, recognition of transitions, ability to follow directions, immediate recall, and the retention of facts from a lecture. The single largest correlate, congitive ability, was not utilized.

The Brown-Carlsen test has been used as a measure of listening ability as an independent variable by a few researchers (Ernest, 1968;

Petrie & Carrell, 1976) and a similar test published by the Educational Testing Service (1957) was used by Dickens and Williams (1964) as an index of listening ability. Whether or not the separate subscales of the Brown-Carlsen actually do vary independently (to be correctly termed "factors" in a statistical sense) still is not known.

However, these studies demonstrate that persons do indeed vary in their ability to retain information following spoken messages, and often that instructional efforts to improve this ability were successful.

From this point of view, listening was considered to take place if information from spoken discourse was retained. When a person scored better on a test of retention, that person was assumed to be a better listener. This listening ability was assumed to be a unique skill, that is, not related to other cognitive skills.

The assumption that the ability to listen was a separate and unitary skill was sharply attacked in the middle of the 1960s by Charles Kelly. He reasoned that if listening tests did indeed measure a separate ability, the Brown-Carlsen and the STEP tests of listening would be more highly correlated with each other than they would with other measures of cognitive ability. He found that they were not, and in fact were more highly correlated with tests of intelligence than each other. These data led Kelly, reasonably enough, to the conclusion that the ability that had previously been termed "listening ability" was in fact only an aspect of intelligence, and that the Brown-Carlsen and the STEP test were only different kinds of intelligence tests (Kelly, 1965, 1967). A clue to Kelly's findings was already present in Nichols' (1948) data--the single best predictor was cognitive ability--a correlation of .54 (p. 154). While "intelligence" is clearly not a unitary factor, defining listening as the remembering of facts from a lecture is definitely isomorphic with at least one of them. Gardner (1983), in his theory of multiple intelligences, clearly indicates that verbal processing is one of the many intelligences, and listening as defined as efficient word processing would fit well into this definition. If we take Sternberg's (1985) definition of intelligence as the ability to manipulate the environment, then we probably would not see the same strong relationship exhibited by the Kelly and Nichols data.

The relationship is certainly not clear-cut. Cognitive ability interacts with difficulty of material and rate of presentation in predicting retention (Sticht & Glassnap, 1972). Beatty and Payne (1984) found that retention was significantly related to cognitive complexity, though most research has found little connection between cognitive complexity and typical measures of intelligence (Sypher & Applegate, 1982).

Kelly's discovery that "listening"--as defined by the retention model--is probably not a separate and distinguishable mental ability complicates the problem. Almost everyone involved in the practical study of communication has had experience with persons who are obviouly intelligent but could never be called "good listeners." Most of us know persons of obvious intelligence who listen poorly.

Attitudes and Listening. One method of reconciling Kelly's findings with everyday experience is to redefine listening so that it includes more than intelligence. This approach invokes an "attitude" about listening to others as a part of the explanatory scheme. This attitude, or the "willingness" to listen has been defined as a separate component of the listening construct and is similar to basic interest in others' ideas. Often when we say that someone is a "good listener" we mean that they have a good attitude about the process, rather than retentive ability.

Carl Weaver was one of the first to incorporate this attitudinal dimension into a formal definition of listening. One consistent finding in perception research has been that attitudinal predispositions affect both selection and perception of incoming stimuli. Weaver utilized this finding in his definition. Listening, to Weaver, was "the selection *and* retention of aurally received data" (1972, p. 12). Weaver went on to discuss "selective exposure," an attitudinally and culturally determined activity which expands the listening construct. Weaver also included information seeking as an important component.

An even broader definition was offered by Larry Barker, who defined listening as "the selective process of attending to, hearing, understanding, and remembering aural symbols" (1971, p. 17). The attitudinal aspect of listening was stressed by inclusion of "selective" and reinforced by "attending." This, together with hearing and comprehension, make up an extremely broad definition of listening. Attending to aural symbols is much the same as selecting them, and remembering them is still included.

Barker's addition of comprehension and hearing as "factors" of listening is especially troublesome. To say that hearing is a "factor" of listening is certainly unarguable, but is much the same as saying that phonation is a "factor" in interpersonal communication. Having said this, we are left with the problem of integrating varieties of hearing (phonation) as a part of a theoretical structure. This is a minor point, however, compared to the assumption that "comprehension" is an important part of the listening process.

The role of comprehension in listening is not at all clear. It seems logical that we might listen to something that we do not understand, or even understand fully. Accepted models of creativity stress that many incoming messages are not immediately understood, and that *eventual* understanding and reordering of information is often the goal, not instant comprehension (Haselrud, 1972).

Common sense tells us that we often listen without full understanding--in fact, sometimes the question of understanding is irrelevant. What does it mean to "understand" a telephone number, or an address? We can assign functions to these linguistic elements, and from a strictly functionalist point of view, some types of language usage can proceed without cognitive integration. From this point of view understanding can be irrelevant (Miller & Johnson-Laird, 1976). The question of "understanding" is an interesting one, but understanding is certainly not a precondition of listening. For one thing, when we acquire new information, we certainly do not always understand it.

Nor is the focus on "selective" listening without its problems. Receivers are selective because of basic perceptual habits and as the result of conscious choice. Factors determining the process of selective perception have been exhaustively studied, and to reclassify this important process as a part of "listening" seems to be renaming already well-understood cognitive processes.

The social element implied in the definition gives us even more difficulty. Not to listen to someone is to deny their value as a person, as well as a communicator. Consequently, listening is heavily freighted with emotional baggage. The statement that "No one listens to me," often accompanies severe social malaise, and has been used to justify divorce, kidnapping, and highjacking.

Some time ago, a prominent manufacturer of data processing machines used listening as the basis for a national advertising campaign, alleging that the people who work for their company "listen better" and consequently were nicer persons to do business with. To give this campaign credibility, the company conducted training sessions for its personnel, centering exclusively on listening attitudes and enjoining individuals to pay attention to each other and to their customers. The company feels that the campaign has succeeded beyond their wildest dreams. Whether or not their personnel are indeed better listeners is not known, but they are at least highly aware of the process and apparently are trying to listen better.

In other words, the term "good listener" has become a synonym for a caring, other-oriented person. In fact, this attitude has been elevated to an elaborate philosophical position--called "hermeneutical praxis."

Another real problem of the attitudinal approach is measurement. When one attempts to assess the process, the usual result is an attitude test item such as "I feel that other persons' ideas can contribute a great deal to my life" and the like. It is very difficult to validate such tests, because the definition of the appropriate behaviors that actually constitute "good" listening are hard to find. Beyond acting interested and and not looking at one's watch while the other is talking, there are few behaviors that indicate that one is *really* involved in the receiving process.

Unfortunately, the measurement of interpersonal attitudes, hearing, and comprehension have not attracted a good deal of attention from researchers. In short, the listening construct has been defined more widely in order to deal with the issue of lecture retention, but these wider definitions suffer from serious conceptual and methodological problems. Some other approach seems to be needed.

In the next section, we will discuss some of the possible approaches to classification of listening behavior. There are a number of possible directions that classification might take.

Possible Approaches to a Typology of Listening

One serious problem that has affected thinking about listening has been the assumption that receiving behavior is the same regardless of differing situations and messages. The "retention" model, for example, is entirely appropriate for a "lecture" but probably not as useful for routine interpersonal interactions. In many situations, the relationship between persons is the principal outcome of a communicative interaction, and retention of specific content is less important. For example, self-disclosure is typically done to strengthen an interpersonal bond (Miller & Steinberg, 1975, p. 324) and the bulk of communication between couples seems aimed at relational issues rather than objective content (Fitzpatrick, 1983).

Everyone agrees that communication is a multipurpose activity, sometimes focusing on information and at other times behavior or attitude change, or both. The ancients distinguished among several types of rhetoric (deliberative, forensic, and epideictic), and modern rhetorical criticism is usefully divided into *genres*. If communication (or sending) has so many distinguishable types, it seems curious that we have assumed that receiving is a simple, univariate activity. It seems obvious that listening to a commencement address, for example, would differ markedly from listening to a political speech or even a sermon.

Nor are distinctions among varying types of communication confined to formal speaking. Informal communicative interactions probably vary even more widely. Descriptive linguists have been able to identify a substantial number of separate functions in the verbal behavior of children. Halliday (1973) identified instrumental, regulatory, interactional, personal, heuristic, imaginative, and representational language behavior in children. Stohl (1983) drew on some of these functions in constructing a communication "competence" scale: dividing communicative activity into controlling, informative, heuristic, and expressive functions.

Regardless of which communication typology is subscribed to, almost everyone agrees that there are a number of differing communicative activities, with differing purposes, differing ideas of success or failure, and differing techniques. It seems only reasonable to ask if listening can be examined from the same kind of "functional" approach. In other words, if ordinary "sending" behavior is of many types, should not the receiving activity associated with it also vary?

How can listening differ? What basic forms could listening take? One method of attacking the problem might be the approach taken by Blaine Goss (1982), who approached the definition of listening from a temporal, or "process" point of view. Goss hypothesized that there are three steps in information processing: signal processing, literal processing, and selective processing. Goss' "processing" steps, however, are somewhat similar to Barker's functions: signal processing and hearing are quite similar, and selective processing (critical analysis and appreciation) seem much the same as "understanding." Further, Goss makes the assumption that all listening involves all of these processing steps, and does not distinguish among types of listening.

We have now reviewed a number of different points of view about the process--and it might be helpful to integrate them somewhat. Certainly if the process is sequential, as Goss and others seem to imply, the nature of the sequence would be the most important aspect of the formation of a listening typology. Figure 1-1 illustrates how the sequence might look.

Basically, the figure is a linear model that might well serve as a basis for a typology of listening. But on the other hand, the more traditional communication typologies might also serve just as well. A third approach would be to look more deeply into some of the contributions of cognitive psychology, and and see how this research might help us. Probably the most productive is the large body of research conducted on human memory systems.

Memory and Listening. An interesting question about listening arises from exploration of the question: once the information is processed, what do we do with it? Remember it momentarily, retain

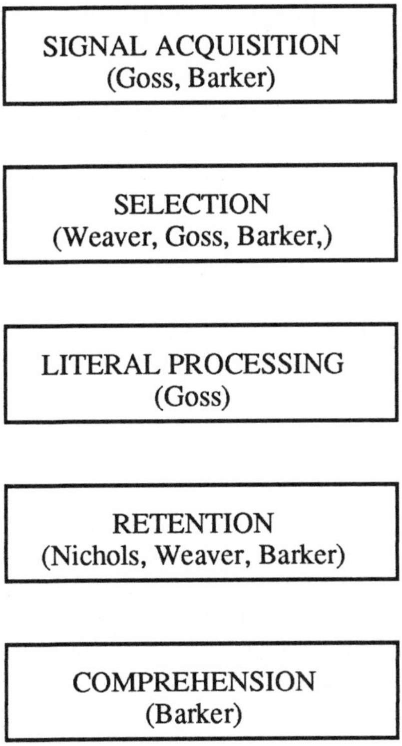

SIGNAL ACQUISITION
(Goss, Barker)

SELECTION
(Weaver, Goss, Barker,)

LITERAL PROCESSING
(Goss)

RETENTION
(Nichols, Weaver, Barker)

COMPREHENSION
(Barker)

FIGURE 1-1. A linear model of the listening process.

forever, or something in between? In a short conversation, it is certainly not important to retain every detail of the exchange--but in a "briefing" session, memory may be so important that we resort to aids such as tape recorders and notebooks to assist us. In other words, the kind of memory involved may be extremely different.

The varying kinds of memory (typically short-term and long-term) have been an object of investigation for some time (Loftus & Loftus, 1976). One reason why few communication researchers have been interested in the memory models is the almost universal assumption among psychologists that memory is relatively mechanical and that individual differences are not a central issue for investigation. Research in listening, however, convinces us that persons do indeed differ in the retention of messages.

The word "storage" is often used to describe the memory system. Visual memory, for example, is usually attributed with three major levels or stages of storage--sensory, or perceptual, short-term, and long-term (Baddely, 1976, p. 76). In both visual and auditory memory systems, sensory storage is the most immediate and the least permanent of the stages; however, visual and auditory memory systems apparently function differently. Visual sensory storage probably lasts no longer than 500 milliseconds (Sperling, 1960). Auditory sensory storage seems to vary in length depending on disruption or masking of the stimulus, but may last up to three or four seconds (Darwin, Turvey, & Crowder, 1972). It is not clear whether there is a separate auditory system for speech and nonspeech sounds. It is widely believed that the left hemisphere is specialized for speech processing and the right for nonspeech processing, and it is assumed that speech sounds are remembered in terms of nonspeech sounds (Baddely, 1976, pp. 236-237).

Short-term memory (STM) involves pattern recognition. Transfer from sensory storage to short-term memory is usually described as "attention." STM seems to consist of a brief component that vanishes after 15 seconds, and an intermediate component that can last as long as 60 seconds if there is an opportunity for "rehearsal," (or storage in a special segment that many have called a "rehearsal buffer") (Baddely, 1976, p. 242; Peterson & Peterson, 1959).

Long-term memory is what most persons commonly mean when they use the word "memory." Usually long-term memory is not activated until at least 60 seconds after the presentation of a stimulus. Actual entry into long-term memory may be dependent on both rehearsal and organizational schemes.

Even though we may be interested in the attention and comprehension processes involved in listening, when we get right down to it, memory is still the crucial process. Most of us would agree that it makes little sense to hear, attend to, or comprehend oral discourse unless we remember it or use it in some way. And since most memory researchers agree that memory has at least three components (short-term, rehearsal, and long-term), we might suspect that these three are involved in listening behavior in different ways.

To investigate this idea, Bostrom and Waldhart (1980) devised listening tasks that involved short-term tasks, intermediate tasks with rehearsal, and a long-term "lecture." The assumption that individual's memories are substantially the same was not borne out in this study: individuals varied considerably in the three types of listening task. The usual approach to memory would predict that an individual who was good at short-term listening (STL) would also be good at lecture listening. In Bostrom and Waldhart's study, the actual correlation was .30. Further, the lecture listening task was found to relate much more strongly with the respondents' ACT composite (a measure roughly corresponding to intelligence), while STL and STL-R (short-term with rehearsal) did not. Finally, and most interestingly, STL exhibited a closer relationship to speech grades than did lecture listening. This relationship has been reaffirmed in a number of instances, but more recent studies seem to indicate that STL-R has the stronger relationship with oral skill (Bostrom, 1980; Waldhart & Bostrom, 1981).

The differentiation of listening skill into short- and long-term components addresses a fundamental issue in communication theory: the delineation of communication into "interpersonal" (dyadic and small group activities) and "public" (more formal speaking). Clearly the good listener in a conversation should not be expected to remember specific data from the conversation, but is expected to hold the data in a short-term buffer just long enough to respond sensibly and continue the interaction. This does not mean, of course, that long-term retention is not important, but it does point out that long-term retention is not always the best definition of successful listening in all situations.

These data would seem to indicate that any definition of listening should include both short-term and long-term components, but does not address the question of whether listening is a unique skill or ability or whether listening merely invokes memory skills. This question is partially answered by a study conducted by Bostrom and Bryant (1980), in which listening was compared to standard characteristics of memory. In this study, listening was found to differ from standard memory models in several important characteristics, leading to the conclusion that listening is indeed a unique ability. In addition, there is evidence that persons with different listening skills use them differently. Persons who are relatively skilled in rehearsal listening (STL-R) may suffer losses in retention when they are forced to take notes on a lecture, while persons who are poorer in STL-R benefited from notes (Waldhart & Bostrom, 1981). In addition, STL and STL-R are enhanced by motivating instructions more than lecture listening (Bostrom, Waldhart, & Brown, 1979).

Our review of memory research shows us that memory is a much broader concept than we might have initially thought, and that the acquisition of a signal is actually a function of a short-term memory process. Into our model on page 9, we should now add STL and STL-R--perhaps instead of acquisition and selection. We will return to this question later in the book. Let us now turn our attention to another kind of information present in oral signals--the interpretive, or "vocalic" information.

Interpretive Listening. Clearly listeners can gain more than linguistic information from an interaction. "Nonverbal" signals are present in face-to-face interactions, and can significantly modify the message.

But the distinction between "verbal" and "nonverbal" is not always clear. One aspect of nonverbal communication has been typically called "vocalic." Voices convey meaning through pitch and rate changes; through differences in rate and timbre. These cues have been demonstrated to affect the perception of communication significantly (Pearce, 1971). The ability to discern these "messages" has long been an assumption of communication researchers, but they have not been considered "listening" in the strictest sense. The discovery that the ability to discern this kind of message varies widely with individuals and does not covary with the other kinds of listening performance (Waldhart & Bostrom, 1981) implies that any comprehensive view of listening must include this kind of ability.

A total picture of information processing, of course, would include the interpretation of visual stimuli as well as vocal ones. Shapiro (1968) found that in situations where facial expressions and vocal messages were inconsistent, receivers processed linguistic cues or nonverbal cues, not both together. Leathers (1979) found that in those kinds of situations, the nonverbal (facial expressions) were clearly dominant over the verbal messages. Leathers and Emigh (1980) demonstrated clearly that individuals do vary in their ability to process the meanings conveyed in facial expressions.

In spite of the similarity of these types of abilities, most persons consider the decoding of nonverbal cues as something other than "listening" behavior, and for the time being, we will defer this issue. Chapter Three will discuss the use of the visual channel in greater detail. In Chapter Six, more specific discussion of interpersonal schemata will also be introduced.

Another important aspect of the selection process is involved when more than one signal is present and individuals must choose among them. This is a distinctly different act from the kinds of "selection" mentioned earlier, but certainly is an important type of it. Let us next look at a simple form of it in the next section.

Discrimination, or Focus. Individuals might well vary in their ability to perform in a situation when two simultaneous messages are presented. This ability has been described as the "cocktail party" phenomenon where persons hear two equally audible conversations and are able to attend to only one. This would seem to correspond to Goss' "selective" processing, and has been demonstrated to differ among individuals and to be somewhat different from STL and STL-R (Waldhart & Bostrom, 1981).

Other Factors. Up to this point in this chapter, we have identified at least five different ways that we might define listening: short-term listening (STL), short-term with rehearsal (STL-R), interpretive listening, lecture listening, and selective listening. These particular factors, however, do not include language processing--decoding, or schematic decoding. It may well be that linguistic ability and schematic ability are aspects of ordinary intelligence tests, as hinted earlier.

But before we can make judgments about the relationships of these various aspects of listening, we must be able to observe the separate elements, examine how they fit together in actual groups of people, and how they relate to other aspects of communicative behavior. The measurement problem is central to the process. In the next chapter, we will examine some of the particular problems inherent in measuring a concept like "listening," and then look at some possible solutions to the problems. Following that, we will report the results of these solutions, including operational definitions, specific approaches to measurement, reliabilities, validity, possible utility. In addition, the results from a large sample of persons will be presented, to offer some idea of the "norms" one can expect in this kind of task.

CHAPTER TWO

Measuring Individual Differences in Listening

GLENDOWER: I can call spirits from the vasty deep.

HOTSPUR: Why, so can I, and so can any man;
But will they come when you do call them?

...Henry IV, Part I

In the previous chapter, we saw that the traditional approach to measuring listening behavior involved the assessment of number of factual items recalled from a lecture, and that this recall is probably more accurately described as one of the "intelligences." However, integration of a number of different definitions of listening (page 9) showed that signal acquisition, selection, literal processing, retention, and comprehension have all been considered as important aspects of listening. Review of recent research in memory, however, shows us that signal acquisition and selection are, in one sense, aspects of the memory system. If this is so, then research into the characteristics of the memory system will shed much light on the listening process, and vice versa. The use of the term "retention" without specification of the type of retention involved may be too simplistic for an accurate description of listening.

Further, other processes related to this kind of cognitive decoding, such as interpretation and selection, are clearly involved. But these conceptualizations are useless if there is no way to determine if individuals differ in each of these processes in any systematic ways. It is one thing to conceptualize a number of different types of communicative behavior, but quite another to demonstrate whether or not the differences are real and can be measured. We set out to investigate whether or not these distinctions were amenable to measurement, and whether our notions about the complexity of listening behavior were were practical ones. Our first task was to devise stimulus material that would serve as instances in which individuals might differ systematically in the reception of information. These stimuli should be repeatable, sensible, and represent actual instances of the phenomena involved.

Construction of Scales

One good way to test memory is to assemble letters and/or numbers in a sequence called a "string," and read them to respondents. Then after this reading, a respondent is asked to remember one or more of the letters. Recording strings on audiotape is an excellent way to control number of units in the sequence and the exact time the sequence takes. This procedure has been used by a number of researchers, notably Baddely and Warrington (1970). By presenting a number of strings, the time for a response can also be carefully controlled. Since Baddely and Warrington had demonstrated that serial position was a strong determiner of the rate of recall of word strings, our initial task was to devise strings that did not demonstrate this serial position effect. Using strings of five and six words, letters, and numbers proved to eliminate serial position effect. Strings of more than six showed positional differences. In other words, long strings tended to induce respondents to choose from initial or final position in the string. We also decided not to use words, since repondents tended to remember "high-impact" words, such as "sting" better than "low-impact" words such as "wash." The possibility of individual differences among the potential respondents led us to eliminate words altogether. Preliminary study had indicated that those who could remember strings of letters could also remember strings of words with equal facility. The strings that we retained approximated the percentages of correct responses in Baddely and Warrington's study.

A second memory task was created by the insertion of an interval of silence between presentation of the string and the presentation of the question about the string. A variety of intervals was used, from 20 to 40 seconds, with the average "rehearsal" being 30 seconds. The assumption is made that individuals must hold the string in working memory for the time period in order pick out a successful answer.

A third variation in remembering strings was introduced by supplying a distracting sound--in this case, a scene from a previously recorded radio drama--which would make the string more difficult to remember. The distracting stimulus was added to the second half of each of the strings. This addition made it possible to look at the responses to different parts of the strings depending on the interest of the scorer or researcher. In practice, however, the responses on the distracted strings is properly defined as a more difficult version of the same task. Sometimes it is useful to look at the distracted portions alone, since persons apparently do differ in their abilities to perform this task.

Another scale was created by writing and recording an imaginary dialogue between a man and a woman in which varying vocal cues could convey strong affective meaning. After parts of the dialogue, respondents were asked to complete the statement "What he (she) *really* means is..." and could respond in a number of ways. The "correctness" of these responses was agreed to by a panel of experts in the Department of Communication at the University of Kentucky. This scale was called "Interpretive Listening."

Lastly, we felt that we should continue to include the more traditional "lecture" listening by constructing a short, information-filled presentation and asking multiple-choice questions about it. Even though previous research showed that this kind of task is more properly labeled "cognitive ability" (or intelligence), we felt that its inclusion was reasonable. Beatty and Payne (1984) discovered a strong relationship between this kind of listening and cognitive complexity, a measure that had previously been associated with a number of communicative skills. Kelly's contentions that lecture listening is isomorphic with generalized cognitive abilities might lead us to believe that cognitive complexity may be strongly related to intelligence. O'Keefe and Sypher (1981), however, report that a number of studies have exhibited only weak relationships between complexity and more generalized cognitive abilities.

Medium of Transmission. In the measurement of listening, one has to confront the issue of whether face-to-face, audiotape, or videotape would best serve as a medium for the stimuli in question. Delivery plays such an important part in a standardized test that face-to-face delivery must be ruled out on the basis of consistency. Each person varies so widely in delivery skills that little, if any, comparison is valid among different "deliverers." In order to "standardize," or establish reasonable bases for comparison from place to place, some sort ot recorded message is vital. But whether to use audio or video recording is an important question.

Searle and Bostrom (1985) demonstrated that messages presented on audiotape more closely resemble messages presented face-to-face than do messages presented on videotape. Searle (1984) had previously demonstrated that this similarity seemed to hold regardless of whether the face-to-face presention was an uninterrupted lecture or involved interactive techniques such as questions. Since a "live," face-to-face interaction is probably the standard against which any taped stimulus should be compared, and given the cost of good videotape production, audiotape seems to be the best way to present the information. However, it must be noted that Searle's data showed small but significant interactions between gender of respondent and medium of transmission. This interaction was consistent with the gender differences reported by Gunter and his associates (Gunter, Furnham, & Gietson, 1984; Gunter, Barry, & Clifford, 1982), so one must keep in mind that real differences in gender (though small) are being ignored here.

These five different audio tasks--short-term retention, short-term with rehearsal, interpretation, lecture, and overcoming distraction--represent a good beginning set of measures of "listening" skills. The list is certainly not exhaustive, but will provide a good foundation for beginning work, and especially for comparisons to other factors, such as language and schemata.

Stimulus Tape. For the sake of convenience and to suit the needs of other users, we assembled the five into a single tape with a one-page optically scanned answer sheet. The tape has twelve items in the first part, which measure short-term listening (STL) and twelve items in the second part which measure short-term listening with rehearsal (STL-R). The third part concerns interpretive listening and has ten items. The fourth part is a conventional short lecture with fourteen multiple-choice items to answer about content of the tape. A fifth scale is created by scoring the last six items from Parts One and Two separately, creating a scale in which overcoming distraction is primary.

In viewing listening from a functional point of view, the five-factor model has a number of conceptual benefits. First, it provides a comprehensive theoretical model based on fairly well-known memory functions; and fits well into private-public models of communicative behavior. Second, it provides a comprehensive alternative to the use of tests which really measure IQ--the problem originally raised by Kelly and ignored by researchers since the middle 1960s. Third, it points to new directions in listening research, an area substantially ignored by researchers for a number of years. All this is predicated on the assumptions that the scales are reliable and valid. Our next task was to examine the general reliability and validity of the scales, and see if they could hold up in a statistical sense.

Statistical Properties of Scales

We have now administered varying forms of these scales to over 20,000 respondents and have some good ideas of their properties. Since the versions of the tapes and the questions have changed a good bit over the years, we report here the results of the most recent representative population of respondents. In this group, the scales constituting Part One had a mean of 7.866 and a standard error of 2.02. Part Two had a mean of 9.574 and a standard error of 1.91. This scale is strongly skewed to the right. Part Three has a mean of 5.704 and a standard error of 1.83. Part Four, lecture listening, has a mean of 8.039 and a standard error of 2.21. The last part, obtained by scoring the last six items of Part One and the last six items of Part Two, has a mean of 8.132 and a standard error of 1.82.

Reliability of Scales. Reliabilities of the varying scales can be estimated in a number of ways. Table 2-1 shows the separate scale reliabilities for differing versions of the test. EXP designates the first version of the test, begun in 1977 and tested extensively in 1978. FR-1 and FR-2 are the test versions that were successively refined in 1979 and 1980, and C-1 is the first version utilizing optical scanning in the

TABLE 2-1
Relialibities of Scales

Test Version	Scales					
	STL	STL-R	Interp	Lect	Dist	Total
EXP	.63	*	*	.58	*	.71
FR-1	.66	.57	*	.71	*	.77
FR-2	.62	.58	.46	.73	*	.83
C-1	.67	.53	.52	.69	.46	.78
C-2	.67	.55	.57	.76	.51	.82

* indicates that this version of the test lacked this scale.

scoring procedure. This version formed the basis for a broadly based standardization program, using responses from different universities. The most recent version of the test is version C-2, the second scanning phase and is the population mentioned below. All reliabilities reported in Table 2-1 are Cronbach's *alpha* measure, a relationship of "unexplained" variance to total variance. Test-retest reliability was measured in FR-1 for three scales and was found to range from .78 to .87.

Table 2-2 presents the percentile distributions of the C-2 version for the "standardizing" population, consisting of 3721 respondents[1] drawn from a variety of institutions. Recent studies show no real deviation from these percentiles.

Another important aspect of reliability is "test-retest" reliability. This normally consists of giving the same individual the test again, to see if the scores are standard. Unfortunately, sometimes persons learn from one administration of the test, and consequently the researcher cannot tell whether the learning is being measured or the test's variability.

We used this approach and devised another form of the entire test. In the Fall of 1985, a second version of the entire test ("Form B") was devised. This alternate form was administered to 168 students who had already taken the first form ("Form A"). For these students, the overall reliability assessment for the total test was .72. Subscales were slightly less than that, with the exception of the "Interpretive" scale, which was only .36. Either the semesters' experience changed the students in significant ways, or the second form is quite different from the first. Another explanation might well be that this kind of data is inherently unstable. But the other subscales showed acceptable reliability.

Validity. There are a number of approaches to validity. Each of the scales represents an actual instance of the performance of the skill in question. Part Four is an actual lecture, Part One is an actual short-term listening task, and so forth.

---

[1] This is a group of respondents who have taken the most recent version of the test and for whom complete, usable data are available. They represent students and adults from a number of different geographical areas, but were all involved with higher education in one form or another. They certainly represent a good cross-section of an undergraduate population.

TABLE 2-2
Percentiles of Listening Scores

Percentile	Total	STL	STL-R	INT	LECT	DIST
99.8	43	12		10	14	
99.5	42			9	13	12
98.4	41					
97.0	40	11	12		12	
95.7	39			8		11
91.6	38				11	
86.6	37	10	11			10
81.1	36			7	10	
73.2	35	9				9
66.0	34			6	9	
60.0	33		10			
53.0	32	8			8	8
45.7	31					
39.0	30		9	5	7	
32.3	29	7				7
24.9	28		8	4	6	
19.5	27	6				6
16.0	26					
12.7	25	5	7		5	5
9.4	24			3		
7.2	23		6		4	
5.2	22	4				4
4.2	21			2		
2.6	20	3	5			3
1.8	19		4		3	
1.5	18			1	2	
.9	17					
.6	16					

One of the first characteristics of validity is uniqueness. A scale that purports to be unique should not be obviously isomorphic with other scales that are similar. It would seem that if these scales are not simply another version of a test of cognitive ability (as other listening tests seem to be), then they ought to be different in obviously different groups.

Second, we should see that a specific mental measurement fits into a logical scheme of other abilities and measures, based on a reasonable theoretical scheme. Specifically we need to know how these scales relate to other kinds of communicative abilities.

Another approach to validity is the use of intact groups which are different in many important characteristics. Taking this approach, we administered the test to university students from several institutions, regular army colonels enrolled in the National Defense University, and high school students. The results of these various groups are presented in Table 2-3. Clearly the colonels were better in lecture retention and STL-R than others. High school students, on the other hand, were better than anyone in STL. The scores of the different groups are convincing evidence that the separate kinds of listening tasks are indeed different ones. Recall that the tape has twelve items in the first part, which measure short-term listening (STL) and twelve items in the second part, which measure short-term listening with rehearsal (STL-R). The third part concerns interpretive listening and has ten items. The fourth part is a conventional short lecture with fourteen multiple-choice items to answer about content of the tape. Unfortunately this comparison did not include the "distraction" items in STL and STL-R. We might have found some interesting differences among the groups.

TABLE 2-3

Percentage of Correct Responses Achieved by
Various Groups

	STL	STL-R	Interp	Select	Lecture
University Students	65	80	54	66	49
Army Officers	61	84	65	63	60
High School Students	74	87	53	76	45

Intelligence, achievement, and reading ability are common measures of cognitive ability. If our scales represent unique abilities, we would expect the correlations to be low with these other measures of cognition. Table 2-4 presents the results of such a comparison, of the varying scales to ACT subscales and two measures of reading effectiveness (an adaptation of the Nelson-Denny). These data, first reported by Waldhart and Bostrom (1981), show definitely that reading skill, ACT scales, and our scales are quite different.

So much of our thinking about communication rests on the assumption that communication is processed almost perfectly. However, it should be obvious that definition of the kind of processing is of utmost importance. Whether the communicative goal is attitude change, relational change, or simple information retention, the general importance of receiver behavior and the ultimate storage and use of information are of sufficient importance for us to give the subject more than a cursory glance. Some reconceptualization might well stimulate more research and provide more useful information about listening.

TABLE 2-4

Intercorrelations of Listening Subscales, ACT Subscales, and Reading Rate and Comprehension

	STL	STL-R	Interp	Lect	Total
STL-R	.375				
Int	.083	.105			
Lect	.038	.207	.187		
Total	.628	.683	.549	.586	
Reading Rate	.122	.221	.215	.071	.258
Reading Comp	-.138	-.003	.022	.023	-.051
ACT Eng	.302	.224	.219	.260	.415
ACT Math	.282	.252	.162	.262	.394
ACT SocSt	.216	.191	.270	.290	.403
ACT NtSci	.091	.223	.127	.148	.238

Summary

In summary, we are convinced that these five scales do indeed show acceptable reliability and are valid measures of the acquisition of information. In addition, they are not a measure of academic achievement or reading ability, and fit comfortably into a multidimensional model of communication attitudes and abilities. Because each of the scales tests a different aspect, the overall total (or percentage) is probably less meaningful.

While our original purpose was to construct a research instrument that did not have the deficiencies that Kelly noted, we have found that these scales combined into a single test serve very well in classes as a diagnostic instrument, as a demonstration, and as a motivator. Students find it useful to compare their abilities with others in a systematic way.

But most importantly, we are discovering new relationships about various aspect of listening behavior. How these receiving skills relate to other cognitive abilities should tell us much about the basic nature of communication.

CHAPTER THREE

Encoding, Media, Affect, and Gender

Robert N. Bostrom

D. Bruce Searle

> People sometimes think that if it's
> not on television, it's not real.
> ....Daniel Schorr

No matter how one defines listening, one cannot escape the fact that the demands of technology occasionally produce situations in which we have to force the normal interpersonal interaction into some "mediated" channel, such as the telephone, where only one part of the signal is processed. We are so accustomed to this process that we often forget that in more natural situations, audio and visual messages are transmitted at the same time. In these natural settings, the visual, or "nonverbal" messages, are normally consistent with the linguistic elements of the message. Burns and Beier (1973), for example, studied situations in which the visual messages were inconsistent with the linguistic messages, and discovered that in this processing, most persons tend to opt for one channel over another. Leathers (1979), on the other hand, demonstrated a distinct tendency for persons to choose the visual channel in these conflicting situations. Whether or not it is sensible to treat listening as aural processing alone is a vital question. It may be that no real differences exist in the presence or absence of "video," as Hsia (1968) seems to indicate.

The "technological revolution" presents interesting challenges to our understanding of listening, because of our assumption that the use of technology in and of itself has an effect on message understanding. This assumption is firmly rooted in the supposed presence or absence of "social presence." This interesting concept, as defined by Short, Williams, and Christie (1976), is similar to the "mere presence" effects as earlier researched by Zajonc (1965). The presence or absence of another human being is motivating (or stimulating, depending on how we define it), and should be included in any description of communicative effects. Obviously, then, messages delivered face-to-face are high in social presence, televised messages are less so, and audiotaped messages are barely better than reading. Williams and Rice (1983) argue that the need for new communication technologies stems from a feeling that this "presence" is an important communication characteristic and that interactive media represent an important method of supplying the social presence that less interactive media have.

If this social presence is indeed a vital part of the communicative interaction, we would certainly expect its presence or absence to have some effect on communication. At the least, social presence should affect the way the information is acquired (and retained) as a result of listening to a message.

This is not a new subject in communication research. For many years, researchers, both in communication and education, have investigated the relative effectiveness of different media used in the educational setting for the transmission of information. In addition, the presence or absence of affect in the receivers has been studied, as have varying kinds of encoding activities. In this study, the relative effects of medium of transmission, encoding activity, receiver affect, and receiver sex were investigated, to determine what, if any, possible interactive effects the varying factors might have on information acquisition and retention.

Early Research on Media Effects

The medium of transmission of messages has been extensively studied and the results have been varied. For example, many studies have been conducted on the use of "media" in classroom settings. Jamison, Suppes, and Wells (1974) surveyed the research on the comparative effectiveness of traditional instruction, instructional television, programmed instruction, instructional radio, and computer-assisted instruction, and found that few studies indicate any significant advantages of one medium over another. Most of these studies took place in an "instructional" setting and compared varying measures of student performance at the end of a semester or even a year. These "experiments" used relatively crude methodology, and the fact that in most cases the null hypothesis was retained should surprise no one.

Direct and careful comparisons of the efficacy of media in information retention are rare. In one such, Brandon (1956) examined the presentation of factual information by television in which a televised lecture, a televised interview, and a televised discussion were compared. Receivers found that the interview and discusssion methods were more interesting but the three methods of presentation did not differ significantly in their ability to communicate information. In another, Taylor, Lipscomb, and Rosemier (1969) found no significant differences between a videotaped interactive lecture and a live interactive lecture. Popham (1961) and Menne, Klingensmith, and Nord (1969) found similar results when comparing live lectures to audio-taped lectures. At both the graduate and undergraduate levels, taped lectures were as effective as live lectures in terms of information transfer.

In a study focusing on the persuasive process, Frandsen (1963) examined taped, televised, and live presentations with different levels of threat appeal. He found that none of the media produced significantly different scores on an immediate recall test. Miller, Bender, Florence, and Nicholson (1974) compared the responses of jurors in a live trial to those of jurors in a videotaped trial. Of particular importance to this study was their intention to determine whether medium of presentation had a significant effect on the retention of trial-related information. They found that jurors' retention of trial-related information was not significantly influenced by the medium of presentation. However, Miller and Fontes (1979) reported that oral presentations were slightly superior to video presentations in retention of information. However, they also reported a more rapid decline in retention among the viewers of the live presentation. The differences disappeared entirely after a 12-day interval. Taylor, Lipscomb, and Rosemier (1969) also found that there was no significant difference in the effectiveness of a video-taped interactive lecture when compared to a live interactive lecture.

Possible Interactive Factors and Media Effects

All in all, those who believe that the "medium is the message" receive little comfort in the research literature, at least where the acquisition and retention of information is concerned. If real differences exist in the media, they have apparently been obscured by other factors that affect information retention, such as the setting or uncontrolled content. It may be true that for information acquisition at least, there are truly no differences among the media.

Still another explanation is at least plausible: the differences are subtle, and are importantly affected by other factors. In the studies cited above, media effects, if any, would have had to appear strongly across a number of subgroups in a consistent fashion, to have made a difference. It is entirely possible that media effects are interactive ones; i.e., effects that appear in one subgroup and not in another. If so, "main" effects would not appear; nor would the subgroup effects. Some possible factors that might contribute to these interactions are intelligence, sex, encoding activity, and immediate affect.

Comprehension or Retention? You will recall from Chapter One that a lack of clear definition has characterized much "listening" research. Only Barker included comprehension in his definition of listening, and this definition was not highly specific. Probably the best way to approach the definition of comprehension would be to invoke larger cognitive structures, such as "constructs" or "schemas" (Sypher & Applegate, 1984). These structures are extremely varied, and at the same time essential for "comprehension" in a real sense. Most of these schemas belong in differently ordered hierarchies, and are highly individual in nature.

When we lack knowledge about simple retention, it makes little sense to study the more complex phenomenon of comprehension. Further, the measurement of information acquisition in almost all previous research has been accomplished by the use of multiple-choice tests, in which "test-wise" respondents are able to excel. These skilled test-takers also do well on the tests of cognitive ability. Better measurement of the presence of information would include some mechanism for confidence weighting, in which a respondent is allowed to indicate how confident he or she is of the answer. In addition, if some penalty for guessing is added, then the randomness of this assessment procedure is diminished.

Re-Encoding: Notetaking. Receivers in a communication interaction almost always *appear* to be attending to messages, but most of us know well that appearances are deceiving. The most attentive-looking participant is often engaging in cognitive wheel-spinning and not attending at all. There are various devices for externalizing encoding behavior, but one of the most common is notetaking. In addition, notetaking reinforces the encoding process by repeating it. Many researchers have studied notetaking behavior and find, not surprisingly, that it operates at two levels: as an external storage mechanism, and as a cueing and encoding activity (Lashbrook, 1976). DiVesta and Gray (1982) found evidence of both sources of retention aids, and Aiken, Thomas, and Shennum (1975) found similar effects.

Notetaking may enhance memory by enabling the receiver to transform the message so that it corresponds more closely with his or her own cognitive structure. Lashbrook (1976) notes that such a restructuring probably includes several subprocesses including repetition or rehearsal, selectivity (in which the notetaker selects the information to be recorded based on such factors as its relevance and unfamiliarity), and adaptation (involving the notetaker in syntactical/lexical reorganization in correspondence with his or her own preferences).

Howe's (1970) study of retention and notetaking is instructive. In that study recall was tested immediately following the presentation of a short, taped lecture with no opportunity for review. Howe found that notetakers had a probability of .34 of recalling informational items while non-notetakers had only .047.

Fisher and Harris (1974) similarly sought to clarify the effect of notetaking on immediate and delayed recall and its role with respect to the encoding and external storage propositions. In their study, college students were subjected to different notetaking and review combinations including notes/review own notes, no notes/review lecturer's notes, own notes/review lecturer's notes, notes/mental review, and no notes/mental review. Recall was measured immediately and three weeks later without additional review. The results showed that the combination of taking and reviewing one's own notes produced the most recall, while not taking notes and reviewing mentally produced the least recall. The study in fact supported both the encoding and external storage hypotheses. Aiken, Thomas, and Shennum (1975) examined the effect of notetaking procedure, information density, and speech rate on delayed recall. Three notetaking conditions were tested--spaced, where notes were compiled during periodic breaks in the lecture, no notes, and notetaking during the lecture. Retention was measured after 48 hours without further opportunity being given for review, and was found to be superior when notetaking was separated from listening. Howe's (1970) finding that information in notes had a higher probability of recall was confirmed.

Another study supporting the facilitative effects of notetaking was undertaken by Carter and Van Matre (1975). They investigated the relationship of notetaking and review to retention of information presented by lecture, measuring the results immediately and after a one week delay by means of free recall and verbatim and paraphrase completion tests. Taking and reviewing of notes yielded maximum retention and recall efficiency, while listening only without review resulted in poorest performance. The benefit of notetaking appeared to be derived from having an opportunity to subsequently review notes, and not from the act of notetaking itself. Encoding differences as a function of notetaking were minimal, while the external storage function assumed primary importance.

Peters (1972), on the other hand, found that those who did not take notes did better than notetakers in recalling content from a taped lecture, although it seems that individual ability, rate of presentation, and complexity of the lecture material may not have been sufficiently controlled to place any great weight on the findings.

Individual differences are a clear source of explanation in examining notetaking effects. Waldhart and Bostrom (1981) found that those who were better in short-term listening did more poorly when forced to take notes than those whose short-term listening abilities were not so good. Clearly notetaking as forced encoding is an important factor in the retention of information from messages.

Probably the most obvious question that follows, however, concerns the possible interaction of forced encoding with media effects. In face-to-face situations we may be accustomed to notetaking, simply because we feel that the presenter might well stop or slow down when we are taking notes. Most of our educational experiences have been face-to-face, and simple association may be a strong facilitator. This kind of encoding is not so common in video or audio presentations. In addition, we may also associate the face-to-face mode with informational presentations and mediated messages with entertainment.

Gender. Another common interactor with media usage is gender. Patterns of media usage, informational utility, and many others differ importantly with the sexes. The evidence for differences, if any, in information acquisition and retention is less clear. Some research associated with the influence of gender on comprehension emanates primarily from a consideration of the apparent physiological differences between male and female brains. Maccoby and Jacklin (1974) were among the first to hypothesize that the evident difference between men and women in visual and spatial ability appeared to have a genetic component. They also noted that women are superior to men on tests of verbal ability, while men perform better on tasks involving visual and spatial abilities. Shucard (1982) reported that females activate the left hemisphere more readily than males and that this hemisphere dominates mastery of linguistic, sound recognition, mathematical, and analytical skills. Goleman (1978) has been one of the most prominent researchers in this field. His research has shown that females perform particularly well on verbal tasks that involve hearing, while males perform better on tasks that involve seeing. This is particularly curious in the light of research that has consistently shown few differences in the sexes (Bostrom & Waldhart, 1980). He postulates that it is easier for females to perform simultaneous tasks which are cognitively similar. Males, however, find it easier to separate cognitively different activities when performed simultaneously. These findings ought to indicate clear media differences in men and women, especially when forced encoding is a part of the process. In addition, specific affect differences ought also be observed.

Previous research in information acquisition shows little difference in the sexes. Kibler, Barker, and Cegala (1970) found no differences, either in immediate or delayed recall. McCracken (1969) found no retention differences nor any affect differences as indicated by GSR. Heinberg (1961), on the other hand, found that women were superior to men in perceiving implications from dialogue, but Heinberg did not control for other abilities, such as intelligence. Kramer (1974) makes a convincing case for differences in linguistic usage, but these usages do not always translate into acquisition and retention.

Affect. Classical learning theory associates the acquisition of new responses with psychological arousal and subsequent "satisfaction." This ubiquitous reinforcement theory has received much support in studies of learning. More recent thinking has focused on "attribution" of affect and other interpretations. McCracken (1969), as mentioned above, did indeed study GSR differences and found none. One reasonable first step toward looking for specific differences in affect ought to be a first-level self-report--if nothing else, to sample how participants in varying information-acquisition situations describe their feelings.

In summary, little, if any, previous research shows differences in the media, despite many indications that such differences are real and probably more complex than we suspect. Part of the problem is that much previous research has focused on "comprehension" which usually is confounded with familiarity with schema or construct structures, and has failed to control for cognitive ability, such as intelligence or scholastic aptitude. In addition, encoding behavior has received little attention as it interacts with varying media, and receiver sex has also not been studied. All of these ought to interact with one another in the acquisition of information, and also ought to produce varying affective changes as receivers attempt to gain information from messages.

A Specific Test of Media Interactions

To test some of these general notions, 460 students at the University of Kentucky were designated as a sample group. The large number was used because previous calculation of power curves (Feldt & Mahmoud, 1958) using estimates of expected means and variances produced a value for Φ' of .43 for $K = 3$ and $\alpha = .05$. Power of .9 required at least 26 respondents per cell. Each person was asked to attend three sessions, all of which were conducted during regularly scheduled class periods, for the collection of data.

The Message. The experimental message consisted of a 13 minute lecture on the subject of TV news, delivered by a skilled television news reporter from a local television station. An accurate assessment of comprehension demanded that the content of the message be sufficiently novel to ensure that subjects would not have an inordinate degree of prior knowledge. The message was structured to answer five specific questions:

1. Why is TV news important?

2. What are the basic sources of TV news?

3. How is TV news formulated on a daily basis?

4. What is the most significant recent development in TV news?

5. What are the current trends for TV news?

The design of the message was such that information was transmitted in a variety of ways including verbal, statistical, and by means of illustration.

First the message was delivered (live) to a large group. During this delivery, the speaker was videotaped by a camera with a long lens. Then another group viewed the videotape and a third heard only the sound track of the videotape. Each of these large groups was made up of a number of intact groups (classes) because of particular scheduling problems. However, *post hoc* analyses showed that these groups did not differ from one another on ACT composites or any of the ACT subscales.

Dependent Variables. Measuring the retention of information was accomplished by a test which utilized a number of different kinds of responses. Rowley (1974), for example, has shown that certain responders who are accustomed to risk-taking are favored by traditional multiple-choice tests because of their propensity to take risks, while other students with equal knowledge and ability are penalized. Goodyear and Behnke (1976) demonstrated that "test-wise" respondents did no better in confidence-weighted tests than did those who were less apt to guess.

The test used included short-answer items (not more than one sentence), fill-in-the-blank items, (one or two words), confidence-weighted multiple-choice items, confidence-weighted true/false items, and cloze procedure. Multiple choice questions required students to provide an estimate of accuracy and also of confidence. True/false questions included a penalty for guessing. Respondents were told that they should not guess, as scoring procedures would penalize them for incorrect answers.

A pretest was administered seven days prior to the experimental treatment, consisting of six confidence-weighted multiple choice and two fill-in-the-blank items designed to test general knowledge of the message topic. Retention was operationally defined as a score on the questionnaire immediately following the experimental treatment minus the score achieved on the pretest. Long-term retention was measured by administering the same test twelve days after the experimental treatment. Respondents were not informed prior to this test of the intention to measure retention. As with immediate retention, the pretest score was subtracted.

Affect. Affect, or the individual's emotional state, was used as a predictor of the level of activation in relation to the respondents' optimal level in a manner similar to that incorporated by Donohew (1981). The direction of affect was measured by a 20-item mood scale originally developed by Green and Nowlis (1957). Participants marked a four-point scale ranging from "definitely applies" to "definitely does not apply" according to how well each item described mood "at this moment". A four-point scale was selected to eliminate the tendency of some persons to choose the median in a five-point scale. Responses were coded according to whether they represent a pleasant or unpleasant affective state, and then summed to produce a mood score. The mood scale was administered immediately prior to the experimental treatment and then again immediately after the experimental treatment before comprehension was measured.

In addition, American College of Testing (ACT) scores were obtained as a measure of each subject's academic ability.

Experimental Procedures. Seven days prior to the experimental treatment, the TV news test was given to all respondents.

Participants were randomly assigned to engage either in listening only or listening while simultaneously taking notes. Notetakers were given three blank lined pages on which to write their notes. Each page contained 28 lines, all of which were numbered. Each respondent's notes were scored by counting the number of lines completed. Those who did not complete at least 14 lines were not included in the note-taking group in subsequent data analyses.

At the beginning of each experimental session, participants were given instructions on the procedure. Those assigned to a notetaking group were given a set of instructions relating to notetaking procedure, including three pages on which to take notes. Notetaking instructions were read and clarified as necessary. All were then handed a packet of instructions which included the first mood scale. The instructions in the packet were read to the group and opportunity given for any questions. Respondents were then instructed to complete the Mood Scale, following which the initial packet was collected.

Each group was then exposed to the experimental message via the appropriate medium. Immediately following the completion of the message, the notes taken were collected, and the second packet including the second Mood Scale and the comprehension instrument was distributed for immediate completion. When everyone had finished the task, the packets were collected and the experimental session concluded.

Twelve days following the experimental treatment, the retention instrument was administered in regular classroom sessions. No prior warning was given.

The size of the mean differences was not quite as large as had been initially estimated, but the mean square within was smaller, so the initial estimates of power were considered to hold for the principal comparisons. The posttest version of the retention test was analyzed for its internal consistency, using Cronbach's *alpha* statistic (Cronbach, 1951). For the immediate posttest, *alpha* proved to be .91. Previous research indicates that the confidence weighting procedure used here usually produces tests with high internal consistencies of this type

(Goodyear & Behnke, 1976). 438 respondents returned usable data. The pretest showed that almost all respondents had very little previous knowledge of the content of the message.

The first test integrated cognitive ability, medium, encoding, and sex. Cognitive ability was defined by by the ACT composite. The high and low quartiles were used as a basis for a series of interactive analyses. ACT proved to be a powerful predictor of immediate retention ($F = 47.8$, $p < .001$) and of delayed retention ($F = 48.3$, $p < .001$) . However this measure did not interact with encoding, sex, or media. The composite correlated .40 with immediate retention and .41 with delayed retention. Accordingly, the remainder of the analyses were analyses of covariance using ACT composite as a predictor. First a four-way analysis of covariance was performed using media, encoding, sex and time of administration of the test (immediate vs. 12 days later). Time of administration was a large effect, but did not interact with any other variables. Therefore, two separate analyses of covariance were performed on each of the measures of retention. These analyses both produced a three-way interaction among medium, sex, and encoding condition. For immediate retention, the three-way interaction produced an F of 14.56, which, with 2 and 471 degrees of freedom,[1] was significant at the .0001 level. The 12-day retention scores' three-way interaction produced an F of 4.89, which, with 2 and 407 degrees of freedom, was significant at the .008 level. The adjusted means for each of these variables are presented in Table 3-1.

Figure 3-1 shows how these three-way interactions are constituted. In the face-to-face groups, marked sex differences are present in the note-taking group, but are diminished when notes were not taken. In the video group, very straightforward effects are present, for both sex and notetaking. But in the audio group, an entirely different effect is exhibited. Males are considerably better than females in the notetaking group, but the effect is reversed in the non-notetaking group. The similarity of the two separate three-way interactions is striking, lending strength to the belief that these are not random effects. Means of the groups were compared without the correction factor introduced by the ACT composite and produced configurations very similar to those in Figure 3-1.

---

[1] This and all subsequent F statistics have varying degrees of freedom due to spoiled tests, absences, and other factors which made each analysis of covariance differ slightly.

TABLE 3-1

Adjusted Means of Information Recalled Immediately and After 12 days

Medium	Gender	Encoding	Immediate	12-days
Audio	F	Notes	10.04	3.79
Audio	F	No Notes	11.39	6.48
Audio	M	Notes	13.11	4.13
Audio	M	No Notes	7.93	2.76
Face-to-Face	F	Notes	13.27	7.45
Face-to-Face	F	No Notes	11.41	6.79
Face-to-Face	M	Notes	10.24	4.45
Face-to-Face	M	No Notes	12.54	5.51
Video	F	Notes	14.17	8.55
Video	F	No Notes	10.62	5.23
Video	M	Notes	13.14	6.97
Video	M	No Notes	9.13	3.15

Affect. Both initial and post-experimental self-descriptions of mood were also analyzed, in order to see if self-report of affect provided any explanation for the unusual three-way interactions. These means are presented in Table 3-2. Analysis of variance was performed on the change scores, since this measure ought to be a rough indication of message effects. However, some differences were present in pre-message mood scores. Figure 3-2 illustrates these means.

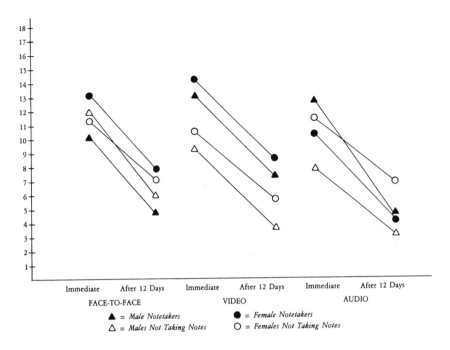

FIGURE 3-1. Information Retention.

For the change scores, a large main effect ($F = 9.12$, $p < .001$) was observed for medium. The face-to-face group changed 1.81 units, the audio group -.04 units, and the video group -.04 units. Essentially this meant that the mediated messages produced no mood change, but the face-to-face group changed in a direction of a "better" mood as measured by these self-reports. In addition, there was an interaction between Sex and Encoding condition ($F = 7.61$, $p < .006$). This interaction showed that women gained in mood when they took notes, but lost when they did not; and that men exhibited an opposite trend. The actual differences in men and women are slight, but they are clearly present, and should not be ignored in future examination of listening effects. The large number of respondents, together with the precision of the method, gives the finding a good deal of believability. It is not clear from any of the previous literature whether or not "androgyny" or biological gender is responsible.

TABLE 3-2

*Means of Self-Report of Mood
Before and After Communication*

Medium	Gender	Encoding	Before	After	Change
Audio	F	Notes	4.75	5.33	.58
Audio	F	No Notes	6.61	5.15	-1.46
Audio	M	Notes	6.00	8.55	2.55
Audio	M	No Notes	3.30	2.36	-1.33
Face-to-Face	F	Notes	2.13	4.50	2.36
Face-to-Face	F	No Notes	3.20	3.89	.68
Face-to-Face	M	Notes	1.17	1.58	.41
Face-to-Face	M	No Notes	3.60	6.36	2.76
Video	F	Notes	4.40	5.75	1.29
Video	F	No Notes	4.42	3.56	-1.09
Video	M	Notes	7.00	6.68	- .31
Video	M	No Notes	9.16	8.69	.27

The analysis of variance performed on the pre-message mood scores also exhibited the large main effect ($F = 9.15, p < .001$) that was shown in the mood change scores. This effect was the opposite of the effect shown in change, in that the groups hearing the mediated messages began with higher scores than did the face-to-face groups.

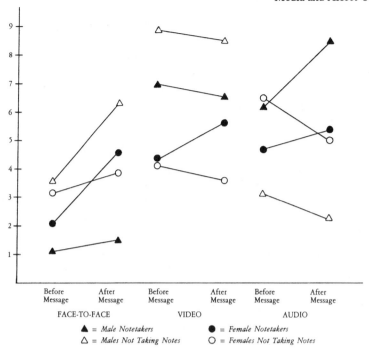

FIGURE 3-2. Changes in Affect.

This would appear to mitigate the mood change exhibited in the previous analysis. No other differences were observed.

Further analysis was performed on the amount of notes taken in the note-taking conditions. A weak ($F = 2.96$, $p < .053$) interaction was observed between sex and medium. In general, women took more notes than men, but in the audio condition this difference was not observed. The main effect for sex was a strong one ($F = 48.31$, $p < .0001$). The mean for women note-takers was 27.7 lines of notes, while the mean for men was 21.4 lines.

DISCUSSION

The finding of all the previous research indicating no media differences was certainly replicated if we examine only main effects due to media. However, this investigation demonstrated that media differences are interactive ones, in this case varying with respondents' sex and the amount of forced encoding behavior present. Forced encoding seems to enhance retention in the video condition but not in the audio or face-to-face conditions. Women retain information better than men in video conditions but not in the audio or face-to-face conditions. Male notetakers were clearly superior in the audio condition, but males who did not take notes in this condition fared far worse. The complexity of these interactions is a strong temptation for the researcher to consider the possibility that these respondents represented an anomalous sample and the differences were simply due to chance. This explanation is supported by the use of intact groups in this study and the possibility that previous differences in media preferences or study habits might have been present. But the fact that none of these groups differed in ACT scores and that the principal method of comparison involved adjusted means as determined by covariance, the possibility of differences in the original groups seems diminished. In addition, the differences in affect and the quantity of notes taken indicate that one must strongly consider the possibility that these results represent real differences among men and women in the acquisition of information from media.

Among respondents who were forced to take notes, women took more notes than men in the face-to-face and the video condition. In the audio condition, men and women took about the same number of notes. The amount of information gained in the immediate posttest, however, is much greater for male notetakers, leading us to look for some other explanation. In Figure 3-2 we see that postmessage affect in that group (male notetakers) is more positive than in any other group in the study. Postmessage affect had the strongest predictive value of any of the affect measures in immediate retention ($R = .41$). But why males in this group should report this kind of mood is certainly not clear.

Goleman (1978) had predicted that women would do better in tasks where simultaneous but related cognitive activites were performed. This certainly ought to explain the propensity of women to take more notes than did men. This does not help us explain why the difference did not appear in the audio only group. It may be that the task was viewed as a greater challenge by the men in this group, and a lesser one by the women. This kind of mindset would lead to the equalizing of the notetaking and the subsequent differences in retention. Clearly the men benefited more from the combination of more notes and greater postmessage affect than did women.

Postmessage affect change obviously has a facilitating effect in the retention of information. This measure correlated .22 (overall) with immediate retention but only .13 with longterm retention. It is interesting to note, however, that premessage affect is higher in the video condition, lower in the audio condition, and lowest in the face-to-face condition. This may well be a novelty effect, since these respondents were students, and lectures are old hat to them, even guest lectures. Caution must be taken, however, in the interpretation of any absolute value in this self-report data of mood. Someone who describes himself/herself as "happy" may vary widely in other measures of affect. However, postmessage affect has a higher correlation with postmessage retention than either premessage affect or affect change.

In addition, we need to be careful in applying Goleman's conclusions to media. Women were better than men in face-to-face and video conditions, a finding directly opposite to that of Goleman. But we need to remember that the information tested was presented by voice, not visually, and the visual elements were peripheral to the task. The amount of notes taken and the differences in affect would indicate that some rethinking of the previous positions about media and sex is needed.

In conclusion, we need to be extremely careful about global generalizations about men, women, and media. The processes involved in information acquisition are complex ones, and need careful study. At the very least, we can conclude that decisions involving varying media use should consider not only cognitive ability, but situation, enconding level, and respondents' sex.

CHAPTER FOUR

Listening, Communicative Skill, and Attitudes about Communication

Nothing is remembered without emotion.

....Israel Rosenfield

Few of us would disagree with Spitzberg and Cupach's assertion that communicative competence is primarily composed of motivation, knowledge, and skills (1984, pp. 119-137). These three factors are so central to communication that further iteration of their importance seems tautological. But while research in communication education has studied parts of these factors in some detail, information is still lacking about ways in which these factors relate to one another.

Listening is such an obvious part of everyone's model of communicative skill, that the relationships among these three factors is of great theoretical and practical interest.

"Motivation" to communicate is an excellent example. Spitzberg and Cupach's description of motivation seems to imply a motivational "trait"--a general tendency to approach or avoid communicative situations. The most prominent of these traits, of course, is avoidance, and the one that has attracted the most attention from researchers. This is reasonable, since communication apprehension, shyness, and reticence, constitute a significant social and educational problem (Daly & McCroskey, 1984). The opposite of avoidance, of course, is "approach," which has attracted less attention.

There is an obvious relationship between skills and the "avoidance" vector of motivation. VanKleeck and Daly (1982) propose that the realtionship is a causal one, stating that "anxiety comes about and is maintained because of failure to acquire the necessary skills" (p. 65). One of the most prominent approaches to the treatment of apprehension has been called "rhetoritherapy" because of the acquisition of rhetorical skill (Phillips, 1977). But we are not at all sure if the relationship holds for positive motivation rather than negative motivation. Nor is it

42

known whether or not the reduction of apprehension leads to more effective communication (Kelly, 1984).

Relationships among knowledge and motivation are suggested by Freemouw and Scott's description of "Rational-Emotive Therapy" (1978). This form of cognitive restructuring is not exactly the sort of "knowledge" proposed by Spitzberg and Cupach, but the relationship observed would seem to support the general principle.

In this chapter, we will examine some of the previously defined factors of apprehension, attitude, and evaluation of communication, to see if they can be consistently described as "motivation" in the sense proposed by Spitzberg and Cupach, and second, to explore the ways in which motivation is related to the various measures of listening as we have defined them.

Motivation. If there is a broad, underlying schema generally motivating persons to communicate, there is no question but that its negative vector could be little else other than communication apprehension. Communication apprehension possesses a strong affective component and has been shown to mediate a variety of communication activity. Daly and Stafford (1984), for example, cite 18 examples of research in which anxiety was found to be inversely related to the frequency and duration of communication. But most of these studies do not clearly indicate whether the communicative behavior is *inhibited* by a negative evaluation or *facilitated* by a positive evaluation.

The studies cited by VanKleeck and Daly probably represent instances of negative affect, which logically ought to inhibit communicative behavior. An examination of the items in typical tests of communication apprehension reveals that they are phrased in terms of negative affect, such as fright, dislike, and the like. Although one version of the communication apprehsion test has been described as including positive and negative items (McCroskey, 1970), these "positive" items only describe the lack of affect. In this version of the test, only four items contain words like "enjoy" and "like."[1] Probably if one were to contend seriously that an item should reflect positive affect, the language of the item ought to reflect some sort of "enjoyment" or

---

[1] Item 2, for example, reads "I have no fear of facing an audience," which is essentially indicates lack of affect. Only items 4, 17, 18, and 25 of this version contain words like "I like" or "I enjoy" and other descriptors of positive affect.

pleasure. The version that McCroskey reports probably does not meet this requirement. However, in some circumstances, lack of fear may well be enjoyable!

Motivation to communicate might also be described as communication "attitude," if attitude is a generalized evaluative schema with both positive and negative vectors. Studies of communication evaluation using "attitude" as a basic conceptual scheme have been undertaken by Knower (1938), Bostrom (1970), Hart, Carlson, and Eadie (1980), Cegala (1981), and many others. If attitudes do indeed mediate behaviors, then communicative attitudes ought logically to be one way of describing motivation to communicate. Since attitudes are usually acquired through reinforcement, it should follow that skilled communicators might well evaluate communication highly, since the act of communication may often provide them with social rewards. But it does not necessarily follow that those who lack ability will possess negative attitudes about the communication process. Persons who are not so skilled might also enjoy the communicative process highly. In addition, some attitudes might facilitate communication while others might not.

This feeling that attitudes importantly mediate communicative skill is exemplified by Hart and Burks (1972), who, in describing an attitude they called "rhetorical sensitivity," contended that "this mode of thought makes effective social interaction manifestly possible (p. 75). In other words, the attitude itself is seen as a primary facilitator of successful interaction. While relationships among communicative attitudes and such factors as personality, age, socio-economic status, and sex have been studied extensively, there have been fewer investigations of the relationships that might exist between attitudes and abilities. Attitude structure and skill--especially cognitive skill--has been well documented in other areas (Staats, 1975). The dimensions of this relationship in communication activity are less well understood. The purpose of this chapter is to explore the relationships among communicative activities and communicative skills, and see what, if any, patterns might exist among these relationships.

We can see that motivation to communicate shares certain common definitional difficulties with attitude research. The broadest way to define this motivation would include affective, conative, cognitive, and behavioral components. While not everyone agrees that attitudes should be thus broadly defined--O'Keefe (1980), for example, would prefer that we confine ourselves to evaluative responses when using the term attitude--there is certainly no reason not to look at the broadest possible starting point while examining motivation to communicate. The cognitive component of such motivation would consist of positive and negative beliefs concerning communication activity, and the conative would, of course, be a general "intention" to communicate. Behavioral manifestations of communication motivation would be specific behaviors relating to communicative activity, such as volunteering or participation. Finally, the affective dimension would be an individual's tendency to be emotionally aroused by communication.

Negative affect has been extensively studied (Daly & McCroskey, 1984), but positive affect has not had as much attention. The conative dimension--"behavioral intention"--has also been studied as "willingness to communicate" (approach or avoidance of communicative acts) and has usually been termed "reticence" (Phillips & Metzger, 1973; Burgoon, 1976; Lustig, 1974).

Cognitive aspects of communicative attitudes are less familiar, but have been studied by Knower (1938), Bostrom (1970), and Hart, Carlson, and Eadie (1980). However, the cognitive elements studied by each of these four researchers are quite different. Knower studied general evaluation and "adjustment" to speaking situations, Bostrom utilized evaluative dimensions of the semantic differential, and Hart, Carlson and Eadie were interested in "sensitivity" as a kind of communication attitude.

"Behavioral" aspects of communicative attitude are not as familiar as the other dimensions. Cegala (1981) and Cegala, Savage, Brunner, and Conrad (1982) have studied self-reports of interaction activity and perceptiveness. These reports of attending and responding behavior might well be viewed as possessing a "motivation" component, but Cegala's theoretical framework seems to be grounded in a competence model, rather than an attitudinal one. However, high scorers on his scale (IIS) also proved to be low scorers in communication apprehension, so self-reports of interactive behavior cannot be ruled out when discussing motivation to communicate. Communicative behavior of other types has been studied in small groups and in volunteering situations (Burgoon, 1977; Bostrom, 1970; Wells & Lashbrook, 1970). A positive motivation appears in one of these scales. Burgoon's scale, while described as a measure of "reticence," actually contains elements of approach to communication and the rewards inherent in communicative activity (Burgoon, 1976).

Motivation to communicate, then, ought to consist of several elements; a broad underlying structure of evaluation, ranging from positive to negative, and more specific manifestations of this underlying structure which show themselves as affective, cognitive, conative, and behavioral responses. The affective and conative elements ought logically to be related to behavioral elements, with the cognitive element less so. Communicative skill ought to play an important part in all of these relationships, as well as other cognitive structure, "knowledge" about communication.

Attitudes about Communication

Hart, Carlson, and Eadie (1980) devised a test of the "rhetorically sensitive" person, which essentially measures a cognitive element of communication attitudes. This test contains elements of this kind of sensitivity, as well as measures that test tendencies to be "noble selves," and "rhetorical reflectors." These last two are probably best described as conative elements, while the first is more aptly described as a cognitive element.

We would expect all of these measures to be interrelated. However, Hart, Carlson, and Eadie found no relationship between RHETSEN (the acronym for rhetorical sensitivity) and communication apprehension. Daly found that communication apprehension was significantly related to both cognitive and conative measures.

One of the most interesting questions is the relationship of all of these measures to instances of communicative behavior. In this respect, not as much has been done as one would like. McCroskey (1978) cites six studies that indicate that high apprehensives engage in less oral communication behavior than do low apprehensives. However, each of these studies cited were instances of communicative behavior in small groups and none were assessments of a predicted tendency of high apprehensives not to communicate when a real choice is offered. Burgoon demonstrated differences in small group behavior as predicted by her test. McCroskey and Richmond (1977) demonstrated that communication apprehension was signifantly related to a conative measure of self-disclosure, and McCroskey and Sheahan (1978) demonstrated a similar effect between communication apprehension and a conative measure of social interaction. The use of conative scales as validators of the behavioral effect of communication apprehension led Page to conclude that "Abundant evidence indicates that the correlations would be higher if *actual* avoidance measures had been used" (1980, p. 96). Porter (1979) agreed with Page, stating that "These studies have yet to confirm a direct behavioral link between CA and communicative behaviors." Porter is correct in that the research he cited fails to show such a direct behavioral link. However, Bostrom (1970) demonstrated conclusively that the PRCS (shown by Daly, 1978b, to be a direct equivalent of the PRCA) had a strong effect in predicting both volunteering behavior and time taken in an unstructured communicative interaction.[2] No direct evidence linking the RHETSEN scale to other communicative attitude measures is available, but one would predict some similarity in the attitude structures.

Communication Attitudes and Communication Skills. One would expect some relationship between attitudes and skills to be present. For example, Phillips' highly successful "rhetoritherapy" program has centered around the acquisition of skill as a means of dealing with reticence. Phillips (1977) also has stated that reticence might be related to listening skills, defining reticence as the "inability to follow the thread of a discussion or to make pertinent remarks in discussions." McCroskey reports that persons high in communication apprehension are perceived as "less socially attractive, less task attractive, less sexually attractive, less competent, less sociable, and less composed" (p. 88). Most of these certainly hint at differences in communicative ability. The most common approach to handle apprehension has been termed "desensitization."

Whether "rhetoritherapy" or "desensitization" should be used in treating emotional problems of communicators is not an easy question. Phillips and McCroskey deal with essentially different kinds of communication attitude and understandably make different kinds of recommendations (Phillips, 1980; McCroskey, 1980). In addition, both are primarily concerned with communication competence, but cheifly those of speaking rather than listening. One would suppose that listening skills would have some relationship to communicative attitudes, but Bostrom and Waldhart (1978a) found no difference between good and bad listeners in apprehension.

Most everyone would agree that we have established a relatively strong relationship between two kinds of communication attitude (affective and conative) and oral communication competence. But what

---

[2] Whether communication apprehension is a "state" or a "trait" is not generally agreed on. Many persons seem to be apprehensive in general, and others are not. For most persons, apprehension is something that is experienced as a function of communicative situations. For a good review of the issues involved, see Beatty, Behnke, and McCallum (1978).

of the other dimensions of communicative attitude? Most teachers of communication would list the enhancement of "positive attitudes about communication" as an important educational goal. But most teaching is aimed specifically at the enhancement of skill rather than the building of attitudes. The connection, if any, between attitudes and skill, then, is an important one. If skills are associated with positive attitudes, then present teaching methods are certainly adequate to teach attitudes.

Listening is probably the most important of the communication skills, and, as Phillips indicated above, would seem to be logically related to reticence. Exactly how listening skills relate to communicative attitudes is not known. Accordingly, this study was designed to provide a comprehensive investigation of the relationships among a number of measures of communication attitudes and communication skills.

Measures of communication attitude were given to 156 students in the introductory public speaking course. These included the short form of the PRCA, Burgoon's reticence scale, a short form of the RHETSEN scale (items selected by using those items having the highest index of discriminability),[3] a measure of self-esteem (Rosenberg, 1962), a self-rating test of communicative ability (similar to Cegala's perceptiveness factor), and a measure of the degree to which respondents enjoyed communication as a social activity.[4] This "communication recreation" test and the "R" scale of Burgoon's test can be thought of as measures of positive affect associated with communication. Burgoon's approach-avoidance scale (AA) can be thought of as a conative measure of communication attitude, or "behavioral intention."

Measures of the students' abilities were also collected. These included their semester totals for their speech grades, written examination scores on course content, and three listening test scores. The listening tests were measures of "short-term" listening (STL), "short-term listening with rehearsal" (STL-R), and traditionally oriented "lecture" listening (Bostrom & Waldhart, 1980).

The intercorrelations among all these measures are presented in Table 4-1. Since there are 66 correlations in Table 4-1, the significance level was corrected, using z transformations. No systematic

---

[3] The effect size for volunteering predictions was reasonably large ($\phi = .535$).

[4] These were items numbered 13, 20, 23, 26, 28, 33, 34, and 38 in the original study.

relationships among measures of ability and measures of attitude appear among the correlations in the table.

TABLE 4-1

Intercorrelations Among Measures Of Communicative Ability And Communication Attitudes

	STL-R	Lect.	Ex.	Speech	CA	Ret.(R)	Ret. (AA)	Self-Esteem	Ability	Rec.	RHETSEN
STL	.33	.20	.16	.16	.02	.08	.00	-.15	.01	.04	-.03
STL-R		.26	.41	.05	-.19	-.19	-.19	-.10	.23	.27	.19
Lect.			.43	.20	-.12	-.10	-.11	-.10	-.07	.15	-.03
Ex.				.41	.01	-.06	-.22	-.05	-.03	.16	-.09
Speech					-.26	-.03	-.21	.04	.20	.01	.13
CA						.40	.15	.25	-.33	-.29	-.36
Ret.(R)							.13	-.01	-.10	-.74	-.14
Ret. (AA)								.44	-.16	-.42	-.30
Self-Esteem									-.28	.04	-.25
Ability										.20	.83
Rec.											.30

R of .25 is significant at the .05 level, an *R* of .29 is significant at the .01 level.

Most of the significant correlations are within each of these two factors, rather than between them. This tendency is not universal, however--STL-R was significantly correlated with the tendency to enjoy communication as recreation, and communication apprehension was significantly though negatively correlated with speech grades. Some correlations are interesting in that they confirm relationships between measures and add to their validity. For example, the high correlation between the "reward" portion of Burgoon's reticence scale and the "recreational communication" measure is certainly what we would expect. The significant relationship between communication apprehension and Burgoon's "expected reward" scale is also what we would expect. Not so obvious, however, is the high positive correlation between RHETSEN and one's estimate of one's own ability in communication. In addition, RHETSEN was significantly related to apprehension, to the "approach-avoidance" measure of reticence, and to "recreational" attitudes.

TABLE 4-2
Factor Loadings--Rotated Factor Pattern

Measure	I	II	III	IV	V
STL	.077	.695	.136	.147	-.010
STL-R	.287	.690	-.239	-.003	-.093
Lecture Listening	-.230	.598	-.161	-.069	.319
Examination	-.110	.584	.002	-.369	.357
Speech Grades	.032	.202	.080	-.018	.816
Comm. Apprehension	-.390	.085	.443	-.129	-.626
Reticence (R)	-.312	.027	.921	-.028	.114
Reticence (AA)	-.137	-.010	.230	.864	.001
Self-Esteem	-.263	.313	-.132	.636	-.360
Ability Estimate	.925	.050	-.041	-.083	.070
Recreational Comm.	.139	.173	-.867	-.245	-.102
RHETSEN	.888	.031	-.131	-.191	.066
Contribution to common variance	*2.07*	*1.85*	*1.99*	*1.47*	*1.46*

To further test the relationships between the measures, factor analysis was performed. A two-factor solution, however, accounted for only 34% of the variance in the matrix. This would indicate, of course, that a simple model of attitudes and abilities does not describe the relationships present here. To account for at least 65% of the variance, a five-factor solution was necessary. The factor pattern for this solution is presented in Table 4-2. Some of the factor loadings in this table are quite interesting. The ability estimate and the RHETSEN scale form a separate factor, as one would predict from examination of the correlation table. The cognitive abilities (the listening measures and the examination score) group together, and Burgoon's reticence scale (R) form a third factor with the recreational measure. Not so obvious, however, is the fourth factor, which is Burgoon's approach-avoidance scale and the self-esteem measure. Apprehension and speech grades form the fifth factor.

Factor analysis, of course, is only one of the many methods of exploring the relationships among measures. Another way of examining these relationships is canonical correlation, which assumes that the "global" dimensions of attitude and ability have greater coherence within dimensions than they do between dimensions. Canonical analysis, however, produced disappointing results. The canonical correlation produced by the first set of canonical variates was only .32. This probably could be interpreted to mean that the structure of the attitudes-skill relationship is more complex than the model assumed by canonical correlation. This statistic presumes situations where variables group themselves into two main categories (Tucker & Chase, 1976), and the variables in this study do not seem to fit such a model.

Another way of analyzing the relationships among these variables would be to explore the "distances" between them. Correlation, of course, is a measure of association, and can be considered a measure of "distance" between measures, directly analogous to physical distances between objects (Woelfel & Fink, 1980, pp. 59-84). Accordingly, the correlations in Table 1 were converted to distance scores and these distances subjected to multiple-dimensional scaling analysis.[5] Figure 4-1 illustrates the two-dimensional model produced by this analysis.

---

[5] The ability test consisted of ten items, and contained statements such as "I am a better communicator than most persons" and "I can usually see through most sales talks." The recreational test consisted of ten items and consisted of such statements as "My idea of fun at a party is good conversation" and "Sometimes arguing can be fun."

The groupings are slightly different from those produced by the factor analysis. Burgoon's approach-avoidance scale, for example, is positioned in the same quadrant as her reward scale, but the two are not closely related. Apprehension, speech grades, ability estimates, and RHETSEN grouped together quite closely. These differences are not unexpected.

In an attempt to clarify the relationships further, three-dimensional analysis was perfomed. These relationships are illustrated in Figure 4-2. The addition of the third dimension significantly reduced the

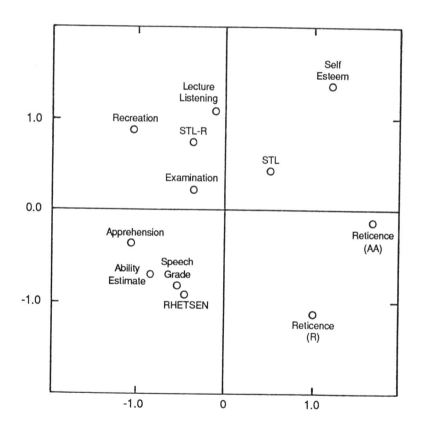

FIGURE 4-1. Two-dimensional analysis of factors.

"stress" in the model and acounted for a great deal more of the variance (R^2 = .926 for three dimensions, R^2 = .801 for two). In the three-dimensional model, apprehension, RHETSEN, recreational attitudes and short-term listening (rehearsal) form a clear cluster, while speech scores, examination scores, lecture listening, and short-term listening form another clear cluster. The two measures of reticence, as well as the self-esteem measure, seem to exhibit complete independence of the other measures and of one another.

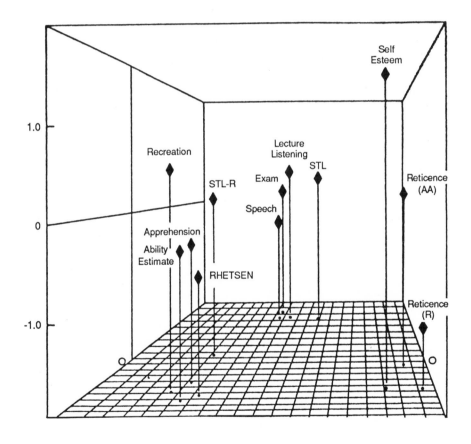

FIGURE 4-2. Three-dimensional analysis of factors.

The implication of these findings seems fairly clear: that communicative attitudes, at least as measured by these tests, are probably not merely different manifestations of a common underlying structure, but are apparently different in interesting ways. No systematic relationship to communicative ability seems to be present. The close relationship of communication apprehension to oral communication grades is logical, as is its grouping with the RHETSEN and ability estimates. The dimensional scaling produced different groupings than did factor analysis. This is logical, since factor analysis depends upon simple association between measures and dimensional scaling not only depends upon these associations but also upon each measure's relationship among all other measures in the analysis. So both methods of grouping are of interest, but the dimensional scaling probably contains more relational information than does the factor analysis. However, different types of multidimensional scaling can often produce slightly different results (H. Sypher, 1980). The tendency of good listeners (as measured by STL-R) to report that they enjoy communication as a recreational activity is intriguing. It may be that one of the factors that facilitates the enjoyment of conversation and other recreational communicative activites is the ability to store the immediate contents of the conversation in the short-term memory. This relationship bears further investigation, especially in the light of evidence that short-term listening and short-term memory are apparently different processes (Bostrom & Bryant, 1980).

While Burgoon had reported that her reticence scale correlated .531 with communication apprehension, this investigation produced significant correlation for only the reward portion of the scale (.402). The conative portion of her scale (approach-avoidance) and communication apprehension were not significantly related. But the scaling analysis, which depended on the overall relationships among the various measures, places this scale in almost the same position as communication apprehension. These anomalous findings might be resolved by decomposing the PRCA scale into private and public components. Certainly this would be an interesting analysis. The conative scale had a strong (.435) relationship to self-esteem, and the tendency to use communication as recreation (-.737).[6] Burgoon's "R" scale is clearly an important aspect of the process of evaluating

---

[6] Since a high correlation would indicate that the two measures were closely associated, positive correlations were subtracted from 1.0 to determine their "distance." Thus distance from RHETSEN to the ability estimate was .167. The distance between RHETSEN and STL was 1.032. The procedure ALSCAL was used to perform the

communication, while the "AA" (approach-avoidance) may be related to other personality factors. It is worth noting that Burgoon's two scales depict clearly different factors and the concept of "reticence" should be separated accordingly.

Rhetorical sensitivity (RHETSEN) exhibited a number of predictable relationships--it correlated negatively with the "AA" factor of the reticence scale (-.295) but not significantly with the "R" scale. It also was negatively correlated with apprehension (-.395) and with self-esteem (.295). In addition, it was significantly related to recreational attitudes and with ability estimates. All of these relationships transcend the "unselfishness" notion that underlies RHETSEN and add support to its authors' contentions that this attitude is of fundamental importance in describing communicative orientations. In addition, the close relationship between the RHETSEN items and the ability estimate items hint at a possible relationship between Cegala's IIS and the RHETSEN scales. The underlying rationale of both of these scales (communicative competence) certainly contributes to similarity.

However, one must be cautious in overinterpreting these data. The scales used in this investigation were attenuated versions of the ones presented by Hart, Carlson, and Eadie (1980) and Cegala, Savage, Bruner, and Conrad (1982).

The interrelationships among the cognitive measures of ability seem rather stable, being very similar to earlier reports of these tests. (Bostrom, Waldhart, & Brown, 1979; Bostrom & Waldhart, 1980). But the speech scores seem to be more strongly related to some of the attitude measures than were the listening scores.

No simple structure apparently underlies the measures of commmunication attitudes, which argues strongly against an interpretation af these measures as different manifestions of a more generally held evaluation structure concerning communication. But the relationship of this general evaluation to communication abilities is not as clear. Affective communication attitude is definitely related to oral performance, and short-term listening is interestingly related to a certain form of positive affect concerning communication. But there

---

analysis, using the Euclidean model. At the suggestion of James McCroskey, the sign of the apprehension measures were reversed before entering the dimensional scaling analysis. Thus, in Figure 4-1, CA appears to be in the same cluster as ability estimates, grades, and RHETSEN. "Lack of apprehension" would be a better label for Figure 4-1.

seems to be no definite overall pattern between abilities and attitude.

Almost all those involved in communication education list the acquisition of positive attitudes about communication as an important educational objective. "Rhetoritherapy" and "desensitization" are two techniques that make specific predictions about narrowly defined types of communication attitude and communication skills. Most pedagogical theory, however, depends on the assumption that the acquisition of skills will probably bring about the enhancement of attitudes. The data presented here clearly indicate that we must be more careful in our specification of what we mean by both attitudes and abilites, as well as what specific relationships we attribute to them. While there are some specific connections between skills and attitude, it is probably safe to say that we cannot depend on the acquisition of skills to build positive attitudes about communication.

CHAPTER FIVE

Semantic Decoding, Short-Term Storage, Sensation Seeking, and Recall of Information

> And should we not study grammar, which knows
> how to control everything, even Kings?
>
> ....Moliere

In the previous chapters, we have examined the role of media in the presentation of information, methods for assessment of listening skills, and the conceptual foundations of listening. Obviously, one of the most important factors in listening is the decoding of the signal once it is acquired and retained. In this chapter we will examine some of the factors relating to semantic decoding and listening skill.

Decoding

It is typical to assume that the apprehension of the signal and its immediate storage are the first step in receiving behavior. Most assume that the second step is decoding, or matching phonemes to lexical and grammatical structures. Many have described these structures as "semantic memory." Squire (1986) has detailed some of the ways in which semantic memory differs from episodic memory, and Chang (1986) has reviewed some of the different phenomena that semantic memory models have been invoked to explain. He concludes that both "network" and "feature" models are equally defensible.

Some of the aspects of semantic memory that have been studied include "category sizes" (Collins and Quillian, 1972), "relatedness," (Kintsch, 1980), and "familiarity" (McCloskey, 1980). And though Baddely and Dale (1968), Kintsch and Busche (1969), and Squire (1986) consider semantic memory to be part of long-term storage, Schulman (1972) has demonstrated that some semantic decoding does take place in shorter temporal situations. Further evidence is furnished by Pellegrino, Siegel, and Dhawan (1975), who showed that short-term memory for words was different than it was for pictures. Camden, Motley, and Baars (1982) deduce that in encoding behavior, graphemic elements may have a priority over phonetic elements. Whether this difference is due to structural/organizational elements, or merely habit, is not known. And whether the temporal organization in encoding is the same as decoding is also not clear. Woodall and Folger (1981) have illustrated how encoding is influenced by context; specific nonverbal cues influence the "episodes" that they examined. They argue for an increased role for context effects in encoding models. If semantic processing is generally involved in encoding, it ought logically to be so in decoding as well, and the strictly linear relationship of storage and decoding may not be accurate.

That short-term processing is implicated in decoding seems logical, but the nature of this relationship is far from clear. Apprehension of phonemes clearly involves short-term listening, and if it is true that semantic elements are simultaneously employed, and nature of short term listening is affected. On the other hand, if the linear model of listening (p. 14), is accurate, then we would expect little semantic encoding to take place in the first few seconds of the process.

One instance of semantic processing that seems obviously connected to short-term storage is complex grammatical decoding, where input must be stored before the relationships of the individual words can be retained and further processed through invoking some grammatical principle.

The work of Astri Heen Wold (1978) offers striking evidence for the operation of differential grammatical structures. She examined the retention of adjectives in "free" and "bound" grammatical contexts. "Bound" adjectives were retained better, indicating that significant amounts of semantic structure were involved in initial processing. Her sentences were of the following types:

I. When the sun goes down, it is beautiful, cool, and pleasant.

II. It is beautiful, cool, and pleasant when the sun goes down.

III. Beautiful, cool, and pleasant it is when the sun goes down.

In the first sentence the phrase "When the sun goes down" binds the adjectives and gives them a potential structure for subsequent processing. In sentence III, the three adjectives must be held momentarily in short-term storage before any semantic structure can be invoked. Heen Wold's subjects successfully processed over fifty percent of the adjectives in the first type of sentences, but only thirty-seven percent of the adjectives in the third type of sentence. In other words, the semantic networking[1] assisted processing to a significant degree.

Listening: Decoding, Storage, or Both?

Obviously, both short-term processing (STL) and semantic decoding are involved in the acquisition of information. Writers in communication have traditionally assumed that "style," or language choice, can play an important part in retention of information (Shamo & Bittner, 1972), but explanations about why this should be so are conspicuous by their absence. Monsell (1984), for example, speculates that it is the job of the "input register" to hold the words or phonemes long enough for semantic encoding processes to be brought into play. If this is the case, then persons who cannot activate the input register would either encode immediately or lose everything. If they do the kind of grammatical processing suggested by Heen Wold's data, material presented in a grammatically sensible structure would be easily processed, while material not having structure would be more difficult.

The standard description of how items are precessed into long-term storage is highly linear (Loftus & Loftus, 1976). If this is an accurate description, then a deficiency at one point of the process would clearly result in deficiencies at later temporal stages. A good way to identify such deficiencies would be to compare persons with differential aptitudes at each stage in the process and see how the end product is affected.

If the procedure is an orderly one, then it should follow that persons who show high aptitude for any of the intermediate steps logically ought to do better on the final step--long-term retention. In fact, they do (Bostrom & Waldhart, 1980; Bostrom, Waldhart, & Brown, 1979; Bostrom, 1980; Waldhart & Bostrom, 1981), but the relationship is a

---

[1] "Networking" is only one of the many descriptions of semantic memory. Heen Wold's invocation of grammatical sctructure is also consistent with "features," "relatedness," or "category" views of semantic memory. Chang (1986) presents a detailed description of each of these interpretations.

weak one (R^2 = .09). Perhaps semantic decoding intervenes in the process in a way that is not clear. Assessing differences in decoding ability might help us understand how the process works. One interesting explanation might be that one process is temporally prior to another, that is, one is definitely needed before another. We might look at the process by inferring temporal relationships from the presence or absence of specific skills.

Affect and Information Processing

The sharpening of certain types of affect has been shown to influence encoding behavior (Motley & Camden, 1985). It seems reasonable to assume that decoding might similarly be affected. Although most affective arousal is situationally determined, sometimes personality differences also produce particular affects. One kind of personality factor of great interest would be that which creates affective reactions to new information. Zuckerman (1978) has identified individuals who are "sensation seekers," whose lifestyle represents tendencies to seek arousal. Part of this sensation seeking often includes the search for information. Donohew, Nair, and Finn (1984) have detailed some of the ways that arousal is implicated in information-seeking behavior. This kind of arousal might well explain some of the internal dynamics of short-term storage and semantic processing.

The specific interactions among semantic processing, short-term storage, and arousal would seem to be of great interest. We might ask the following specific questions: Do persons who exhibit less ability in storing phonemes in short-term memory (those who are poor in STL) correspondingly show difficulties in semantic decoding when the decoding task is more difficult; and less when the decoding task is less difficult? Do those who decode (semantically) more efficiently and those who are more efficient in short-term storage show correspondingly better retention in a long-term information acquisition task? Does long-term retention consisting of factual material only affect STL, STL-R, and semantic encoding ability more than a retention that involves some implicative process? Do individuals who have positive affect associated with the acquisition of new information ("sensation seekers") retain better in a long-term task, depending on STL and decoding ability?

Answers to these questions can be obtained by examining interactions between STL and semantic encoding and by interaction effects involving type of recall, STL, STL-R, and encoding ability. In addition the interactions among both short-term tasks and long-term tasks is also of great interest.

Experiment I

Method

Respondents were 226 students enrolled in an introductory communication course at the University of Kentucky. Soon after the beginning of the semester, they listened to a tape with strings of letters and numbers in order to measure "short-term" listening (STL), "short-term" listening with rehearsal (STL-R), interpretive listening and lecture listening (as described in chapter two). The short-term strings consisted of both letters and numbers, and were randomly ordered. Measurement was accomplished by asking questions which required the respondent to hold the entire string in mind. The procedure was exactly same as that devised by Sternberg (1969), and the size of the strings, reaction times, and criterion for success were adapted from his data. The test "success rate" was set to match the findings of Baddely and Warrington (1970), who found that at least six elements were needed in each string. A specific test item might sound like "In the series of letters S A Y L E, the fourth letter is _____." An immediate response was necessary, and no more than ten seconds was provided for a response. STL-R was measured in essentially the same way, except that respondents needed to keep the string in mind for at least forty seconds before the question was asked. All of the test items were presented by audiotape. In addition, a distracting stimulus was dubbed on the tape to make the task more difficult. Following this task, a short (eight minute) lecture was presented to each of the respondents and multiple choice questions asked immediately following.

Delivery plays such an important part in a standardized test that face-to-face delivery must be ruled out on the basis of consistency. Each person varies so widely in delivery skills that little, if any, comparison is valid among different "deliverers." In order to "standardize," or establish reasonable bases for comparison from place to place, some sort of recorded message is vital. But whether to use audio- or video- recording is an important question.

You will recall from chapter three that messages presented on audiotape more closely resemble messages presented face-to-face than do messages presented on videotape. Searle (1984) had previously demonstrated that this similarity seemed to hold regardless of whether the face-to-face presentation was an uninterrupted lecture or involved interactive techniques such as questions. Since a "live," face-to-face interaction is probably the standard against which any taped stimulus should be compared, and given the cost of good videotape production, audiotape seems to be the best way to present the information. However, it must be noted that Searle's data showed small but significant interactions among gender of respondent and medium of transmission.[2] This interaction is consistent with the kinds of gender differences reported by Gunter and his associates (Gunter, Furnham, and Gietson, 1984; Gunter, Barry, and Clifford, 1982). All this means is that there are real gender differences which vary according to medium used. The differences, however, are so small that ignoring them for the purpose of this analysis is probably not going to affect the ultimate outcome.

Semantic decoding was measured by repeating Heen Wold's sentences. These sentences were presented to all of the respondents approximately forty days following the listening assessment. In a pilot study, the exact sentences (with three adjectives) proved to be relatively easy for American students, so a fourth adjective was added to each. Eight sentences were used.

Results

Though the initial testing of the Heen Wold sentences had been done in Norwegian, the relationships held good for responses in English. Table 5-1 illustrates the percentages of correct responses in the Heen Wold data and the present study. The proportions are roughly comparable.

Table 5-1 shows that the performances of American students were slightly better, a phenomenon for which no ready explanation is available. In addition, the differences between Condition II and Condition III were not apparent in the subjects in the present study. Perhaps the American students were more highly motivated than the Norwegian students. Great care was taken to reproduce the stimuli as nearly as possible, though we should recognize that without an original audiotape (not possible from the Heen Wold stimuli) an exact reproduction wasn not possible. The percentile differences, however, were very close (about 7% in each case).

---

[2] Women were consistently better at decoding information presented on videotape and men were better at encoding information presented on audiotape.

TABLE 5-1

*Correct Responses by Condition (Sentences)
in Norwegian and American Students*

Condition	Norwegian	American
I	51.3%	61.7%
II	44.1%	53.2%
III	37.6%	51.3%

Having determined that the grammatical structure had approximately the same effects in English as it did in Norwegian, the next task was to examine what realtionships, if any, existed between grammatical structure presented and the ability to take in material in the short-term task.

There are many ways of investigating this relationship, but the one chosen here was to create a bivariate classification using the scores in short-term listening. Respondents, therefore, were divided into high and low scorers on the short-term task. A high score was defined as one equal to or better than 9 out of 12 correct and a low score was defined as equal to or worse than 6 of 12 correct. The reader might wish to compare these distributions to those in Table 2-1 in chapter two. This division is approximately equal to a separation of one standard deviation away from the mean of these scores. This classification, along with gender and sentence type, formed the basis for a comparison of good listeners and poor listeners, and differential effects of the varying grammatical structures on each . An interactive analysis of variance was used to test for differences.

TABLE 5-2

Correct Responses by Condition (Sentences)
and Performance on STL (Short-Term Listening)

Condition	High STL	Low STL
I	16.83	23.75
II	19.16	18.92
III	17.11	17.40

The results of this analysis were not as expected. The three-way interaction among short-term listening ability, gender, and grammatical form was not present. However, a two-way interaction between listening ability and grammatical form was exhibited ($F = 5.83$, $p <$ .003, $df = 1,145$, $E = .173$).[3] The means are presented in Table 5-2 and are described in Figure 5-1. Poor scorers in STL encoded much more efficiently in Condition I, while no real differences were apparent in the other conditions. Duncan's test revealed that the mean of the low STL-Condition I respondents was significantly different from all other means, but no other mean differences were significant. Apparently, those who were poor in STL apparently did something that enhanced their effectiveness in storing the adjectives in short-term memory. One would not expect those who were poor in STL to be more effective in storing information, but could only do it when the task was more easily processed grammatically.

---

[3] All tests in this study used Type III sums of squares, since the design reflects random, rather than fixed effects (Hays, 1973, pp. 524-533).

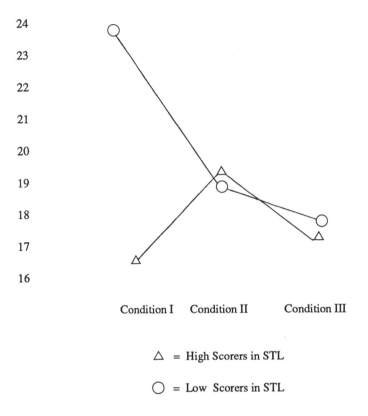

FIGURE 5-1. Interaction between Semantic Decoding and STL.

This finding was so surprising that specific analyses were undertaken to examine this effect further. Within Condition I all scores (including those originally excluded from the analysis) were analyzed to test this relationship. A strong linear relationship was observed in these scores (R^2 = .42). While certainly not conclusive, the linear nature of this relationship adds credibility to an interpretation of immediate decoding. In other words, within the affected cell, STL scores and grammatical decoding were inversely related.

In other words, the low inverse correlation within the group of scores seems to indicate that some systematic relationship exists between those two variables. It is certainly not the relationship that was originally expected, however.

TABLE 5-3

*Retention of Information Presented by Lecture
as a Function of Gender, STL, and Decoding Ability*

Encoding Ability	Males		Females	
	High STL	Low STL	High STL	Low STL
High	7.38	9.00	7.99	7.13
Low	8.45	8.63	7.36	8.63

Following that test, all of these analyses were then repeated for high and low scorers in STL-R. No interactions were present, nor did STL-R apparently affect any of the simple effects. This outcome certainly casts doubt on the notion that difficult grammatical decoding is importantly mediated by STL. If, then, that decoding is an independent skill, its interaction with STL in longer-term tasks would be of great interest. Accordingly, the scores on the Heen Wold task were used to divide respondents into two groups (High and Low) according to decoding "ability."

One would expect that both STL and decoding skill would enhance retention on lecture material. Analysis of these data did not support this notion. Table 5-3 presents the means for lecture retention scores analyzed by gender, decoding ability, and STL. The three-way interaction among these variables was significant ($F = 4.22$, $df = 1$, 159, $p < .04$, $E = .08$). Figure 5-2 illustrates this interaction. For males, the good short term listeners who were poor decoders did worse than all other groups. For females, a crossed interaction was present--for good short-term listeners, encoding skill facilitated retention on the lecture, but for poor short-term listeners, encoding skill had the opposite effect.

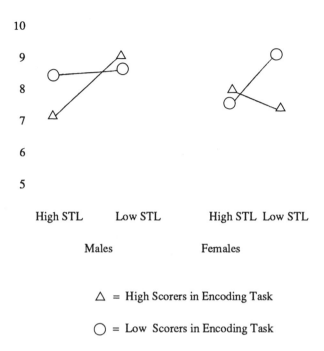

High STL   Low STL   High STL Low STL

Males   Females

△ = High Scorers in Encoding Task

○ = Low Scorers in Encoding Task

FIGURE 5-2. Interactions among Gender, STL, and Decoding.

To examine the effect further, the types of lecture retention items were divided into two groups: those requiring only memory of facts; and those requiring some implicatory principle. A similar three-way interaction was observed ($F = 3.82$, $df = 1, 150$, $p < .05$, $= .066$). While the effect size was approximately the same, the nature of the three-way interaction was more extreme than it was in the total scores. For items containing an implicatory step, however, no significant effects were observed.

The means are presented in Table 5-4. One cell (factual questions, high decoding ability, and low STL-R) is considerably higher than the rest, probably causing a good deal of the three-way interaction. If this difference is a consistent one, the hypothesis of a linera processing model is proably not going to be tenable. It seems as if the decoding ability may be the more powerful predictor of the factual question. Why this should not have been present in implicative questions is not clear.

TABLE 5-4

Retention of Information presented by Lecture as a Function of Question Type, STL-R, and Decoding Ability

Decoding Ability	Factual Questions		Implicative Questions	
	High STL-R	Low STL-R	High STL-R	Low STL-R
High	2.94	4.13	3.33	.39
Low	3.45	3.35	3.06	3.37

Ability in short-term listening with rehearsal (STL-R) did not exhibit the same effects as were shown in STL. The interaction between grammatical form and listening ability that was present in STL was not present for STL-R. The interaction among gender, encoding ability, and STL in affecting lecture scores (overall) was not present when STL-R was substituted for the listening ability measure. However, an interaction among the different types of retention, STL-R, and decoding ability was evident ($F = 5.13$, $df = 1, 231$, $p < .024$, $E = .063$). These means are presented in Table 5-4. The interactions are described in Figure 5-3. Although this is three-way interaction, inspection of Figure 5-3 shows that the principal differences appear in the factual questions condition and among those respondents who were high scorers in the encoding task. Among these persons, being low in STL-R ability actually helped them recall lecture items.

In short, the results of Experiment I are not in agreement with a linear explanation of information processing. Previous findings indicate that the ability to store information in the short term affects other kinds of information processing. This would seem to preclude good processing in a second step. These data indicate that this does not seem to be the case when grammatical structure is invoked.

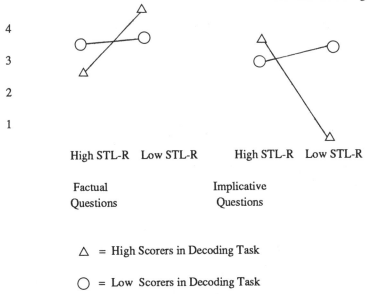

High STL-R   Low STL-R   High STL-R   Low STL-R

Factual   Implicative
Questions   Questions

△ = High Scorers in Decoding Task

○ = Low Scorers in Decoding Task

FIGURE 5-3. Interactions among STL-R, Question
Type, and Decoding Ability.

Experiment II

Method

Subjects were 232 students drawn from the same subject pool as those in Experiment I. They too listened to a tape with strings of letters and numbers in order to measure "short-term" listening (STL), "short-term" listening with rehearsal (STL-R), interpretive listening, and lecture listening.

Semantic decoding was measured by repeating Heen Wold's sentences, but in this instance only two grammatical forms were utilized (Condition I and Condition III from Experiment I).

In addition, respondents completed Zuckerman's (1978) 40-item inventory of sensation seeking. These 40 items represent a fairly broad range of activities, so the entire scale was subjected to factor analysis. Three distinct factors emerged: seeking physical danger (hang gliding, sky diving), recreational activites (loud music, drugs, party people), and less specific items (unpredictable people, art with clashing colors, exploring new plans). The latter set of 11 items was used as an indication of affect associated with new information. Respondents were divided into high and low groups, with each determined by a score at least one standard deviation away from the mean. This reduced the respondent pool to 87 respondents.

Results

The differences in condition (grammatical form) were not identical to those in Experiment I, in that respondents in Experiment II achieved greater accuracy. Condition I respondents achieved a 95% accuracy rate, and Condition II (Condition III in Experiment I) achieved a 78% accuracy rate. The two, of course, were significantly different ($p < .001$).

As in Experiment I, respondents were divided into high and low scorers on the short-term task. A high score was defined as one equal to or better than 9 out of 12 correct and a low score was defined as equal to or worse than 6 of 12 correct. This division was approximately equal to one standard deviation away from the mean of these scores. Then this designation, along with gender, sentence type, and sensation-seeking, was entered into a four-way analysis of variance to predict the number of successful retentions in the Heen Wold task.

The results of this analysis were different from those shown in Experiment I. The four-way interaction was not significant, nor were any of other interactions. Main effects for sentence type were present, and a main effect for STL was also present. This main effect was the opposite of that in Experiment I. Good short-term listeners exhibited a mean of 21.9 adjectives remembered and poor ones exhibited a mean of 20.76. This difference was small, but significant ($F = 3.71, p < .04$ $df = 1, 231, E = .094$). The anomalous (at least to the author) effects in Experiment I were not present in Experiment II. No interactions of the previous type appeared, and the means for STL were more in keeping with a facilitation role for STL as it relates to the adjectives remembered.

Next the effects of gender, grammatical encoding ability, sensation seeking, and STL were tested to see how they affected the longer term retention in the lecture task. An interaction was observed between sensation seeking and STL ($F = 4.88; p < .01; df = 1, 86; E = .11$).

TABLE 5-5

Lecture Retention Scores as a
Function of STL and Sensation Seeking

	Sensation Seeking	
STL	High	Low
High	9.07	10.51
Low	9.17	8.15

Another interaction was observed between decoding ability and sensation seeking (F = 3.85; p < .04; df = 1, 85; E = .08.) The means for this interaction are presented in Table 5-5. A clear interaction is present in this table, attributable to the cell in which STL is high and sensation seeking is high.

Initially, the interaction seems odd, but when we remember that the lecture task consisted of listening to a relatively boring lecture and remembering details from it, the interaction presented above makes better sense. Essentially it indicates that the best listener is an individual who does not bore easily and has some fundamental acquisitive skill. This acquisitive skill seemed to make no difference to those who were high in sensation seeking. This interaction is equal to one standard deviation away from the mean of these scores. Then this designation, along with gender and sentence type, was entered into a three-way analysis of variance to predict the number of successful retentions in the Heen Wold task, graphically presented in Figure 5-5.

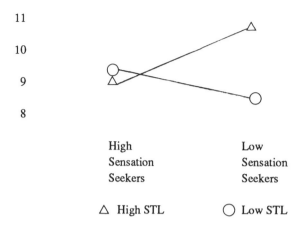

FIGURE 5-5. Interactions among STL and Sensation Seeking.

The next comparison involved lecture retention scores arranged by decoding ability and sensation seeking. In this comparison, we look to see if good decoders who were also high in sensation seeking did as well as poor decoders who were high in sensation seeking. The reverse was true for those who were low in sensation seeking. This interaction is presented graphically in Figure 5-6. Clearly sensation seeking is implicated in the process, but certainly not in the predicted direction.

If one would simply examine the means of the sensation seeking scale, one would miss a good deal of information about these interacting abilities. The sensation seeking scales produce no visible effects at all when viewed as a main effect. When interactions with STL and decoding ability are examined, interesting relationships appear. For example, the retention scores in the high sensation seekers show no differences due to STL, but in the low sensation seekers large STL differences are apparent. In other words, low sensation seeking and high STL combine to produce better retention of lecture items. This is certainly not in accordance with earlier predictions.

The same tests were separately performed on test items which were primarily of a factual nature as opposed to those of an implicative nature (see pages 18-19). The interaction between sensation seeking and STL (presented in Table 5) was present for both factual and implicative items, while the interaction between grammatical decoding and sensation seeking (presented in Table 6) only occurred in factual recall rather than implication. The selection of tests in this fashion is only intended to be suggestive, rather than conclusive.

TABLE 5-6

*Lecture Retention Scores as a Function
of Decoding Ability and Sensation Seeking*

Decoding Ability	Sensation Seeking	
	High	Low
High	8.73	9.71
Low	10.25	8.81

Discussion

Phonetic Storage and Grammatical Decoding. The assumption that phonetic storage is a prior condition to decoding cannot be maintained, if one assumes that those scoring poorly on this kind of scale are truly not storing phonemes in other tasks. It is possible that the "string" task does not reflect the kind of phonetic storage that is hypothesized in conventional views of information processing. The fact that the string task does have some relationships with other kinds of short- and long-term processing leads me to the concusion that short-term storage and immediate grammatical decoding are not simply related. Experiment II demonstrated the predicted relationship, but when combined with the data from Experiment I no differences can be maintained. Apparently the decoding tasks were easier in Experiment II, but it is difficult to see how this would have created a differential effect.

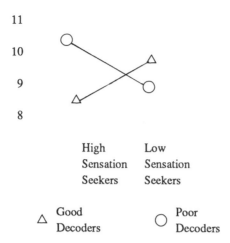

FIGURE 5-6. Interactions among Grammatical
Decoding and Sensation Seeking.

Decoding and STL as Predictors of Lecture Retention. Obviously
both STL and decoding do affect subsequent retention of lecture
material, but when these two factors alone are relied on, only shaky
assertions can be made. Experiment I demonstrated a number of
differences that are probably not dependable, since Experiment II
shows us the strength of the personality factor in this process. The
easiest interpretation of the data in Experiment I is to say that the
sensation seekers were not identified and that the results are therefore
suspect. Important gender differences are involved in the entire
process, and the data present above do not show these consistently in
this context. We might examine this factor in greater detail as we
continue to study listening.

Sensation Seeking. The most promising outcome of this study is
the identification of an interesting interaction among this personality
variable and two kinds of immediate processing and lecture retention.
Being a good phonetic storer only helps you if you are a low sensation
seeker; and being a better decoder only helps you if you are a high
sensation seeker. Normally we would expect high sensation seekers to
do more poorly on the lecture task as presented, since it is a truly boring
lecture (devised that way because it is a test, and made to be difficult.
The high sensation seekers are probably victims of the "wandering
mind" phenomenon so familiar to teachers of listening, and are not able
to benefit from their abilities in STL. The semantic decoding task is
more difficult to interpret. Just what these good decoders who were
also high sensation seekers found in the lecture to help them store

factual items better is puzzling. An obvious explanation is that the good decoders were characterized by other language processing skills (such as rapid reading). While previous research has showed only modest connections between reading and lecture retention (Bostrom & Waldhart, 1988), it may be that the addition of the sensation seeking scale might illuminate this process.

Nonetheless, the discovery that sensation seeking plays a major role in data processing gives a clue about why so much of previous listening research seems so erratic. Other personality and attitude measures ought to researched in this fashion. Some of these might include communication apprehension (McCroskey, 1977), reticence (Burgoon, 1976, 1977) self-esteem (Rosenberg, 1962), ability estimates, recreational communication, and RHETSEN (Hart, Carlson, and Eadie, 1980). The most obvious candidate however, is "receiver apprehension (see chapter seven).

Clearly something happens in the first few seconds of data processing that is quite interesting and has effects on subsequent facilitation. One explanation might be that those who process well in the first few seconds are actually performing too well, taking in much more data than the task demands. Running speech has an information content that is much lower than these STL string processors, and those who are good at it might well be also taking in irrelevant data that inhibits long-term retention of speech content.

The conjectures raised by these data are interesting, but need to be tempered by careful study. Different types of semantic decoding (other than the Heen Wold task) need to be compared, as well as associational aspects of semantic encoding.

Nonethless, the prospects involved in the study of short-term retention and semantic decoding are exciting ones. Since they represent the most basic elements in receiving behavior, their study promises to reap great rewards. How these psycho-physical differences might interact with personality and motivation factors could contribute importantly to our understanding of the process of receiving information.

CHAPTER SIX

Making Sense of Data:
Constructs, Schemas,
and Concepts

Margaret Fitch-Hauser

> Remembrance and reflection, how allied!
> What thin partitions sense from thought divide!
>
> ...Alexander Pope

As communicators we have long been concerned with organizing messages in order to make them more coherent. Now we are discovering that our brains seem to organize information as we perceive, interpret, and recall messages. When the brain organizes information, we have typically called the process "schematic" processing. This assumes that the processing uses a systematic organizational hierarchy called *schema*.

Linguists and psychologists have studied schemas for over 50 years, but only recently have scholars begun to realize their importance as they affect the way we understand and interpret information that we receive.

Schemas are large units of knowledge that organize much of what we know about the world around us. As such, they provide a basis upon which we make sense out of incoming stimuli. Without such a basis, information has little relevance to the person on the receiving end of a message. The importance of schemas in our intellectual functioning has been clearly brought home in the recent book, *Cultural Literacy*. In this book, Hirsch (1987) promotes the idea that education must establish a common body of knowledge. He suggests, however, that it is not the individual details that are important, instead it is the categories or schema that are important for these categories are essential to understanding the details. For example, Appomatox Courthouse has little significance to one who has no schema for the Civil War.

As large units of knowledge that help us interpret and understand information, schemas are an important concern of anyone who studies how we take in information. One such means of taking in information is listening. This chapter focuses on schema and the role of schemas in listening.

Schemas

Research in information processing strongly supports the notion that we use some type of plan or blueprint to interpret, store, and recall information. These plans have been variously labeled scripts, schemas, prototypes, and stereotypes. A close examination of each of these labels, however, will reveal that each refers to something slightly different than the rest.

The most generalizable difference appears to be in how general or specific the plan is. Schemas, in the realm of receiving information and perceiving the world around us, are large complex units of knowledge that organize much of what we know about general categories of objects, events, people, and information. Another term which has sometimes been used synonomously with schema is prototype. However, prototypes are much narrower in focus than schemas. Instead of being large, broad categories, prototypes are much narrower in scope. For example oration could be considered as a prototype while oral communication might be classified as a schema. As the example shows, prototypes are more specific in terms of the details of the plan than are schemas. Consequently, the broader schema is more widely generalizable.

Two more categories of plans are scripts and stereotypes. Scripts are blueprints of textual information such as stories or events. Scripts serve the role of providing organized structures which are used to perceive and recall information presented in stereotypic patterns. Romance novels provide an excellent example of a script. Aficionados of this entertainment genre have a script of how the stories should be structured. Similar to scripts only in that they establish expectations used on perceiving and storing information, stereotypes are yet another information plan that we use to encode messages. Stereotypes, however, apply to our expectations of people instead of messages.

Although we have discussed four different types of blueprints that we use in taking in, interpreting, and storing information, we can easily argue that what we have actually been doing is discussing a single system that contains several identifiable subsystems. The general system is schemas and the other types of plans can be considered as merely subsystems of that general construct.

Thorndyke and Hayes-Roth (1979) surveyed the various memory models which utilize the schema construct and found that four elements are essential to any notion of schema:

1. A schema represents prototypical abstraction of the complex concepts it represents.

2. Schemas are induced from past experience with numerous examplars of the complex concept it represents.

3. A schema can guide the organization of incoming information into clusters of knowledge that are "instantiations" of the schema.

4. When one of the constituent concepts of a schema is missing in the input, its features can be inferred from "default values" in the schema. In general, Thorndyke and Hayes-Roth feel that a schema is an abstraction of a set of concepts and relationships that explicitly occur in a number of unique contexts. This abstraction of concepts and relationships provides a pattern for the individual to use in processing information.

Schank (1982) suggests that schemas not only provide prototypical abstractions of events, they also provide a means of linking the prototype with situational variables. In his system, Schank redefined scripts as "memory organization packets" or MOPs. The MOPs are made up of generalizable clusters of events in which the MOP specifies the organization of the scene and adds information from the specific context. The second part of his system is composed of "thematic organization packets" or TOPs. A TOP is an interaction pattern of goals and plans which function as structures in memory and take into account the specific conditions of the event.

Based upon these conceptualizations of schema, we can present a generalizable definition. Schema can be defined as data structures for representing generic concepts which are stored in memory as well as those structures used to put the information together for transmission. Keeping this definition in mind, Rumelhart and Ortony (1977) found four characteristics of a schema which qualify it as a means of representing knowledge in memory. The first characteristic is that schemas have variables. Secondly, schemas can embed one within the other. Thirdly, schemas represent generic concepts which vary in their levels of abstraction. The fourth characteristic is that schemata represent knowledge areas and definitions. These four aspects seem to explain a schemata's ability to cope with encoding and decoding information. This is especially relevant in light of postulations about how information is processed in memory.

Schema and Information Processing

One such notion about memory was postulated by Bobrow and Norman (1975). They theorized that the human is guided by a central, limited processor which utilizes schemas. They felt that three reasons justify this conclusion:

1. The central processor gives the system coherence. "Without purpose, the system will fail to pursue a line of inquiry in any directed fashion" (p. 146).

2. The central processor controls the number of purposes thus minimizing confusion. In other words, there must be some type of "central motivational process" which can select among different purposes.

3. Some mechanism with access to all memory schemas must guide the interpretive process. This guide is needed to know when a schema is filled out and to judge the goodness of fit between information and schemas.

Bobrow and Norman felt that information is processed by using this central limited processor and that the central processor is needed for the system to respond to the environment in a rational, coherent manner. Based on information available on how the human being functions, they felt that the central processor allocates the resources among the various functions of the system. However, the system is limited. First, the system is data-limited. This limitation occurs when quality of input confuses the mapping process. Due to such confusion there may be some difficulty in mapping input into the memory structure. Secondly, the system is resource-limited. This limitation occurs when the mapping procedure is obstructed by lack of appropriate memory structures. When this limitation exists the demands may exceed the system's ability to cope.

Because the system is limited, it utilizes techniques which allow it to process information in the most efficient manner. The use of schemas is one such technique. Bobrow and Norman (1975) felt that their central processor utilizes schemas in at least two situations. First, schemas are used when the system attempts to reduce any ambiguity or fill holes in an existing information category. In other words, schema provide the guidelines for the system's search for the information needed to complete a category so it can achieve closure. Secondly, the system utilizes schema when it tries to associate new information with existing information categories. In this capacity, the schema help the receiver be sensitive to novel information or help confirm or dispute hypotheses (Rumelhart, 1975).

By taking this approach to schematic processing, we can take into account our ability to process many different types of information. According to Tulving (1985) and numerous others (i.e., Seifert et al., 1985) any consideration of how human beings receive and process information must take into account the multifaceted nature of human information processing. Tulving (1985) developed a ternary classification which includes episodic, semantic, and procedural classifications. Episodic memory allows one to remember past events and relate them to present or future events. (Schemas as defined earlier could easily be considered as episodic in nature.) Semantic memory helps us to construct mental models of the world, including events that are not perceptually present (prototypes and scripts help us do these things also). Procedural memory allows us to retain learned connections between stimuli and responses. These connections include complex stimulus patterns and response chains (scripts and stereotypes will provide some ability to respond to response chains).

Whether or not we agree with the specific elements of Tulving's (1985) ternary system, the soundness of his argument for multiple subsystems of memory is unavoidable. This chapter does not claim to address all the different ways that humans process incoming information. Instead, it focuses on the way a schema can provide a multifaceted system of information processing that allows us to perceive, process, and remember many different types of information. By taking this approach then, we see that schema serves as the central cognitive structure (Bartlett, 1932) which is multilevel and multidimensional in nature. As such, schemas provide plans or blueprints for perceiving, interpreting, and remembering incoming information. It is doubtful whether we should ever use words like "understand" or "comprehend" without invoking schemas. But since these terms are often invoked in listening, let us next examine how schemas and listening might interact.

Schema and Listening

By defining a schema as the central processor with the properties presented above, we can easily see how a schematic processing system (a memory system using schemas) can digest linguistic information. Aaronson and Scarborough (1977) felt that an underlying structure exists into which incoming linguistic information is integrated. They felt that since evidence indicated that chunking occurs in the recall of sentences, individuals must be identifying, organizing, and integrating linguistic information. Their model suggests "that there is a level of linguistic processing at which words must be integrated into a larger context across phrase units" (p. 301). Schemas can provide such a context.

When we listen, we take in large amounts of linguistic information. If we define listening as the process of receiving and assigning meaning to incoming stimuli, we must view listening as an information processing activity. Goss (1982) took this perspective when he proposed a listening model composed of three interlinking parts: signal processing, literal processing, and reflective processing. If we examine each of these steps we can see how we use schema as listeners.

Signal processing (SP) is auditory perception. This step entails the listener being aware of physically receiving sound. During this step we engage in an on-the-spot analysis of the stimulus. To do this we probably store the sound in our short-term memory while we search for an appropriate schemas which will make the sound meaningful to us. If no such schemas exists in our memory, we expend no further energy trying to assign meaning to the noise. However, if we find an appropriate schemas, we enter the next step in the listening process.

The next two steps in the Goss model are subdivisions of message comprehension. During these phases of listening, we call upon our long-term memories and will utilize the memory system, i.e., episodic, semantic, or procedural, which is appropriate for the incoming information.

The initial assignment of meaning to a message occurs during the literal processing (LP) step. During the LP step, listeners attempt to understand the meaning with little or no evaluation of the information. Consequently, at this stage, the listener probably calls on a broad, general schema. An example of this level of listening might occur during a casual social conversation. During this type of pleasant exchange, we do not need to analyze the information and tend to fall into using well learned scripts (Shiffrin & Schneider, 1977) that we have stored in our schema system. Langer (1980) explicated this point further when she suggested that people who engage in a particular behavior repetitively develop a pattern or script for the situation. So, if we as listeners find ourselves in a typical social exchange, we do not devote a great deal of conscious effort in processing the information. Instead, we probably use familiar scripts to process and respond to the exchange. Langer suggests that people often respond to social situations by using these well-learned scripts rather than using new, incoming information. If, however, the event and the complexity of the information call for a deeper understanding, we enter the next stage of listening.

The final state in the Goss model is reflective processing (RP). During this step the listener strives for a deeper understanding of the incoming information. In doing so, the receiver makes extensive inferences about the information and evaluates both the message and the speaker. At this level, the listener will explore the depths of long-term memory for the schemas that are most appropriate for understanding what is being said. The listener uses existing schema to both make the predictions and the inferences (inference making is discussed in greater detail later in this chapter).

By looking at the listening process in the three steps presented in Goss's model, we can see that the use of schema has a strong bearing on all levels of listening. This suggests, then, that good listeners make effective use of their schema system.

To illustrate more clearly how we use a schema system to process incoming information, we will look at a type of message that has very clear schema structure--stories.

Story Structure

When a message's sentences are put together to form a wholistic idea--a story--an underlying organization holds the sentences together. This underlying structure will be referred to as story structure or the idealized internal representation of the parts (Mandler & Johnson,

1977). According to Mandler and Johnson (1977) the structure of a story provides a framework for the comprehension of the ideas expressed in the story. This framework provides several functions:

1. It directs attention to certain aspects of incoming material.

2. It helps the listener keep track of what has gone before. In this capacity the story structure provides a summary that increases the predictability of what information will immediately follow.

3. It tells the listener when some part of the story is complete and can be stored, or is incomplete and must be held until more material is encoded.

The pioneer in the study of story structure was Bartlett (1932). As he studied memory he tried to find some explanation for the memory of prose information. He felt that "perceiving, recognizing, and recalling were all functions which belong(ed) to the same general series" of information processing (p.187). Bartlett's notion indicates that the original form of a message as the receiver perceives it influences how the story is stored and recalled. Research seems to bear out this conclusion. Bartlett found that his subjects had a much easier time recalling stories that were presented in an organized format than stories that had little organization. The same finding had been repeated by others (Mandler, 1978; Mandler & Johnson, 1977; Rumelhart, 1975). In order to establish a particular grammar, the researchers originally used the folk tale as their model. Their rationale for using this material was that folk tales are handed down through the ages orally. The researchers felt that in order for these stories to be transmitted as accurately as they have been, they must be highly structured.

Recently, however, research in this area has been expanded to include additional formats or structures. Mandler (1978) and Mandler and Johnson (1977) felt that some story grammars were incomplete and that some categories are artificial. In an attempt to correct these weaknesses, they expanded story grammar. They felt that a successful theory of story structure must provide a clear "parsing system which can be used to divide a story into structurally important units" (p. 111). This type of system should be able to predict which units tend to be remembered and which units tend to be forgotten. The grammar that these researchers originally developed was geared for simple stories, or stories with only one protagonist in each episode. Mandler (1987) has recently expanded this basic structure to include complex grammars in which multiple episodes are imbedded within each other. Both the simple and the more complex grammars can handle a limited amount of conversation if the emphasis is on the reactions of the protagonist. The story structure then represents the underlying structure of a story as a tree structure which designates the explicit constituent structures and the relationship between the constituent parts. An event which occurs in the story is an example of a constituent structure. That is, the story structure is concerned with underlying information units not just surface structure sentences.

Using such an operationalization of story grammar and structure, Mandler and Johnson divided a story into two very general categories: the setting and the event structure. Each category could be used to analyze the characters and events of the story. When Mandler and Johnson tested their grammar, they found that stories which fit the grammar very closely were recalled in more detail and with more accuracy than stories that were not as closely structured. However, the structure of the original story and, as later research has shown, the one that is evident in the stories that are recalled did not seem to be the same (Rumelhart, 1975; Mandler & Johnson, 1977). The discrepancy between the two structures for the same story may contain part of the explanation for information distortion which occurs in the inferential recall of information. Mandler and Johnson (1977) believe that recall "comes to approximate the idealized [story structure] more than the actual form of the input" (p. 112). They feel that this shift to the ideal may occur because people can follow more twists and turns in incoming material and irregularities in information can be retained briefly in short-term memory. Long-term memory is not quite so flexible. They feel that memory tends to simplify information and make it conform to logical structures. The story structure provides logical patterns for the information.

Mandler and Johnson's (1977) analysis of their study showed strong support for the idea that well structured stories result in well structured recall. They found that fewer distortions occur in the recall of stories that have strong structures. Their analysis also revealed that information distortion occurs in certain types of situations. The first type of situation occurs when an important part of the story structure is weak or missing. For example, if the protagonist's reaction to an action is missing, subjects tend to fill in (infer) the missing or unclear information. Another distortion occurs when a subject reverses the order of events in the story. This occurs when two similar nodes occur in the same story, e.g., two action sections. The final type of distortion that occurs is the addition of information. This happens when the subjects elaborate upon something in the story. This type of distortion usually involves using more adjectives or adverbs as a subject describes a story. These findings were further verified by Mandler (1978) and Stein and Glenn (1979).

Even though story structure is used in both encoding and decoding a story, the rules may not be the same in both incidences. This difference in the rules for the two story structures has led researchers to conclude that neither the amount encoded, nor the level of processing at which the information is received can predict recall (Craik & Lockhart, 1972; Mandler & Johnson, 1977). Mandler and Johnson feel that recall is partially a function of the goodness of the story structure itself, but they agree with Bartlett's (1932) assertion that information is continuously being rearranged as new information is forthcoming. Spiro (1977) found that incoming information does seem to influence the stored knowledge. He also found that incoming information is selectively remembered and affected by selective perception and context. He felt that the content includes pre-existing information (or prior linguistic context) and the actual context of the situation.

The discussion of story structure indicates that the more highly a story is structured, the more accurately the story is recalled. However, the story structure does not remain static from input to recall. This change clearly indicates that although structure certainly affects the storage and recall of a story, it may also interact with an underlying schema. This interaction between the structure or organization of the message and existing schema may explain some of the distortion that occurs as we retrieve information from our memories.

Schema and Information Distortion

The schematic processing system is not static and changes so that new and old information can be integrated during information processing. Because the system does change to accommodate new information, or fit the new and old information together, inferences often become part of the information that is recalled.

When a message is presented to the schematic processing system, it has a structure of its own. If the structure is strong enough, the system integrates the story structure into the mind's system. If, however, the story structure is weak or has missing or incongruent parts, the mind seems to change the message. This phenomenon is evident if we look at the difference between the original message and the recalled version. By examining these differences, researchers have been able to discover where we as receivers make inferences or distort information.

By once again looking at stories as an example, researchers have identified certain information elements that seem to be crucial to the accurate recall of the gist of the story. These elements are a setting, a goal, a beginning, a simple reaction, an attempt, an outcome, and an ending. Paris and Upton (1976) collapsed these elements into two general categories when they modified the list of story elements. Their categories were setting and event. Any background information is labeled setting while the event category includes causes, the actual action in the story, and any outcomes and reactions.

Studies by Bartlett (1932) and Mandler (1978) found that as long as the above categories of information or nodes were present in a story, the story is easy for subjects to recall. Those stories that are not parsable into some version of these categories are not remembered very easily, and in fact are distorted in recall.

The entire process of inference making appears to be an attempt on the part of receivers to make information fit expectations. Schank (1975) functionally defined inference as a "process in which an individual tries to represent incoming information fit into existing information categories." In this capacity, inferences serve to fill in gaps in the structure of the incoming information (slot-filling) and connnect events in the structure with other events in order to provide a higher level of organization (text-connection).

Warren, Nicholas, and Trabasso (1979) feel that inferences are based primarily upon three identifiable sources of information. The first is logical relations between events in the text. The relations are causes, motivations, and conditions allowing the events. An example of an inference based on logical relations occurs if a receiver infers why a particular act is done. The second source of inferences is the informational relations between events in the text. Examples are specific people, instruments, objects, times, places, and contexts of events; in other words, who, what, when, and where. If a receiver infers that an act in a story is performed by using a particular tool, the inference is based on informational relations. The third source is world knowledge. This includes knowledge about vocabulary, items referred to and the functional relations among them. This category is based upon prior knowledge and perceptions and it affects the other two categories. Using these sources of information, an individual (listener or reader) focuses on the present (focal point) and uses this focal point to connect events from the past and to predict future events.

Warren, Nicholas, and Trabasso (1979) also theorized that these same sources of information are used to fill empty slots in a story. They felt that individuals use their world knowledge (past experience and knowledge) to infer information missing in a story.

The slot filling and connections are made with various types of inferences which occur with such regularity that they can be categorized. Warren, Nicholas, and Trabasso (1979) place inferences into two categories. The first category is logical inferences. Inferences in this category are bi-directional. They can predict forward or connect things from the past. Logical inferences answer the questions "why" and "how." The second category of inferences is value inferences. These are evaluative judgments on the actions of characters, intentions of the sources, or the validity of the events.

In addition, the researchers theorized that inferences will be produced in four degrees. The first is called first-order inferences. These are consistent with but undetermined by information in the text. This category consists of straight additions to world knowledge such as elaborative inferences and any guesses at nonindicated causes and motivations. This group of inferences is not used to connect parts of a story, they merely add information. Second-order inferences are determined but irrelevant. This means that the inference is implied by the text but does not specifically contribute to the flow of the story.

The next two orders of inferences are relevant to the flow of the story. Third-order inferences, however, are only relevant to the flow of a narrative. In addition, these inferences are determined by the text as being relevant and function in the interpretation of information on the basis of one's world knowledge and determining what happened and why. Unlike third-order inferences, fourth-order inferences are not relevant to the story event, and thus add nothing new to the progress of the story text.

A review of some studies which have examined the production of inferences in the recall of information will show more convincingly when and where inferences occur.

One place inferences occur is in the listener's integration of pieces of information. Bransford and Franks (1972) tested this notion in a study in which they presented a group of related sentences to their subjects. The stimulus sentences presented were either four simple sentences or combinations of two or three simple sentences:

    a. The ants are in the kitchen.

    b. The ant ate the jelly.

    c. The jelly was sweet.

    d. The jelly was on the table.

    e. The ants in the kitchen ate the jelly.

    f. The ants in the kitchen ate the sweet jelly.

After the memory phase of the study, the subjects were asked to (1) identify sentences which they had heard and combined sentences which they had not heard, and (2) tell how confident they were about their choices. The subjects all stated their claims with a high level of confidence. In many cases, however, subjects claimed that they had heard sentences which combined four simple sentences when in actuality none of these was presented in the experiment. An example of one of the "remembered" sentences was "The ants in the kitchen ate the sweet jelly which was on the table." The subjects thought that they had heard a combination of sentences a, b, c, d, and e presented above. This strongly suggests that information gathered from the semantic interpretation of related sentences is stored together and integrated in memory. However, as the information is integrated, inferences are made. As the subjects remembered the information they also inferred relationships among the parts of the whole. These inferences seemed to be a spontaneous part of the reconstruction of information in memory.

Paris (1965) likewise found that even his elementary school age subjects spontaneously constructed inferential relationships which were integrated in their memory representations of a story. This study revealed that comprehension is a constructive process, and that inference making is a constructive process. Further evidence of this was found by Paris and Carter (1973) when they used a semantic integration paradigm similar to that used by Bransford and Franks. They presented brief stories to elementary age children and instructed them to remember the exact story. However, the children did not recall the stories exactly as they had heard them. Instead, they integrated information and drew inferential relationships during recall.

Other research indicates that inferences are made by adding information to the original messages. Several studies have found that when certain types of information are not explicitly stated, the subjects will infer the information when they are asked to recall the message. In one such study, Paris, Lindauer and Cox (1977) read sentences to 7- and 11-year-olds. The sentences either implied or stated an instrument of action in a story. (An example of the statements used is "the workman dug a hole in the ground [with a shovel].") Even when the tool was not stated explicitly (as in the non-parenthetical portion of the sample sentence) the children could "remember" the tool used as well as if it had been named in the sentence.

Paris and Upton (1976) conducted a similar study which tested the production of contextual and lexical inferences. Lexical inferences were operationalized as remembrance of an implied tool while contextual inferences focused on "remembering" the consequences which were not stated in the stories. Their findings agree with those of Stein and Glenn (1979). Stein and Glenn found that four categories of information were most likely to be inferred in the recall of a story. The categories were major settings, initiating events, major goal statements, and consequences. Paris and Upton's tools can be found in the initiating events category, and their consequence category is the same as Stein and Glenn's.

Kintsch and Monk (1972) reported similar findings. They presented their subjects with sentences like "The man was shot" and asked them to specify other information that was true of the statement. Most subjects indicated that the man had to be shot by something which was probably a gun. Thus, the subjects inferred an instrument or tool which was part of the setting and used in initiating the event.

Johnson, Bransford, and Solomon (1973) supported Kintsch and Monk, finding that their subjects inferred instruments along with consequences when the actual information was missing from the story. Furthermore, Kintsch and Monk (1972) found that their subjects made similar inferences regardless of whether their stimulus material was presented in a simple or complex manner.

Further research by Fitch-Hauser (1984) also lends support to the interplay between the structure of incoming information and the way information is stored and recalled. By manipulating the structure of narrative information, she found that she could also manipulate the type of inferences, or distortion, that the receiver made. Her study found that if certain parts of a narrative are deleted, the subjects infer the missing part of the narrative. In her study, Fitch-Hauser manipulated the cause node and the consequence node of three narrative passages. The results of her study showed that if either of these nodes is deleted from a passage, receivers will infer them when they recall the information.

All of the research discussed so far indicates that inferences occur when information is either missing or is implied by a message. Another cause of inferences seems to be the presence of an inconsistency or contradiction in a message. Research indicates that when incoming stimuli are consistent with the expectations of the receiver, the information is assimilated and recalled with relative ease. However, when information is only mildly inconsistent with one's expectations the information is rejected as not being valid. However, when information is only mildly inconsistent with expectations, the information is easily recalled in short-term memory but tends to be converted to fit the expectations in long-term recall (Taylor & Crocker, 1980; Kintsch & Van Dijk, 1978). In other words, the presence of a mild inconsistency in a message will cause a receiver to make an inference in order to attain consistency. This information also implies that any message which is contradictory to a receiver's expectations is subject to distortion by inference.

Fitch-Hauser (1984) also found support for this conclusion. In her study, she manipulated the consequence node, making it incongruent with the cause node in a particular narrative sequence. Her subjects "inferred" a congruent consequence when they were asked questions about the story.

Conclusion

As we begin to focus more on the receiver in the communication process, we are compelled to look at the act of receiving and listening. This chapter has attempted to do just that by focussing on one aspect of that process, the use of schemas in information processing. Schemas are a functional part of listening and information processing. As such, it provides a means for the receiver to make sense out of incoming sounds by providing meaningful categories in which to place information. These categories help us as listeners interpret, store, and reconstruct the message.

CHAPTER SEVEN

Affective Responses in Listening: A Meta-Analysis of Receiver Apprehension Outcomes

Raymond W. Preiss

Lawrence R. Wheeless

> Fear is a rot--that cankers root and fruit alike.
> Strive for new beginnings and new shoots.
>
> ....Robert Graves

Affective responses in the listening process are not well researched. Perhaps we are not accustomed to thinking of listening as an activity that evokes an emotional reponse. However, communication in general is often associated with a specific emotional response--communication apprehension--so it is certainly logical to look at the process of receiving in terms of its potential for particular affect. One line of research has done just that. Wheeless (1975) advanced receiver apprehension as an affective variable relevant to listening effectiveness. Noting evidence for reticence (Phillips, 1968) and communication apprehension (McCroskey, 1970), Wheeless reasoned that an individual's communicative role (source or receiver) should function relatively independently in fear or anxiety arousing contexts. Specifically, he suggests that the fear of sending messages was related to social approval, while the fear of receiving messages was related to processing information. Termed receiver apprehension, the variable was linked to "...the fear of misinterpreting, inadequately processing and/or not being able to adjust psychologically to messages sent by others" (Wheeless, 1975, p. 263). Our next task should be to examine the conceptual basis for receiver apprehension.

The Conceptual Basis for Receiver Apprehension

Wheeless (1975) designed the Receiver Apprehension Test (RAT) and found that receiver apprehension functioned relatively independently of source related anxiety. Wheeless and Scott (1976) developed the "Revised Receiver Apprehension Test" (RRAT) and replicated the independence of the construct. Factor analysis revealed a primary vector associated with the fear of not understanding a message.

There is evidence that receiver apprehension affects information processing. In the classroom, Scott and Wheeless (1977) found that receiver apprehension was negatively related to student achievement on tests and projects, with student performance on class projects producing the major differences. The authors concluded that "high receiver-apprehensives...have lower levels of effective information processing than low receiver-apprehensives" (Wheeless & Scott, 1976, p. 9). Based on these early findings, few generalizations were established about the consequences of receiver apprenhension and little insight was gained into the nature or antecedents of the anxiety. We believe that studies may be interpreted in the context of three explanations: Primary anxiety, secondary anxiety, and communication logics.

The Primary Anxiety Explanation. The primary anxiety explanation asserts that receiver apprehension occurs as the function of a fear of encountering new information. Wheeless and Scott (1976) made this case when they advanced two distinctions between source- and receiver-based communication anxieties: (1) encoding versus decoding functions, and (2) specific versus general contexts. Receiver apprehension was conceptualized as a more situational-type anxiety associated with message decoding. Like oral communication apprehension, receiver apprehension appeared to be more of a fear or phobic reaction than a generalized anxiety (Wheeless, 1975).

Porter (1973) noted that the difference between fear and general anxiety hinges on the issue of understanding the source of the arousal.

"Anxiety" refers to psychological/physiological apprehension which is not rationally understood by the individual in question: whereas "fear" is characterized by the same apprehension except there is no personality trait accounting for the disruption, and the individual in question probably understands why he is aroused (Porter, 1973, p. 3). Spielberger (1966, 1970) further distinguished between fear and general anxiety on the basis of "state" and "trait" characteristics of the phenomena.

	Situationally Specific	Situationally General
Rationally Known Causes	FEAR I	APPREHENSION II
Rationally Unknown Causes	APPREHENSION III	GENERAL ANXIETY IV

FIGURE 7-1. Situations best described as
fear, general anxiety, or apprehension.

State anxiety, which Spielberger equates with fear, was related with specific things, events, and situations that could be defined (e.g., water, heights, etc.). Trait anxiety, equated with generalized anxiety, was related to a generalized activation level or trait of the individual which applies across a broad spectrum of situations. Figure 7-1 illustrates the differences between fear and pathological, generalized anxiety.

Two conditions are clearly tied to the concepts of fear, Condition I and general anxiety Condition IV. The factor distinguishing between the two conditions is an understanding of the causes of the arousal (receiving information). Figure 7-1 also shows two conditions which are not clearly tied to either the fear or general anxiety constructs. An individual who understands the reasons for his or her apprehensiveness--albeit a specific or general situation--appears to be more fearful than pathologically anxious. Likewise, the person who has a phobic reaction to a specific situation, but does not rationally understand the reasons for the reaction, also seems to be more fearful than pathologically anxious. Therefore, the two conditions labeled apprehension (Conditions II and III) appear to be more allied to the concept of fear than generalized anxiety. This reasoning leads us to conclude that receiver apprehension can be conceptually summarized as a fearful, but not necessarily understood reaction to information processing in both specific and general situations.

Receiver apprehension studies dealing with listening effectiveness and information processing effectiveness appear to be consistent with the primary anxiety explanation. Roberts (1986) found that RAT scores were related to total listening ability and long-term memory as measured by the Watson-Barker Listening Test (Watson & Barker, 1984). However, short-term memory was not associated with receiver apprehension. In the area of short-term memory, Daniels and Whitman (1979) detected a significant effect for receiver apprehension on recall of facts following exposure to an experimental message.

Attempts to equate receiver apprehension with trait listening ability have produced mixed results. In a study of Southern and Midwestern university students, listening comprehension scores following tape recorded messages (Watson & Barker, 1984) were not significantly related to RAT scores. Similarly, Paschall found no correlation between RAT scores and responses on the Sequential Test of Educational Progress-- Listening Test.

In the area of information processing effectiveness, additional evidence has reinforced the early research on classroom performance (Wheeless & Scott, 1976) and academic achievement (Scott & Wheeless, 1977). For example, there is reason to believe that stress plays a role in the processing of information for apprehensive individuals. Bock and Bock (1984) found that, when under stress, highly apprehensive students rated student speakers leniently. When the stress was removed, low receiver apprehensive raters were least lenient in their evaluations. These findings tend to support the primary anxiety explanation because situational demands may suppress or exaggerate existing fears of encountering new information. The variability in leniency errors suggests that receiver apprehension may function as a perceptual screen or filter that affects information processing efficiency.

The Secondary Anxiety Explanation. The second conceptual approach to receiver apprehension maintains that the fear of processing or psychologically adjusting to messages leads to a general response set involving anxiety. Beatty and his colleagues made this case in studies focusing on the information processing consequences of receiver apprehension. In the context of listening efficiency, Beatty, Behnke, and Henderson (1980) found that respondents scoring high on the RAT instrument tended to respond anxiously in situations where incoming information required complex processing or psychological adjustment (p.135). Low processing efficiency was interpreted to mean that receiver apprehensives might have difficulty assimilating new information.

Working from Assimilation Theory (McReynolds, 1976), Beatty (1981) reasoned that inefficient information processing might result in a backlog of unassimilated facts. This backlog was viewed as producing a general anxiety which conditioned the individual to trait-like receiver apprehension. In other words, receiver apprehension may be produced as secondary anxiety, and the "trait" may emerge as response associated with receiving information. As predicted, Beatty (1981) found a significant correlation between cognitive backlog and receiver apprehension.

In an attempt to understand the creation of cognitive backlogs, Beatty and Payne (1981) explored receiver apprehension and cognitive complexity. Conceptually, cognitive complexity refers to the use of judgment categories and decision rules when forming impressions and adopting social perspectives. Because complexity levels set information processing thresholds, cognitively simple receivers should experience a backlog of unprocessed information. The authors found a significant negative correlation between cognitive complexity and receiver apprehension. Employing participants from a different geographic region and education level, Bocchino (1984) replicated this finding. This relationship lends credence to the notion that receiver apprehension is a developmental phenomenon related to information processing efficiency.

There is a body of receiver apprehension research supporting the secondary anxiety explanation. Using a measure of physiological arousal (tympanic temperature), Roberts (1984) found a positive correlation between receiver apprehension and arousal while listening to two tape recorded messages. The stronger, stable correlation associated with the second message suggested that the RAT instrument was measuring habitual, rather than situated, communication apprehension (p. 128). Beatty (1985) made a similar case when he examined the stability of RAT scores after processing complex messages. The "relatively stable" nature of the scores was interpreted as supporting the trait-like characteristics of receiver apprehension. This was consistent with earlier research correlating the RAT with a measure of state anxiety (Beatty, Behnke, & Henderson, 1980).

Because the secondary anxiety approach views receiver apprehension as assuming trait-like characteristics, it is reasonable to expect the RAT to be moderately correlated with other "anxiety-related" personality variables. There is evidence to support this relationship. Studies have detected a small, but significant correlation between the RAT (Wheeless, 1975) and the RRAT (Wheeless & Scott, 1976) and the communication apprehension (McCroskey, 1970). Similarly, Borzi (1985) found a significant positive correlation between the RAT and general shyness (McCroskey & Richmond, 1982). In a study designed to develop a measure of trait information anxiety, Williams (1976) found a moderate correlation between his instrument and the RRAT.

It is clear that the primary and secondary explanations differ in their approaches to receiver apprehension. The primary anxiety approach stresses a situational fear associated with message decoding. The secondary anxiety model broadens the scope of receiver apprehension to include general response tendencies. When differences in information processing abilitites are viewed from the vantage points of primary and secondary anxieties, we conclude that the outcomes of receiver apprehension are pervasive and serious. It appears that apprehensive individuals experience a conscious, unpleasant affect that distorts perceptions of incoming information. This suggests that high and low apprehensive individuals may operate in fundamentally different ways in their social environments. The communication logics explanation was developed to explore this area.

The Communication Logics Explanation. The communication logics approach represents a constructivist account of receiver apprehension (Preiss, 1987). The basic proposition is that individuals rely on interpretive schemes to generate strategies for guiding actions. Furthermore, possession of highly differentiated schemes (of situations and others--perspective-taking) may result in developing a strategic repertoire of appropriate communication behaviors (Delia, O'Keefe & O'Keefe, 1982, p.143).

While most constructivists have focused on patterns of message production, O'Keefe (1985) explicitly identified message interpretation as an outcome of communication logics. She identified distinctly different styles of communication logics: (1) expressive/reactive, (2) conventional/cooperative, and (3) rhetorical/coordinating. Of special interest here is the higher order, rhetorical/coordinating logic (strategic and listener adapted) and the lower order, expressive/reactive logic (mere statement of feeling). Individuals who operate under these logics "may have systematically different implicit definitions of communication and . . . these differences might be reflected in fundamentally different ways of constructing and interpreting messages" (O'Keefe, 1985, p.1).

Preiss (1987) linked receiver apprehension to this perspective when he found a negative relationship between the RAT and O'Keefe's (1985) instrument designed to identify communication logics. Conceptually, an individual operating at a lower ordered logic (reactive and expressive) might, indeed, react anxiously to the possibilities of misinterpreting, inadequately processing, and/or adjusting psychologically to strategic, listener adapted messages. This reasoning provides a basis for understanding situationally based receiver/decoder fear. Viewing receiver apprehension as a correlate of a special logic of communication provides a cognitive explanation for the construct and offers another source of predictions and explanations.

There is evidence that receiver apprehension may embody a special logic of communication. Constructivists (cf. Delia, O'Keefe & O'Keefe, 1982) have long noted the role of cognitive complexity in the interpretation messages and receiver apprehension has been linked to low levels of cognitive complexity (Beatty & Payne, 1981; Bocchino, 1984). The cognitive consequences of receiver apprehension have been isolated in studies dealing with conversational sensitivity, trait argumentativeness, and message processing.

Daly, Vangelista, and Daughton (1987) have provided evidence that receiver apprehension is related to how individuals understand conversations. The authors developed a measure of conversational sensitivity, indicating the degree to which "people attend to and interpret what occurs in conversations" (p.2). Conceptually, conversational sensitivity involves the ability to make high order inferences about verbal and nonverbal messages, to self-monitor the social environment, remember utterances, and detect the power and affinity relationships exhibited in conversations. Consistent with the communication logics perspective, receiver apprehension was negatively correlated to the conversational sensitivity scale.

The possibility that apprehensive people may not understand the intricacies of conversations leads to speculation on how these messages are processed. Widgley (in press) reasoned that the cognitive backlogs associated with receiver apprehension might cause individuals to develop other cognitive traits related to the assimilation of information. He reasoned that backlogs of unassimilated information would reduce an individual's ability to understand the precise nature of positions advocated by others and attend to feedback related to these positions. Specifically, Widgley suggested that trait argumentativeness (Infante & Rancer, 1982), the predisposition to refute ideas offered by others, would be negatively related to receiver apprehension. Results supported this relationship, indicating that anxiety about receiving information "discourages individuals from engaging in activities that require effective listening, such as arguing."

The possibility that receiver apprehension affects the ability to understand another's position and feedback is consistent with the explanation offered by Preiss et al. (1985) as an analysis on low order communication logics. Widgley's results suggest that highly apprehensive receivers may operate in a communication environment where they do not understand the motives that guide messages sent by others. Further, the limited ability to question and argue effectively might result in uncritical acceptance of ideas when the apprehensive individual is under situational stress (cf. leniency errors, Bock & Bock, 1984). This indicates that receiver apprehensives often misperceive some messages while they fail to assimilate other messages.

Preiss, Rindo, Fishfader, and Wickersham (1985) explored the information processing consequences of receiver apprehension. Using the counterattitudinal advocacy paradigm, Preiss and his associates found differences in self-persuasion following message encoding attributable to a receiver apprehension level--information level interaction. Low receiver apprehensives exhibited self-persuasion when they generated their own issues (active participation) against a personally held belief. High apprehensive participants demonstrated the most change when issues against their beliefs were provided as part of the experiment (passive participation). This lends support for the notion that receiver apprehensives are not able to produce arguments contrary to privately held beliefs (cf. low trait argumentativeness) and uncritically process messages.

The communication logics approach to receiver apprehension provides a valuable extension of the primary and secondary explanations. This view subsumes the anxiety issue by framing it as a cognitive style of constructing and interpreting messages. While anxiety is a prominent feature of this style, the communication logics explanation stresses the cognitive processes that allow the individual to understand and function in a social environment.

Summary of Theoretical Approaches

We believe that studies adopting these three explanations have provided insights into the major outcomes and processes related to receiver apprehension. The differences between the approaches are largely attributable to an emphasis on one aspect of a theory. The utility of the approaches will depend upon the interests of the researcher and the nature of the research question. In addition, the literature reveals that no single approach is unequivocally superior to others.

Consequently, it is prudent to develop a theory that unifies the three explanations. The most comprehensive attempt to identify the theoretical nature of receiver apprehension was offered by Beatty (1981) in his application of assimilation theory (McReynolds, 1976). However, Beatty focused exclusively on anxiety as the outcome of inadequate assimilation, *at the expense of the nature of assimilation.* We believe that assimilation theory offers additional potential for increasing our understanding of receiver apprehension. Refocusing attention on the cognitive system that utilizes assimilation may provide a new, rich source of information bearing on the construct.

McReynolds' theory is couched in a medical analogy. He equates the assimilation of new information into a person's cognitive structure to the process whereby nutrients are assimilated into the bloodstream. In this scheme, the "contents of one's conscious experiencing [sic] become part of the overall category system" (McReynolds, 1976, p.46). Primary anxiety is observed to occur when the rate of information exposure exceeds processing thresholds. Secondary anxiety is hypothesized to develop when overexposure creates stressful backlogs of information and this anxiety is associated with a previously neutral stimulus (in this case, receiving information).

At the hub of assimilation theory is the cognitive system which governs an individual's ability to "absorb" new facts. This system is the "mental apparatus which receive, process, transform, categorize, experience, organize, store, and perceive perceptual inputs" (McReynolds, 1976, p.40). The overlooked fact is that assimilation theory is a hybrid of the constructivist tradition. The quantitative and qualitative characteristics of information processing are seen as being governed by cognitive schemas. In essence, the cognitive system postulated by McReynolds is isomorphic with the constructivist interpretation of communication behaviors. Further, McReynolds made a valuable theoretical contribution by specifying assimilation as the mechanism for changes in cognitive schemas. This directs attention away from mere anxiety, toward the cognitive structure that is the precursor of the anxiety. We suggest that the best way to understand the cognitive structure is to survey the outcomes of receiver apprehension. In an effort to understand these, we conducted a meta-analysis of existing empirical literature and cumulated the effects of receiver apprehension.

Method

The literature bearing on receiver apprehension has proliferated since Wheeless' (1975) observation that scholars have ignored receiver-based anxiety in favor of source-based anxiety. Now, a sufficient number of studies exist to allow generalizations to be established about the consequences of receiver apprehension. The appropriate tool for summarizing results across such a research area is meta-analysis (Glass, McGaw, & Smith, 1981; Hedges & Olkin, 1985; Hunter, Schmidt, & Jackson, 1982). By coding and transforming outcomes of the studies into a common metric, it is possible to estimate an overall effect size and detect moderator variables. This technique allows us to cumulate many studies and quantify the empirical results of the body of literature (Cooper, 1984; Light & Pillemer, 1984) on receiver apprehension.

Search Procedures and Selection Criteria. An extensive search of the literature was initiated using four methods: (1) manual and computer searches of *Social Sciences Citation Index, Psychological Abstracts, Resources in Education, Dissertation Abstracts International,* and *Index to Journals in Speech Communication* (2) manual searches of the Speech Communication Association and the International Communication Association convention programs, (3) correspondence with authors conducting primary research, (4) locating all receiver apprehension monographs cited in published studies and convention papers. These efforts resulted in the location of 11 published articles, 9 convention papers, and 4 unpublished masters theses and dissertations. To insure that all of the receiver apprehension literature domain was reflected in the meta-analysis, no studies were excluded on the basis of quality or recency (Glass, 1977). One convention paper (Paschall & Clark, 1984) was dropped from the meta-analysis because it failed to report summary statistics or significance levels. However, Paschall's (1984) dissertation (the basis for the Paschall & Clark paper) was included in the meta-analysis. A second convention paper (McDowell, McDowell, Hyerdahl, & Steil, 1978) was excluded because it employed multivariate methods that are not appropriate for meta-analytic cumulation (Hedges & Oklin, 1985).

Decision Rules for Coding and Computing Effect Sizes. Several receiver apprehension studies tested more than one hypothesis using a single set of respondents. Because reporting multiple tests violates statistical assumptions of independence (Rosenthal, 1978; Strube & Hartman, 1983; Bangert-Drowns, 1986), the decision rule in this meta-analysis was to extract a single effect size for each independent test of of a hypothesis.

Because several statistical tests were often reported in a single study, a decision rule was required for computing effect sizes. For this meta-analysis, a three level rule was developed. (1) If the study involved a single dependent variable, the statistical test for that variable was used in computing the effect size. (2) If the study contained several dependent variables, the statistical test for the variable most directly related to listening was used in computing the effect size, (3) If the study contained several dependent variables and if the variable most directly related to listening could not be determined, the median statistical test for that variable was used in computing the effect size. This procedure ensured that the effects sizes were at least roughly comparable and that collapsing the sizes would be a reasonable procedure.

Results

Application of the three tier decision rule resulted in the isolation of the twenty-four criterion variables identified in Table 7-1.

Table 7-1 reveals that receiver apprehension has been linked to a variety of criterion measures. When summary statistics are converted to Pearson product moment correlations, the magnitude of outcomes attributable to receiver apprehension may be displayed. The meta-analytic procedures and decision rules resulted in twenty-five data points. The criterion variables were categorized into groups based upon conceptual similarities. This process was quite straightforward, as the literature reviews in the primary studies identified the conceptual variables of interest. Five categories were identified: (1) listening effectiveness, (2) processing anxiety, (3) information processing effectiveness, (4) information processing complexity, and (5) education level.

Table 7-2 indicates consistent patterns when primary studies are grouped into these categories. Four effect sizes are displayed for each study: (1) r is the average Pearson product correlation coefficient, (2) z is computed by transforming Pearson product correlations into standard normal deviates and indicates the association corrected for sample size (Cohen, 1977), (3) r^2 is the variance accounted for on each criterion variable, and (4) Cohen's d is the difference in standard deviation units attributable to receiver apprehension on each outcome variable.

TABLE 7-1

Variables Extracted from Receiver Apprehension Studies

Study	Relevant Criterion Variable
Beatty (1981)	Conceptual variable: Self-reports of unassimilated material on salient personal topics. Measurement device: Assimilation Scales (McReynolds & Acker, 1966).
Beatty (1985)	Conceptual variable: Situational listening anxiety. Measurement device: Change in RAT scores when subjects were told they would be tested after listening to tape recorded "complex material."
Beatty, Behnke, & Henderson (1980)	Conceptual variable: State listening anxiety. Measurement device: Spielberger's STAI (A-Trait) inventory (Spielberger, Gorsuch, & Lushene, 1968).
Beatty & Payne (1981)	Conceptual variable: Cognitive complexity as measured by open-ended responses to six sentence stems. Measurement device: Schroder, Driver, and Struefert's (1961) Paragraph Completion Task.
Bocchino (1984)	Conceptual variable: Cognitive complexity as measured by open-ended responses to six sentence stems. Measurement device: Schroder, Driver, and Struefert's (1961) Paragraph Completion Task.

TABLE 7-1 (Cont.)

Bock & Bock (1984)	Conceptual variable: Leniency error as an indicator of information processing efficiency. Measurement device: Induced positional anxiety during the Rating Error Paradigm. (Bock & Bock, 1977).
Borzi (1985)	Conceptual variable: Shyness. Measurement device: Shyness Scale (McCroskey & Richmond, 1982).
Daly et al. (1987)	Conceptual variable: Conversational sensitivity, conceptualized as high order inferences, receiver adaptation, and understanding relational dynamics. Measurement device: Conversational Sensitivity Measure (Daly et al, 1987).
Daniels & Whitman (1979)	Conceptual variable: Message recall. Measurement device: A test for facts presented in experimental messages.
McDowell & McDowell (1979)	Conceptual variable: Education level. Measurement device: High school vs. college scores on RAT (Wheeless, 1975).
McDowell et al. (1981)	Conceptual variable: Education level. Measurement device: High school vs. college scores on the RAT (Wheeless, 1975).
O'Hair (1986)	Conceptual variable: Preference for information in physicians' persuasive styles. Measurement device: Self-reports.
Paschall (1984)	Conceptual variable: Listening effectiveness. Measurement device: Sequential Test of Educational Progress--Listening Test (STEP) (McGraw-Hill).

TABLE 7-1 (Cont.)

Preiss (1987)	Conceptual variable: Integrated communication-constituting concepts that reflect a logic of communication functions. Measurement device: Functional Integration of Communication Concepts (FICC) (O'Keefe, 1985).
Preiss et al. (1985)	Conceptual variable: Self-persuasion following counterattitudinal advocacy. Measurement device: Semantic differential scales completed after encoding a belief-discrepant message.
Roach et al. (1985) Groups 1 & 2	Conceptual variable: Listening comprehension scores for tape recorded messages. Measurement device: Watson-Barker Listening Test (Watson-Barker, 1984).
Roberts (1984)	Conceptual variable: Psychophysiological arousal while viewing video taped messages. Measurement device: Tympanic temperature as a direct measure of arousal (Patterson, 1976).
Roberts (1986)	Conceptual variable: Listening comprehension scores for tape recorded messages. Measurement device: Total listening ability score from Form A, Watson-Barker Listening Test (Watson & Barker, 1984).
Scott & Wheeless (1977)	Conceptual variable: Information processing and academic achievement. Measurement device: Examination and project scores.

TABLE 7-1 (Cont.)

Sheahan (1976)	Conceptual variable: Perception of receiving a large amount of election information. Measurement device: Likert-type scale.
Wheeless (1975)	Conceptual variable: Communication apprehension. Measurement device: PRCA (McCroskey, 1970).
Wheeless & Scott (1976)	Conceptual variable: Information processing and academic achievement. Measurement device: Grade point average and three examination scores.
Widgley (in press)	Conceptual variable: Trait argumentativeness. Measurement device: Argumentativeness Scale (Infante & Rancer, 1982).
Williams (1976)	Conceptual variable: Information anxiety. Measurement device: Information Anxiety Scale (Williams, 1976).

A final step in the meta-analysis is determining the average effect size. Table 7-3 displays five indexes: (1) R is the average Pearson product moment correlation coefficient, (2) R^2 is the average variance accounted for in each outcome category, (3) Z is the average of the standard normal deviates. Z provides a measure of association corrected for sample size, (4) $R(Z)$ is computed by transforming the average Z into the corresponding R, following procedures provided by Rosenthal (1984). This effect size adjusts the average correlation for the skewed nature of the r distribution. (5) Cohen's d is the average difference in standard deviation units attributable to receiver apprehension on each outcome variable.

TABLE 7-2

Classification of Effect Size Metrics

	r	z	r^2	d	N
Listening Effectiveness					
Daniels & Whitman (1979)	-.18	.18	.03	.37	132
Paschall (1984)	-.03	.03	.01	.06	167
Roach et al. (1985)	-.25	.26	.06	.53	112
Group 2	-.17	.17	.03	.35	59
Roberts (1986)	-.21	.21	.04	.42	120
Processing Anxiety					
Beatty (1985)	.63	.74	.39	1.62	50
Beatty, Behnke, & Henderson (1980)	.56	.63	.31	1.35	82
Borzi (1985)	.31	.41	.09	.65	153
Roberts (1984)	.30	.31	.09	.62	54
Wheeless (1975)	.20	.20	.04	.40	234
Williams (1976)	.56	.63	.31	1.35	314
Information Processing Effectiveness					
Beatty (1981)	-.73	.99	.53	2.22	84
Bock & Bock (1984)	-.78	1.04	.61	2.50	217
Preiss et al. (1985)	-.40	.42	.16	.88	40

Scott & Wheeless (1977)	-.36	.37	.13	.82	194
Wheeless & Scott (1976)	-.40	.42	.16	.87	256

Information Processing Complexity

Beatty & Payne (1981)	-.78	1.05	.61	2.51	51
Bocchino (1984)	-.10	.10	.01	.21	401
Daly et al (1987)	-.22	.22	.04	.45	230
O'Hair (1986)	-.12	.12	.01	.25	303
Preiss (1987)	-.38	.40	.14	.82	66
Sheahan (1976)	-.42	.49	.18	.94	194
Widgley (in press)	-.36	.37	.13	.77	67

Education Level

McDowell & McDowell (1978)	-.05	.05	.00	.11	297
McDowell et al. (1981)	-.19	.19	.03	.39	694

The benchmark for evaluating an effect size has been provided by Cohen (1977). He suggested that $d = .2$ be termed a "small effect," $d =.5$ a "moderate effect," and $d = .8$, a "large effect." While these standards are quite crude indices, they have been widely accepted by scholars. The National Institute of Education's Joint Dissemination Review Panel identified effect sizes of between .25 and .33 as being educationally significant (Tallmadge, 1977). Rossi and Write (1977) designated a .5 effect size as the conventional index of practical significance. Regardless of the evaluation criteria, the effect sizes associated with receiver apprehension in Table 7-3 easily exceed minimum standards for meaningfulness.

TABLE 7-3

Receiver Apprehension Across Outcome Categories

	r	r^2	Z	$r(Z)$	d	N
Listening effectiveness	-.17	.03	.17	.17	.35	590
Information processing anxiety	.42	.17	.48	.45	1.00	887
Information processing effectiveness	-.53	.32	.65	.57	1.45	791
Information processing complexity	-.34	.16	.39	.37	.85	1,312
Education level	-.12	.02	.12	.12	.25	991

The results of the meta-analysis indicate that receiver apprehension has practical and theoretical consequences. Across conceptual variables, the impact of receiver apprehension is pervasive and important.

Listening Effectiveness. The effect size discovered for listening effectiveness (d = .352) is consistent with Beatty et al.'s (1980) conclusion that receiver apprehension measures trait listening anxiety. However, the average unadjusted R (-.17) and the average R adjusted for sample size (-.174) reinforces classifying the effect size as "small" using Cohen's (1977) index. This view is underscored by the modest average variance accounted for by the receiver apprehension and listening instruments (.035). In addition, the pattern of effect sizes is consistent across criterion measures (message recall, scores from Sequential Test of Educational Progress--Listening Test, and total listening scores on the Watson--Barker Listening Test).

Information Processing Anxiety. The magnitude of the effect size for processing anxiety (d = 1.004) classified as "large" using Cohen's system and the results are compatible with Wheeless' (1975) original formulation regarding the relationship between receiver apprehension and the fear of processing messages. Further, the unadjusted (.427) and adjusted (.488) average Pearson product moment correlation indicates a moderate relationship between receiver apprehension and various measures of anxiety (changes in RAT scores following listening, STAI A-Trait Anxiety Inventory, Shyness Scale, tympanic temperature, PRCA, Information Anxiety Scale). Also, the average R^2 (.209) indicates substantial shared variance between receiver apprehension and indices of anxiety.

Information Processing Effectiveness. The effect size for effective information processing (d = 1.461) is classified as "large" (Cohen, 1977). The unadjusted (-.536) and adjusted (-.574) correlations indicate a moderate relationship between receiver apprehension and measures of information processing abilities (unassimilated information, leniency errors, self-persuasion, examination scores, GPA). The average shared variance is substantial (.320).

Information Processing Complexity. The effect size for processing complexity (d = .853) is classified as "large" (Cohen, 1977). Further, the unadjusted (-.343) and adjusted (-.378) average Pearson product moment correlation indicates a small relationship between receiver apprehension and various measures of processing complexity (cognitive complexity, conversational sensitivity, perception of adequate information environment, desire for additional information, low order communication logic, ability to formulate arguments). Also, the average R^2 (.099) indicates substantial shared variance between receiver apprehension and indices of anxiety.

Education Level. Level of education appears to be associated with a decrease of about one half of a standard deviation (d = .251) in receiver apprehension scores. This effect size is classified as "small" (Cohen, 1977). The unadjusted (-.124) and adjusted (-.125) correlations indicate a definite, but slight, relationship between receiver apprehension and measures of information processing abilities (junior high, high school, year in college). The average shared variance is not substantial (.020).

Composite Results. While it is not possible to identify a causal sequence of effect sizes, the composite results of the meta-analysis confirm the pervasive influence receiver apprehension. The sheer magnitude of the effect size for information processing effectiveness (d = 1.461) indicates that receiver apprehension plays a meaningful role in the individual's cognitive system. Adding the effect sizes for processing complexity ($d = .853$) and anxiety $d = 1.004$) to the formula suggests that those who experience receiver apprehension may function in a fearful, unpredictable social environment. The small effect size for listening indicates that poor perceiving/recalling of messages may not be a primary outcome.

Discussion

The pattern of effect sizes isolated in the meta-analysis suggests that receiver apprehension is a more complex variable than had been previously thought. The results of the meta-analysis have practical, theoretical, and methodological implications.

Practical Implications. The meta-analysis has clear implications for professionals in the field of education. The decrement in information processing efficiency has been associated with nearly a full GPA loss for high apprehensives when compared to low apprehensives in university classrooms (Wheeless & Scott, 1976). Further, Bock and Bock (1984) found that receiver apprehensives under stress tended to commit leniency errors, overestimating the performance of speakers. Finally, McDowell and McDowell (1978) found that receiver apprehension was higher in primary and secondary schools than in university classes. These results suggest that receiver apprehension must be considered when developing educational curriculum and targeting classroom objectives. However, the treatment implications of receiver apprehension are vague. The real danger exists in poor conceptualization leading to simplistic treatments for the "problem." For example, Wolvin and Coakley (1985) cite Paschall and Clark (1984) to support the claim that the receiver apprehensive listener "may have to learn how to relax before he or she can listen effectively." (p. 106). The Paschall and Clark paper was based on Paschall's (1984) dissertation; that study found no significant relationship between receiver apprehension and listening. Even if such a relationship had been established, we believe that this diagnostic advice may be quite inappropriate, as the role of the "anxiety" associated with receiver apprehension is unclear.

		Satisfactory	Unsatisfactory
Receiver Apprehension Level	LOW	Rational I	Irrational II
	HIGH	Irrational III	Rational IV

FIGURE 7-2. Information processing efficiency.

Figure 7-2 illustrates the potential error of prescribing relaxation as a "cure" for receiver apprehension. This approach assumes that anxiety serves as a barrier that interferes with listening abilities (Condition III). However, the student who is anxious when listening may have a rational basis for the apprehension: poor listening skills. We believe that this student (Condition IV) may not be helped by relaxation. Relaxation training may move this student to Condition II.

Here no concern is exhibited toward unsatisfactory listening abilities. We suggest that treatment programs should focus on apprehension *and* skills. Moving students to Condition I may require systematic desensitization (Goss, Thompson, & Olds, 1978), training in critical thinking, improving the ability to argue (Infante, 1982), and practice in message evaluation (Phillips, 1977).

Clearly, the entire approach to "treatment" for receiver apprehension is poorly reasoned. The meta-analysis revealed a small effect for receiver apprehension on listening effectiveness. However, the large effect sizes for processing anxiety, processing ability, and processing complexity suggest that receiver apprehension is a complex variable that transcends current programs designed to measure and improve listening skills. While the meta-analysis revealed a small overall effect ($d = .251$) for education on reducing receiver apprehension, the limited number of studies precludes us from identifying a preferred educational strategy. Consequently, educational practices must focus upon improving information processing and listening skills at all receiver apprehension levels. For those who experience anxiety, special educational techniques should be developed. These programs must consider the apprehensive student's breadth of information on a topic area, educational background, and reinforcement history related to listening. We believe that irrational fears (Conditions II and III) may not respond to relaxation techniques alone. Also, the optimal "mix" of treatment strategies will vary based upon the theoretical nature of receiver apprehension. Consequently, researchers must devote increased attention to refining a theory of receiver-based anxiety.

Theoretical Implications

Results from the meta-analysis indicate that the effect sizes across conceptual variables are meaningful. Theoretically, decrements in listening efficiency, increases in processing anxiety, inefficient information processing, and cognitively simple reasoning may result from primary anxiety and/or from secondary anxiety and/or from operating on a low level communication logic. In fact, the theory that frequently has been used to explain receiver apprehension (assimilation theory) integrates these sources of anxiety into the individual's larger cognitive system (McReynolds, 1976, pp. 40-52). Thus, we believe that the three explanations should be viewed as complementary approaches, rather than competing perspectives. Additional research is needed to determine the receiver apprehension-type variables leading to inadequte listening. Theory construction is required because the construct contains questionable theoretical assumptions and vague conceptual relationships. Hague (1972) provided four basic standards for evaluating theory: (1) scope, (2) parsimony, (3) precision of prediction, and (4) precision of explanation (pp. 177-181). Applying Hague's standards may clarify the variable of receiver apprehension.

Scope. Scope refers to the number of basic problems in a discipline that are handled by the same theory. Wheeless (1975) argued this issue when he noted, "Although communication scholars have verbalized concern for receiving and processing information (we spend more of our time as receivers than sources), little concern has been evidenced for receiver apprehension, which would most directly affect decoding and response tendencies" (p. 261). He suggested that the functional roles of encoding and decoding were independent dimensions of communication and each role might result in a communication related anxiety. A fundamental problem of scope flows from the use of communicative role (source/encoder or receiver/decoder) as the model for receiver apprehension. On the surface, the role distinction is clear. However, Wheeless (1975) noted that the antecedents were not similar conceptually. The source role and its antecedent of social approval provided no insight into the receiver role and its antecedent, information processing. The source-receiver analog would be more meaningful had Wheeless, at the time, specified a process comparable to social approval operating in the receiver role. Without this addition, the scope of the theory properly focuses on information processing, not communication related social anxiety or apprehension.

Based on the meta-analysis, we suggest psychological self-approval as the mirror opposite of source-based social approval and an antecedent of receiver apprehension. Rokeach (1973) argued that individuals hold salient beliefs and values about themselves that effect their self-concepts. In Rokeach's scheme, the instrumental values of being logical, capable, self-controlled, and intellectual are aspects of the terminal value of "self-regard," a variable we equate with psychological self-approval. Psychological self-approval is consistent with McReynolds' emphasis on an integrated cognitive system that governs assimilation. McReynolds (1976) argues that:

> Each person...develops certain characteristic *conceptual schemata* which serve in the role of enduring plans or programs for the ordering of precepts; e.g., a person may assimilate certain inputs according to the conceptual schemata that he or she is intelligent, or that he or she is unlovable, or that people are untrustworthy, and so on. The notion of conceptual schemata is related to constructs such as attitude, expectation, and belief. (pp. 42-43)

We view psychological self-approval as a cognitive schemas germane to receiver apprehension. It represents a special logic and ordering of precepts; e.g., that incoming messages have unknown, manipulative goals, that other people seem to understand messages in ways that allow them to resist influence, that the topics of most conversations are too complex to be understood, and that discussions of controversial topics should be avoided. We believe that to fully capture the phenomenology of receiver apprehension, a theory must reflect the cognitive and the anxiety dimensions of the construct. Adopting Rokeach's framework of the terminal value of self-regard provides such a phenomenology. Consistent with the primary anxiety explanation (Wheeless, 1975), low self-approval would reduce the individual's confidence in message interpretation and/or psychological adjustment. Over time, low psychological self-approval might lead to a secondary anxiety (Beatty, 1981) associated with listening effectiveness, and result in the individual operating from a low level communication logic (Preiss, 1987). The result would be consistent with findings of our meta-analysis--lower listening effectiveness, higher processing anxiety, lower information processing ability, and cognitively simple reasoning.

Parsimony. Parsimony is a property of theory which deals with explaining as much as possible with as few theoretical statements as possible. For the variable of receiver apprehension, the precise nature of the cognitive components of misinterpretation, inadequate processing, and psychological adjustment (Wheeless, 1975) have not been specified. Beatty and his colleagues have offered McReynolds' (1976) assimilation theory to fill this void. However, this approach adds a fourth and fifth antecedent--persistence and rate of information overload--to receiver apprehension rather than clarifying the original three. While the "secondary anxiety" explanation is appealing, it does not illuminate the primary causes or processes that are the proper scope of the theory. Also, Preiss' (1987) finding that receiver apprehensives may employ low level communication logics has not been replicated or integrated into other theoretical approaches and it is unclear how low level logics are related to other traits (viz., argumentativeness, conversational sensitivity).

Precision of Prediction. This characteristic of theory involves anticipating outcomes, the timing of outcomes, and the qualitites of outcomes. Of Hauge's categories, receiver apprehension is strongest in the area of precision of prediction. The meta-analysis indicated clear patterns of receiver apprehension outcomes. Although Table 7-3 reveals some variance in the magnitude of the study effects, all effect sizes are in the hypothesized direction for each set of conceptual variables. Further, the magnitude of the average effects is meaningful. As research on the antecedents of receiver apprehension accumulates, greater understanding of the processes and timing of events should provide even more precise predictions of receiver apprehension outcomes.

Precision of Explanation. This criterion for evaluating theory involves the ability of premises to explain and interpret a series of events. To date, the anxiety associated with receiving a message has been linked to: (1) misinterpreting, (2) inadequately processing, and/or (3) psychologically adjusting to messages. These cognitive outcomes may well be conceptually independent. For example, misinterpreting a message may be associated with variables such as tolerance for ambiguity (Rotter, 1966) or selfschemas (Mandler, 1982). Inadequate processing of a message may be associated with self-monitoring (Snyder, 1974) or self-awareness (Gibbons, 1983). Psychological adjustment may involve cognitive rigidity (Rehrisch, 1958), cognitive complexity (Beatty & Payne, 1981), or dogmatism (Rokeach, 1960).

In its current state, the receiver apprehension literature is not able to isolate or explain the causes of the construct. For example, there is evidence that apprehensive individuals under stress overestimate the performance of speakers (Bock & Bock, 1984). It is unclear, however, if leniency errors are the result of increased anxiety for high receiver apprehensive raters, if errors result from an interaction between receiver apprehension and situational source anxiety (cf. stage fright), or if the ratings are attributable to deficiencies in information processing abilities. Of course, this problem is not unique to receiver apprehension. Research on source-based anxiety is unable to isolate or explain the series of events producing communication apprehension.

Methodological Implications

While conducting the meta-analysis, we discovered inconsistencies in the use of instruments measuring receiver apprehension. Although Wheeless and Scott (1976) developed the RRAT and demonstrated the superiority of the revised instrument, most researchers have continued to employ the RAT in their investigations. To explore the claims made for the RRAT, a meta-analysis of reliability estimates was conducted. Of the twenty-four studies examined, only fifteen provided information on the reliability of the scales. These figures were categorized by measurement instrument. Table 7-4 displays these data.

TABLE 7-4

Reliability Estimates for the RAT and RRAT

Test	Average Reliability	No. of Studies	No. of Subjects
RAT	.842	10	1,668
RRAT	.854	5	1,987

Table 7-4 does not provide compelling evidence for the empirical superiority of the RRAT. Although the average alpha coefficients are virtually identical, the failure of ten studies to report any reliability figures reduces our confidence in this finding. When 40% of the literature is unavailable, we believe it prudent to withhold judgment.

This is especially important because the RRAT (when compared to the RAT) exhibits a more normal distribution, a more stable factor structure, and a greater sensitivity to the variability of receiver apprehension (Wheeless & Scott, 1976).

An alternative method for evaluating the RAT and RRAT instruments is to examine the effect sizes associated with each outcome category. Unfortunately, when the fifteen data points were grouped according to the five classifications from Table 7-2, there was insufficient data to allow for comparisons. At this time, it is not possible to determine if the RAT and RRAT instruments are isolating similar or different patterns of relationships with oucome variables.

Conclusion

Our main meta-analysis revealed meaningful relationships with conceptual variables. Nevertheless, the variance associated with the studies is not overwhelming. Results from the meta-analysis are unable to support any one explanation for receiver apprehension over other perspectives. Also, considering the modest reliability estimates (Table 7-4) of both instruments, we are cautious in favoring any one theoretical perspective.

The primary and secondary explanations for receiver apprehension differ somewhat on conceptual and pragmatic grounds. Conceptually, the secondary anxiety approach represents an extension of Wheeless' (1975) formulation. The secondary anxiety approach shifts the construct toward a more generalized anxiety explanation, as the secondary anxiety assumes trait-like proportions. Beatty (1985) made this point when he argued that RAT scores represented a trait response to message processing that may be magnified by situation-specific processing tasks (pp. 74-75). On a pragmatic level, the secondary anxiety approach alters the focus of predictions extracted from the receiver apprehension construct. While Wheeless considered the primary impact of receiver apprehension to involve message processing, the new approach places more emphasis on selective exposure. In this frame, Beatty redefined receiver apprehension as a "tendency to avoid receiving information...or to suffer a variety of anxiety type reactions when forced to listen" (Beatty, 1981, p. 279; Beatty, 1985, p. 72). However, if one accepts the information avoidance hypothesis, the logical outcome is lower, not higher levels of cognitive backlogs. Therefore, theory development involving receiver apprehension and secondary anxiety must specify linkages between information avoidance and rate/persistance of information backlogs.

The communication logics explanation bridges the trait-state explanations by returning to the cognitive consequences of receiver apprehension. The finding that receiver apprehension is negatively related to cognitive complexity (Beatty & Payne, 1981) is consistent with Preiss' (1987) conclusion that high receiver apprehensives employed low order communication logics. This shifts the focus of receiver apprehension away from information overload and toward unpredictability. The high apprehensive would operate in an environment where incoming messages do not conform to a predictable model of the ways communication function. Anxiety would be a reasonable response to this situation, leading to backlogs of information and decrements in listening efficiency. From this vantage, however, the individual could understand the situational locus of the anxiety, if that were the "cause."

The notion that high and low receiver apprehensives employ fundamentally different communication logics complements, rather than displaces, the primary and secondary anxiety explanations. In tandem, these three explanations suggest that receiver apprehension is a complex variable with significant consequences for those who experience the anxiety. The sheer magnitude of the effect sizes indicates that it is possible for the individual's self-esteem to be affected by functioning in an unpredictable environment. We offer psychological approval of the self as a new antecedent for receiver apprehension. Just as social approval may lead to communication apprehension, low psychological approval of the self may result in situated anxiety about receiving, processing, and/or adjusting to messages.

Receiver apprehension offers promise for exploring how individuals process and respond to messages. The meta-analysis revealed meaningful effect sizes in areas of concern for educators and communication theorists. Future research must focus on theory development in order to advance understanding and treatments of the receiver-based information processing anxiety. A major finding of the meta-analysis is that the effect sizes for information processing efficiency and processing anxiety were substantially greater than the effect size for listening effectiveness. We urge educators to be cautious when prescribing treatments for apprehensive students with poor listening skills. The average difference for education in the meta-analysis was .124. Considering the modest overall effect for education, we are unsure of the viability of specific treatment programs. Our caution is also based on the fact that the effect size estimate is calculated on only two studies. Finally, there is no research on the desirability or efficacy of any method for reducing receiver apprehension. The complexity of the variable leads us to believe that programs designed to improve listening skills should employ multiple treatment strategies. These programs should be tailored to the rational or irrational nature of the fear experienced by the individuals. When receiver apprehension is identified, a mix of systematic desensitization, cognitive restructuring, and skills training may produce optimal improvement in listening skills.

CHAPTER EIGHT

Listening in the Organizational Context

Joy Hart Seibert

> The most important factor for successful communication
> is not only the ability to use language well or to speak
> well or present one's own point of view; it is rather the
> ability to listen well to the other person's point of view.
>
> Weinrauch and Swanda (1975, p. 26)

Across all areas of communication study, little disagreement exists that communication is best conceptualized as a process. And further, despite our specific areas of interest and focus, most of us agree that communication involves both "senders" and "receivers" (both are better called "communicators," but this term makes distinguishing between them more difficult. Thus, for the purposes of this chapter, the terms "sender" and "receiver" will be used, with the recognition that receivers can simultaneously be senders of information and vice versa). While many contexts of communication study (e.g., organizational, interpersonal, mass, intrapersonal, etc.) can be found within the field, communication researchers can generally be distinguished because of their processual views regarding communication and their focus on messages. For example, in the management literature, communication is conceptualized as one variable in overall organizational functioning. But in the organizational communication literature, much more attention is given to the processes of communicating, and these processes are viewed as much more than "a" variable. Models emphasizing the dual roles of the sender and the receiver and communication as processual have been widely accepted in our field for several years now.

However, despite high levels of agreement on conceptualizing communication as a process with both senders and receivers, we have clearly chosen to emphasize the "sending" aspects. Reviews of the literature in all areas of communication study indicate that much more attention has been afforded the process of sending, rather than receiving. In fact, listening or receiving has generally been taken for granted (Floyd & Reese, 1987; McCroskey, Richmond, & Stewart, 1986). Such a focus has likely occurred for two reasons. One reason is that it is with the sender that the message originates and this person's abilities are key ones in the process of exchanging information. It is clear that the vast majority of communication studies have been sender focused. Another possible reason is methodological difficulties involved in studying and measuring a process. Bostrom and Waldhart (1988) argue that most textbooks include material on listening, and 'standard' models of communication stress the dual importance of both sending and receiving ... (but) researchers in speech communication have shown little real interest in listening, and as a consequence, our knowledge of the process has grown little in the last twenty years" (p. 1).

Further, our general educational system provides much more skill building in sender competencies (e.g., public speaking) than in receiver ones (e.g., listening). For example, public speaking courses are frequently offered in universities across the country, but usually one must reach the graduate level before one can enroll in a course specifically focusing on listening. In addition, a quick glance through undergraduate texts will indicate the amounts of attention given to listening and speaking. Much the same distribution of attention to speaking and listening can be found in the texts and lectures in our elementary and secondary schools. Johnny and Janie may learn how to read and write (and even do some short speeches), but probably the only lesson on listening they receive is the caveat "Sit still and listen."

While it is true that more texts are beginning to focus on listening skills (Goss, 1982; Hunt & Cusella, 1983), few include more than a section dealing with listening. Thus, most individuals, at any point in their educational careers, receive little formal training in the skills associated with listening (Smeltzer & Watson, 1984). However, it is widely believed that listening skills can be taught and further developed (Blewett, 1951; Erickson, 1954; Heilman, 1951; Nichols, 1957; Toussaint, 1960; Wolff, Marsnik, Tacey, & Nichols, 1983). For example, Wolff et al. (1983) posit that all facets of listening skill can be developed and that "neglecting to make the effort to develop our listening power can profoundly affect our ability to communicate" (p.

1). Given the fact that listening has received little research attention and has not been emphasized in the educational systems, it is of no surprise that we know so little about it.

Despite some degree of "lip-service" in our texts about the importance of listening in communication and our own implicit understandings that listening is important (i.e., arising from compliments about our listening behavior, "Thanks so much for listening to my problems" or "It helps just to have you listen," or complaints about it, "You never listen to me" or "You haven't heard a single word I've said"), relatively few studies dealing with listening or the receiving part of the communication process have been published in the communication research literature (Beatty, Behnke, & Froelich, 1980; Hunt & Cusella, 1983; Rhodes, 1985). Of the published work in listening, very little research has been conducted in the organizational realm. A number of recent polls of business executives highlight the importance of listening within organizations (Rhodes, 1985; Smeltzer & Watson, 1984) and several recent organizational studies have examined the importance of communication abilities for success (e.g., Sypher, 1981; Sypher & Zorn, 1986). Thus, it is time we began to examine listening as a communicative skill affecting one's performance in the workplace.

The Importance of Listening in the Workplace

Smeltzer and Watson (1984) felt that the "importance of listening in organizational contexts is well documented" (p. 166). In twenty-five recent studies seeking to identify necessary employment skills, listening abilities were the most frequently mentioned skills (DiSalvo, 1980; Smeltzer & Watson, 1984; Wolvin & Coakley, 1985). Additionally, the general perception of executives and personnel officers was that these necessary listening skills are at present underdeveloped. This underdevelopment is not surprising given the lack of attention to building listening skills throughout the educational system. Wolvin and Coakley (1985) assert that "executives of major corporations also are recognizing an almost universal failure to listen" (p. 4).

Various investigations have indicated that nearly one-half of our communicative day is spent listening (Hirsch, 1979; Rankin, 1929; Steil, Barkder, & Watson, 1983; Weaver, 1972; Wolvin & Coakley, 1982). Some findings have estimated that executives spend at least 63% of each work day listening (Steil et al., 1983). These findings clearly point to the overarching importance of listening in the process of communicating. Within the context of an organization, our own communication has both individual, work group, and organizational outcomes.

Specifically, one's own degree of success (or failure) is dependent on in part on how well one can communicate with significant others (e.g., peers, supervisors, and subordinates) in the organization. Abilities in these types of communication influence whether one stays at the same organizational level, rises in the organizational hierarchy, or even remains employed by the organization. Further, at the individual level, one's ability to communicate successfully with others influences one's satisfaction with the work environment and his/her job. Beyond this, good listeners are generally well-liked (Wolvin & Coakley, 1985), which is an important social reward.

The ability of coworkers to successfully interact is also of key importance in the organizational context. The communication abilities of an individual likely impact upon how his/her work is regarded by peers. In addition, communication in work groups is important in achieving group consensus and identity and working toward common goals.

Further, effective and ineffective communication affect organizational productivity and profit. Estimates reveal that millions of dollars can be lost when organizational members do not communicate successfully. While these profitability concerns may not be of direct interest to organizational scholars, they are of key interest to those directing the course of organizations in our society. Executives "are beginning to realize that inefficient listening is costly to corporations -- costly in wasted money, misused time, deflated morale, reduced productivity, and alienated relationships" (Wolvin & Coakley, 1985, p. 4). Wolvin and Coakley (1985) quote J. Paul Lyet, the chairperson and chief executive officer of the Sperry Corporation, as stating:

> Poor listening is one of the most significant problems facing business today. Business relies on its communications system, and when it breaks down, mistakes can be very costly. Corporations pay for their mistakes in lower profits, while customers pay in higher prices. (p. 4)

In fact, Sperry's interest in listening has received vast amounts of attention. Beginning in 1979, the Sperry Corporation launched a public relations campaign based on their interest in and willingness to listen. Top Sperry officials have applauded the listening campaign as a huge success (see Wolvin & Coakley, 1985, for additional information on the Sperry approach).

The rewards of effective listening are reaped at the individual, work group, and organizational level. For example, Wolvin and Coakley (1985) state that:

> Businesses with effective listeners are rewarded not only with more satisfied customers and increased sales but also with more satisfied personnel and increased productivity, both of which will often lead to increased profits. Through effective listening, we gain more information, up-grade decision-making, reduce the number of mistakes, spend time more productively (in conducting meetings, performing job tasks which are more clearly understood, avoiding misunderstandings, etc.), share more viewpoints, and improve management/employee relations. (p. 15)

Recent bestsellers point out a trend emphasizing listening skills. For example, *A Passion for Excellence*, the followup to *In Search of Excellence*, is filled with numerous references to the importance of listening (Brown, 1987). In fact, Peters and Austin (1985), authors of *A Passion for Excellence*, define excellence as "built ... on a bedrock of listening ... listening and thus adapting ... turning every employee into an outward-focused, adaptive sensor" (pp. 5-6).

The recognition of listening's importance in organizations (e.g., DiSalvo, 1980; Downs & Conrad, 1982; Harris & Thomlison, 1983; Hunt & Cusella, 1983; Muchmore & Galvin, 1983; Rendero, 1980) has lead to the development of a variety of training programs and sessions aimed at increasing worker listening effectiveness. Although few data are publicly available to evaluate their effectiveness, such programs do indicate a general trend toward emphasizing listening skills. However, despite an increase in the implementation of various listening training programs, still little research on listening in organizations has been conducted.

Research on Organizational Listening

Although listening's importance is frequently commented upon by those in business settings and researchers studying such settings (e.g., Steil et al., 1983; Wolff et al., 1983; Wolvin & Coakley, 1982), few actual studies of listening have been conducted in the organizational realm. As Hunt and Cusella (1983) point out, much of the published listening literature is of the "how to" nature and few published works contain research on organizational listening. Given the overwhelming agreement on the importance of listening and the number of training programs developed to improve worker listening, this void seems to constitute a gap in our understanding.

One of the few studies examining organizational listening was conducted by Sypher, Bostrom, and Seibert (1989). This study investigated relationships between listening abilities and various social-cognitive and communicative abilities. Further, it is a continuation of a line of research pursued by Sypher (1981) and Sypher and Zorn (1986) linking such abilities to organizational outcomes. Findings of the Sypher et al. (1989) piece show a number of positive correlations beween listening and social-cognitive and communicative abilities. Specifically, results of the study indicate that total listening scores, on the Kentucky Comprehensive Listening Test, are positively correlated with cognitive differentation, perspective-taking abilities, self-monitoring abilities, and persuasive argumentation skills. These results lend support to Beatty and Payne's (1984) finding that more developed listening abilities (comprehension) are found in individuals with higher levels of cognitive differentation.

In addition, Sypher et al. (1989) examined the possibility of a relationship between listening abilities and individual organizational success. While this analysis produced mixed results, with only short-term memory and rehearsal listening subscales producing significant positive correlations with one's level in the organization, other correlations, although nonsignificant, were in the predicted direction.

Closer examination of the Sypher, Bostrom, and Siebert data is worthwhile. They studied a variety of assessements of communicative abilities and attitudes in middle executives at a large eastern insurance company. Table 8-1 presents part of these data. One of the most interesting findings is the strong relationship between STL and the ability to generate persuasive arguments in a communicative task (.64). Another interesting finding in this study is that women in the sample scored almost twice as well as men in interpretive listening. This is another example of gender differences that persistently crop up in studies of this type. Regardless of the kind of explanation one offers for these differences, it is clear that these separate scales exhibit relationships that are quite different from each other.

TABLE 8-1

Correlations among Varying Measures of Communicative
Abilities and Listening Scales

	STL	STL-R	Int	Lect	Select
Construct Complexity	.08	.45	.07	.32	.36
Persuasive Arguments	.64	.39	.05	.48	.49
Supervisor's Evaluation	.19	.50	-.05	.54	.47
Perspective Taking	.23	.20	.04	.23	.38
Self-Perception (Persuasive)	.11	.07	-.07	.18	.32
Self-Monitoring	.35	.29	.26	.52	.49

Future Directions for Listening

Research in Organizations As previously discussed, listening research in the organizational context has been frequently called for, but infrequently conducted. As such, many avenues of inquiry would be appropriate to advance our limited knowledge. Specifically, research in the following areas is highly needed:

1. Additional research on the relationship between listening and other communication abilities is needed. A number of studies have examined the importance of socio-cognitive and communicative skills in reaching one's goals. Sypher and Zorn's (1986) work has dealt with the importance of communication skills to upward mobility in organizations.

Future research should explore how strongly and in what ways listening is related to other communication abilities.

2. Future research should also examine Bostrom and Waldhart's (1978) five different types of listening in the organizational setting. In line with the research described in point one above, it would be interesting to investigate which type or types of listening are most closely related to other communication abilities.

3. Previous research has suggested that good listeners are more other-oriented. This finding certainly seems an intuitively sound one, but deserves further investigation and replication. Other-orientedness clearly has important implications for communication. Previous constructivist research has focused upon adaptations to the other interactant and their importance. The relationship between listening and other-orientedness warrants further exploration.

4. Examining differences in superior and subordinate listening would also be useful. Such studies might illustrate how power differentials influence what is heard. Further, previous studies of superior-subordinate communication (Jablin, 1979) have indicated that listening is highly important in these relationships.

5. Examinations of an organization's cultural values and norms toward listening would also be useful. During its recent listening campaign, the Sperry Corporation showed a strong focus on this communication skill. The organization spent a large amount of money developing and administering the listening program. Top executives praise the program and its outcomes. This type of commitment illustrates a value in the cultural system of Sperry. Various organizational mottos have come to symbolize the Sperry view and way of conducting business.

Just as at Sperry, cultures in other organizations have indicators of their listening norms. Analyses of organizational culture could provide insight into the existing cultural beliefs about listening or the amount of emphasis given to listening across cultures.

6. Another key role of research would be to evaluate existing

and new training programs in listening. While organizations themselves would likely take an interest in this type of evaluation, it can more importantly be a key in helping us to understand how listening skills are developed and the educational principles involved in fostering such skill development. Understanding how listening skills are acquired is clearly important across all domains of listening research.

Conclusions

Despite a number of comments on the importance of listening in the organizational context and the implementation of several training programs, few empirical research studies of listening in the organizational context have been conducted. The absence of such studies leaves us with a void in the literature and our understanding. This chapter makes several suggestions for areas of future research conduct. Only through the conduct of studies on organizational listening can we advance knowledge in the area.

CHAPTER NINE

Listening to Medical Messages: The Relationship of Physician Gender, Patient Gender, and Seriousness of Illness On Short- and Long-term Recall

Eileen Berlin Ray

Robert N. Bostrom

> When a doctor's patients are perplexed,
> A consultation's in order next.
> ....Oliver Wendell Holmes

A critical component in effective health care is the quality of the interaction between doctors and patients (Kreps & Thornton, 1984; Pendleton & Hasler, 1983; Street & Wiemann, 1987; and others). Most of the health communication research has focused on the relationship of doctor-patient communication to compliance and patient satisfaction and has neglected to examine some potential intervening influences that may effect these outcomes (e.g., Burgoon et al., 1987; Korsch & Negrete, 1972; Lane, 1983; Street & Wiemann, 1987). Certainly the doctor-patient relationship is an important one, and efforts to improve it are laudable. But even if a patient has the best relationship possible with a doctor, effective health care depends on the ability of the patient to remember (and act upon) information given by the doctor.

This, of course, points to communication as an important process in the relationship and message recall as a vital aspect. Part of the ability to comply rests with patients remembering what behaviors they must implement. Message recall is a necessary, though not sufficient, condition for patient satisfaction and compliance (Ley, 1975, 1977, 1983). Both short- and long-term recall of their physician's messages are important. Even though a patient may remember a good deal of information immediately after hearing the message, details may fade by the time comes to comply with the medical regime suggested. Even though some researchers have investigated recall (e.g., Ley, 1983), this critical link has been largely ignored by health communication researchers (cf., Bush, 1985). Accordingly, we conclude that research is needed to discover the characteristics of health messages and the sender to message recall. Recall might vary with low- and high-serious illness messages, physician gender, and patient gender. First, however, we need to examine the way that patients remember messages.

Patient Recall

Effective treatment will be possible only if the patient is able to remember accurately information from the physician (Bush, 1985). Unfortunately, research findings in this area are somewhat contradictory. Some work has focused on recall of written messages. Ley and his colleagues have conducted ongoing work in the area of message recall with much of their focus on written information in the form of leaflets (see Ley & Morris, 1984, for a review of this work). Primarily, they have examined levels of difficulty of material in medical pamphlets and found that greater simplification (shorter words and shorter sentences), repetition, categorization, and using specific instead of general advice all increased patient recall.

Other studies have examined recall of oral messages with a variety of clientele. For example, a review of studies investigating patient recall of medical information presented orally (Ley & Morris, 1984) finds the percentage of patient recall ranges from 37% to 71%. However, Pendleton (in Bush, 1985) found that the amount of information recalled depended on the type of information. Instructions about medication resulted in more recall (83.8%) than "things to do" (76.3%), or general information (61.5%). When more information was added, recall remained the same for instructions about medication but decreased in the other two categories.

Seriousness of Illness

While retention is important with any illness, it is of greater consequence when the illness is potentially life-threatening. It is then that treatment information (i.e., dietary and/or exercise regimens) becomes critical. Bush (1985) noted that "characteristics of the verbal content exert an important influence on the recall of health information"

(p. 104). Once a patient hears a diagnosis of a serious illness, typically they hear nothing else the doctor says (Kreps & Thorton, 1984; Thompson, 1986). The anxiety and fear that accompany such an illness block the patient's ability to hear the message, much less recall it. In addition, anything patients do hear may be forgotten due to their high level of anxiety (Ley, 1983). These findings would lead us to believe that there will be less recall of a high serious illness message than a low-serious illness message.

Gender and Health Communication

With the increase of women entering medical school over the past 15 years (Arntson et al., 1982; Braslow & Heins, 1981), gender issues in health care have become more salient. Research outside the health care context suggests that men are listened to more than women (Pearson, 1985), and are perceived as more competent (Miller & McReynolds, 1973) and more powerful (Cline & Cluck, 1985) than their female counterparts. Even when their professional credentials are the same, males continue to be perceived by both males and females as more intelligent and competent than women (Fidell, 1970; Peterson et al., 1971; Rosen & Jerdee, 1974; Schein, 1975). In addition, both males and females tend to remember more when listening to a male speaker (Gruber & Grebelein, 1979).

Within the health care context, a review by Gray (1982) suggests that female patients prefer female physicians and that males and females find it easier to talk with female physicians. However, research suggests no gender differences on recall of health messages but greater liking of female speakers (Hall, Braunwald, & Mroz, 1982). Bush (1985) examined written messages and found that author gender alone did not result in greater recall of health information but that recall was increased when the speaker was the same sex as the listener. In his review of the recall literature, Bush (1985) notes that "taken together, these studies suggest, given equally rated presentations, more will be retained when the speaker is male" (p. 104).

However, this effect may be mediated by the gender of the listener. In a series of studies, Bush (1985) first had subjects listen to an audiotape on heart attacks presented by a male "doctor" and a female "doctor" and examined nonverbal expressiveness of the speaker on recall. This was followed by subjects viewing a videotape of a female "doctor" delivering the same message. His findings indicate that sex differences may depend partly on the sex of the speaker. Recall of health information appears to be greatest when the doctor is the same sex as the listener. These findings would lead us to believe that recall will be greater when the doctor and patient are the same sex than when they are opposite sexes.

Listening and Retention of Messages

It often surprises researchers to discover that the ability to remember messages is as varied as it is. However, the research reported earlier in this book illustrates how different persons can be in basic listening ability.

Of obvious importance in the acquisition of medical information is the ability of the patient to listen. What is not clear from other studies is whether these factors of importance--patient and physician gender-- and amount of specific medical information interact with the ability to listen in the clinical context.

This study was designed to examine these factors as they interact one with another. The fact that individuals vary widely in their ability to store information presented orally would lead us to believe that individual listening ability will interact with seriousness of illness and gender of both patient and physician in the retention of messages.

METHOD

Design of Messages

First we needed messages that would resemble (as closely as possible) messages that might have been received in a physician's office. Since direct observation of patients in doctors' offices is out of the question, we chose to reconstruct such a situation as closely as possible. This required a number of preliminary steps.

Seriousness of Illness. Obviously, an illness could be considered "serious" from a number of points of view. Our concern in this study was the patient's perspective and knowledge base. An illness had to possess two characteristics: it had to be reasonably familiar to a large group of persons, and it had been judged to be serious in a general way. We therefore proceeded in three phases. Each is discussed below.

Phase 1: Respondents (N =112) were asked to "Write down the names of every illness you can think of." These lists were compiled and resulted in naming 147 different illnesses. Those illnesses mentioned by fewer than 10% of the respondents were eliminated. A final list, which had 25 illnesses, formed the based for the second phase.

Phase 2: A questionnaire was constructed listing each of the 25 illnesses. A new set of respondents (N =122) were asked to evaluate each as to seriousness, ranging from 1 (not serious at all) to 5 (extremely serious). Means were calculated and illnesses were then rank ordered from low to high seriousness. All illnesses that fell below the median were considered low serious and all above the median were considered high serious. Of the low serious illnesses, we chose the median illness, strep throat. Of the high serious illnesses, we chose the median illness, diabetes.

Phase 3: The first author met with a family physician and posed the following question: "A patient comes to see you and you have found that he has strep throat (diabetes). Tell me everything you would tell him." The physician's responses were audiorecorded and later transcribed. The researchers examined the messages and omitted any material irrelevant to the diagnosis, symptoms, treatment, or prognosis. Two basically equivalent messages (one for strep and one for diabetes) were then constructed. Following this, two different physicians examined these written messages for content accuracy and completeness and assessed them as valid. These messages were then used for the basic script for audiotapes. Four audiotapes were made, using professional actors (male physician, strep throat; male physician, diabetes; female physician, strep throat; female physician, diabetes).

Respondents. Respondents were undergraduate students in communication courses at the University of Kentucky. Participation was voluntary and anonymity was assured. Respondents were assigned randomly to one of four treatment conditions. Physician's gender was cued by the following introductory comments on their questionnaire: "Imagine that you have gone to see a physician, Dr. Steven (Marcia) Davis, because you have not been feeling well. Dr. Davis has run some tests and has now called you into his (her) office to tell you the results. Listen to what Dr. Davis tells you about the test results." In addition, of course, the physican's voice on the tape was clearly male or female.

Measurement. Immediately after hearing one of four audiotapes with a medical message, respondents completed a questionnaire asking for the diagnosis, symptoms, treatment, and prognosis. Then intervening questionnaire items were introduced and completed. Short classroom activites were then introduced, and twenty minutes later another questionnaire was distributed which again asked about diagnosis, treatment, prognosis, and symptoms. Scores were determined by counting the number of information items written down by each respondent for diagnosis, symptoms, treatment, and prognosis.

Listening Ability. Students were administered Form A of the Kentucky Comprehensive Listening Test. Scores for Short-Term Listening (STL), Short-Term with Rehearsal (STL-R), Interpretive Listening (Int), and Long-term Listening (Lect) were obtained.

Results

First we were interested in what effects gender of physician, gender of respondent, and seriousness of illness had on retention of information, both on immediate and delayed recall. Table 9-1 presents the results of the analyses of variance on the measures of immediate recall.

TABLE 9-1

Results of Analysis of Variance
on Seriousness, Physician Gender, and Respondent
Gender on Immediate Retention

	Symptoms		Treatment		Prognosis	
	F	p	F	p	F	p
Seriousness (S)	32.05	.001	19.52	.001	31.51	.001
Physician (PG)	7.02	.007	.11	.734	6.86	.002
Respondent (RG)	.87	.875	6.12	.013	.37	.543
S x PG	.21	.651	.00	.984	1.20	.278
S x RG	.09	.766	.01	.966	.09	.762
PG x RG	.08	.773	5.90	.016	6.37	.014
S x PG x RG	2.24	.136	.28	.655	.07	.796

TABLE 9-2

Means of Various Cells
for Immediate Retention

	Symptoms		Treatment		Prognosis	
	Male Doctor	Female Doctor	Male Doctor	Female Doctor	Male Doctor	Female Doctor
Diabetes, Female Respondents	2.77	3.06	3.95	3.91	2.02	1.51
Diabetes, Male Respondents	2.50	2.96	2.63	3.59	1.91	1.81
Strep Throat, Female Respondents	3.90	3.73	2.60	2.73	1.00	.86
Strep Throat, Male Respondents	3.11	4.12	1.67	2.25	.88	1.00

Table 9-2 presents the means of each of the various conditions (cells) of the measures of immediate recall. The "seriousness" variable was a strong one, producing large effects. These effects were inconsistent, however. In the strep throat condition, more symptoms were remembered than in the diabetes condition. The opposite was true for the information about treatment and prognosis. Respondents in the diabetes condition remembered more treatment data and prognosis data than the ones in the strep throat group. Gender of the physician produced main effects in the remembering of symptoms and the remembering of the prognosis. In both cases, the female physician produced better results (for symptoms, the mean for the female voice was 3.30, the mean for the male voice was 2.93, and for diagnosis, the mean for the female voice was 1.72 and the mean for the male voice was 1.37). Women respondents remembered more data about treatment than did men (women's mean was 3.55; men's mean was 2.89). However, in both the treatment and prognosis a significant interaction between respondent gender and physician gender was present. For the treatment information, women remembered the information presented by the male physician better, and men remembered information presented by the female physician better. For prognosis, women remembered information presented by the male physician better, but no differences were present among male respondents. All of these results are presented in detail in Table 9-1.

Table 9-3 presents the results of the analyses of variance on delayed recall and Table 9-4 presents the means for this set of scores. Again, large effects are present for the type of disease that was the subject of the message, but the strep throat symptoms were more easily remembered, while the opposite was true for treatment and diagnosis messages. Again, the female physician produced better retention on the symptoms variable. As with the immediate recall, physician gender and respondent gender interacted. For treatment information, males remembered information presented by the female voice better and female respondents remembered information presented by the male physician better.

TABLE 9-3

Results of Analysis of Variance
on Seriousness, Physician Gender, and
Respondent Gender on Delayed Retention

	Symptoms		Treatment		Prognosis	
	F	p	F	p	F	p
Seriousness (S)	29.3	.001	38.0	.001	28.7	.001
Physician (PG)	5.9	.015	.0	.953	1.9	.160
Respondent (RG)	.2	.635	10.1	.007	3.1	.079
S x PG	1.3	.244	.0	.827	.1	.707
S x RG	.0	.977	.7	.395	1.8	.177
PG x RG	1.0	.302	9.6	.005	5.0	.025
S x PG x RG	2.7	.098	.2	.673	.3	.551

TABLE 9-4

Means of Various Cells
for Delayed Retention

	Symptoms		Treatment		Prognosis	
	Male Doctor	Female Doctor	Male Doctor	Female Doctor	Male Doctor	Female Doctor
Diabetes, Female Respondents	2.77	3.04	4.26	4.11	1.88	1.66
Diabetes, Male Respondents	2.45	3.07	2.63	3.59	1.27	1.48
Strep Throat, Female Respondents	4.10	3.62	2.30	2.48	.91	.93
Strep Throat, Male Respondents	3.11	4.12	1.44	2.25	.88	1.00

When we analyzed the amounts of information remembered concerning the prognosis (the estimated outcome), then females remembered information presented by the male doctor better, and no differences were present for males. In other words, women remembered predictions made by male doctors, but not by female doctors. In men, no such effect was present.

Since the kind of illness produced inconsistent results, it was dropped from the analysis of the data when listening ability was incorporated. Scores from the first two scales of the Kentucky Comprehensive listening test were used to measure listening ability (STL and STL-R). Results of this analysis are presented in Table 9-5.

TABLE 9-5

*Results of Analysis of Variance
on Listening Ability, Seriousness of Disease, and
Respondent Gender on Immediate Retention*

	Symptoms		Treatment		Prognosis	
	F	p	F	p	F	p
Physician (PG)	6.2	.013	.1	.741	6.0	.014
Listening (L)	.0	.797	3.9	.042	6.7	.010
Respondent (RG)	.7	.389	5.6	.011	.3	.566
PG x L	1.7	.187	.1	.733	1.8	.173
PG x RG	.0	.790	5.4	.022	5.6	.018
L x RG	1.7	.193	1.0	.301	.6	.438
PG x L x RG	.0	.930	.0	.765	.1	.686

As before, the female physician produced better scores. In the analysis of the treatment information recalled, listening ability, respondent gender, and respondent by physician gender interaction effects were all present. The gender effects were the same as presented in the above analysis, of course. In the items of prognosis recalled, physician gender was signficant, along with listening, and a physician by respondent gender interaction.

The interactions in Table 9-5 were the same, of course, as those presented earlier. In other words, while listening ability did indeed exhibit differences, no interactions were present that would modify the the findings about physician gender and respondent gender. The differences for gender are marked in the recall of symptoms and prognosis, but not for treatment. Listening ability is a large component of the recall of prognosis but not of the other aspects. The interaction between physician gender and respondent gender shown in Table 9-6 is primarily due to the fact that the male respondents actually remembered less when a male physician presented the information. All of the other conditions were equal.

TABLE 9-6

Means of Various Cells
for Immediate Retention

Ability:	Symptoms		Treatment		Prognosis	
	Good	Poor	Good	Poor	Good	Poor
Male Physician, Female Respondents	2.76	3.17	3.92	3.51	2.19	1.50
Male Physician, Male Respondents	2.77	2.80	2.80	1.60	1.60	1.30
Female Physician, Female Respondents	3.30	3.35	3.60	3.30	1.39	1.14
Female Physician, Male Respondents	3.43	3.05	3.68	2.94	1.68	1.57

In other words, the interaction was due to that one cell only. Normally interactions signal "different differences" where something works at one level but not at another. This interaction, while actually falling into the framework of that definition, is actually the result of something that occured in only one cell. Just why the males in this study should exhibit a memory deficiency of this type at this place in the table is puzzling. Duncan's test indicates that this cell (male respondents, male physician) were indeed different from the others in the table. We will return to this topic later in the chapter.

Delayed retention was examined in the same way. These findings are presented in Table 9-7, and the means for the separate cells in the analysis are presented in Table 9-8. The results of this analysis are quite similar to the results for immediate recall. In other words, the same kind of puzzling interaction took place here as did in the earlier findings.

Our interest in listening ability stemmed from our assumption that good listeners would assimilate more data and that the subsequent gain in knowledge would produce the effects that we were interested in. The above findings indicate that the relationships among data assimilated and listening ability are, at best, complex ones. Accordingly, we next turned to the measure of knowedge obtained and examined it as if it were an independent variable. We then analyzed the "intent to comply" responses to see what, if any, effects knowledge acquisition had on this important response. A two-way interaction was present between knowledge obtained and the seriousness of the disease ($F = 6.01$, $p <$ .01, $df = 1, 323$, $E = .021$). This interaction was an odd one, however. When individuals gained a good deal of information, they indicated lower intent to comply (for the serious disease) than persons who had acquired lesser amounts of information.

TABLE 9-7

*Results of Analysis of Variance
for Listening Ability, Seriousness of Disease, Respondent
Gender on Delayed Retention*

	Symptoms		Treatment		Prognosis	
	F	p	F	p	F	p
Physician (PG)	5.0	.025	.0	.957	1.7	.183
Listening (L)	.0	.764	4.0	.046	6.6	.010
Respondent (RG)	.1	.664	8.1	.004	2.7	.096
PG x L	3.3	.068	.4	.498	2.8	.090
PG x RG	.9	.338	8.5	.004	4.4	.034
L x RG	.2	.597	.0	.895	.1	.632
PG x RG x L	.2	.628	.5	.476	.1	.674

TABLE 9-8

*Means of Various Cells
for Delayed Retention*

	Symptoms		Treatment		Prognosis	
	Good Listeners	Poor Listeners	Good Listeners	Poor Listeners	Good Listeners	Poor Listeners
Male Physician, Female Respondents	2.76	3.24	4.34	3.51	2.04	1.43
Male Physician, Male Respondents	2.70	2.80	2.30	1.90	1.45	0.85
Female Physician, Female Respondents	3.36	3.19	3.61	3.36	1.48	1.27
Female Physician, Male Respondents	3.43	3.22	3.62	3.00	1.32	1.30

The means of this interaction are presented in Table 9-9. While these mean differences are not spectacular ones, there is a definite tendency among those obtaining more knowledge to comply more with the strep throat message than with the diabetes message. It is difficult to imagine why those with more knowledge should be the ones who were lowest on the intent to comply measure in the diabetes condition. This is a puzzling finding, to say the least. It may be due to the kind of person gaining the knowledge, or something in the knowledge itself that would make the difference. Lastly, in this experimental situation, it may well have been that the respondents could not imagine themselves in an appropriate diabetic regimen.

TABLE 9-9

Means of "Intent to Comply" Scores for
Seriousness of Illness and Knowledge Obtained

Illness	Knowledge Obtained	
	High	Low
Diabetes	2.35	2.55
Strep Throat	2.57	2.44

Finally, we asked respondents to evaluate the physician on a number of personal characteristics: "Warm-Cold," "Concerned-Unconcerned," "Friendly-Unfriendly," "Involved-Uninvolved," and "Caring-Uncaring." This analysis produced two interesting effects.

First there was a main effect for respondent gender ($F = 7.44, p <$ .01, $df = 1, 363, E = .031$). Women generally responded that the physician was more personable ($.usX = 14.1$) while men generally responded that the physician was less so ($.usX = 13.0$). A neutral response would have produced a mean of 10.0, so we cannot say that the men saw the physicians as nonpersonable, only that the women tended to do so to a greater degree.

These responses produced a three-way interaction among seriousness of illness, physician's gender, and knowledge obtained ($F = 4.92, p < .02, df = 1, 363, E = .024$).

The means of this interaction are presented in Table 9-10. While there was a general tendency to feel that the physician in the strep throat condition was more caring, there is an interaction among amount of knowledge obtained and gender of the physician. When knowledge obtained was high, female physicians tended to be evaluated higher and male physicians lower in the diabetes condition. The opposite was the case in the strep throat condition.

TABLE 9-10

Means of "Personableness of Physician"
for Seriousness of Illness, Knowledge Obtained,
and Gender of Physician

| | Female Physician | | Male Physician | |
| | Knowledge Obtained | | Knowledge Obtained | |
Seriousness of Illness	High	Low	High	Low
Diabetes	12.75	11.42	11.83	12.50
Strep Throat	13.76	14.24	13.40	12.80

DISCUSSION

It is clear that a number of factors are present in the evaluation of medical messages. One of the most important, of course, is the seriousness of the illness. Other vital items are the gender of the physician and the gender of the respondent. And while listening ability is not as important as we originally hypothesized, it is clear that it is of some importance, and that people would do well to consider this kind of communication skill in medical interactions. In interpreting the "seriousness" manipulation, the fact that the strep throat (nonserious) condition produced better scores than the diabetes (serious) condition in the symptoms remembered seem anomalous. In the treatment and prognosis items the serious condition did indeed produce more retention. It is highly possible, however, that respondents in this study had previous knowledge that could have affected their scores in the strep throat condition. In a *post hoc* analysis, students from the same sample group were asked to indicate their personal experience with each of the two diseases. One in three had personal knowledge of strep throat and one in fifty had personal knowledge of diabetes. Personal knowledge might well explain symptoms knowledge differentials. Treatment and prognosis would not necessarily fall into this category.

The interactions among gender of sender and gender of receiver do not support the contention that same-sex dyads will result in greater retention. These data were more consistent with data reported by Searle and Bostrom (1983) and Bostrom and Waldhart (1988). These differences might well be explained by noting that Rost and Roster's contentions apply to real dyads in an interpersonal situation, however.

All in all, the data reported in this chapter indicate that medical messages do indeed vary with individuals' listening ability, with their gender, and with differing situations. Further research ought to focus on more specific interpersonal factors, such as interaction, setting, and compliance.

CHAPTER TEN

Differences in Motivational Levels and Performance on Various Listening Tasks

Mary Helen Brown

Enid S. Waldhart

Robert N. Bostrom

> Nothing great in the world has ever been
> accomplished without motivation.
>
> ....Hegel

In many instances throughout the book we have seen differences in information processing that seemed to depend on the "importance" or "value" of the information to the recipient. One would conclude that in these instances, the listener was "motivated" to perform, that is, that some inducement was present in the different situations that led to enhanced performance. Whether we call the mental set "involvement," "motivation," or something else, we clearly have some idea that differing performance is the result of a specific situation.

In Chapter Three, we examined the differences in "mood" that might be dependent on the acquisition of information. You will recall that in that data set, the amount of information acquired had little influence on perceived mood. Another approach to "motivation," or affect, is to provide some external stimulation that normally enhances a reaction. In other words, in the data provided in Chapter Three, we cannot really be sure that individuals were different in mood, so our conclusions about mood may be flawed. If we take steps to alter mood slightly, we might get different results.

In this chapter, we will examine some induced differences in performance by trying to "involve" respondents in a specific way.

Involvement has proven to be an important antecedent condition to many communicative efforts (Cegala, 1981; Cegala, Savage, Brunner, & Conrad, 1982). One of the best ways of manipulating motivation is through direct instructions in a classroom setting. In this study, we used "challenging," "relaxing" (or supportive), or "neutral" instructions prior to taking the test.

"Neutral" instructions consisted merely of the standard instructions provided with the test. The "challenging" instructions were intended to raise attentiveness and involvement in the testing situation. Thus, in addition to the standard instructions, the following statements were made: "The ability to recall this information is a good test of your ability to apply course information. The results of this test could very possibly have a positive or negative effect on your class grade. I will be reporting your results to your instructor. Therefore, it is to your advantage to do your best on this test."

While the "challenging" instructions were designed to raise involvement regarding the test outcome, "relaxing" (or supportive) instructions were aimed at alleviating any stress associated with the testing situation. So the researcher added the following statements to the standard instructions on the test: "This is only a preliminary study and I am only interested in determining how long it takes to administer this test and in finding out your reactions to the test items. Your performance on this test is not the main concern." If there is a clear connection between mental set and performance, then, these different instructions would lead to different levels of performance in the listening test.

The second aspect of the study focused on the relationship between modes of acquisition (note taking or non-note taking) and various measures of listening. The first two sections of the test were divided into those items dealing with numbers, letters, and words. The third section was divided into those items asking for number recall, word recall, and general concept recall. If acquisition and recall functions are similar, we might expect short-term listening (STL) for numbers, and short-term listening with rehearsal (STL-R) for numbers to predict number recall in the lecture part of the test. STL on words, STL-R on words, and "lecture" word recall might also be related. In this way we might be able to better understand memory storage functions or to determine if there are separate abilities.

Subjects were selected from the basic public speaking classes at the University of Kentucky. Twelve sections (out of twenty-two) were selected for inclusion in the study. Two sections were chosen randomly to receive the "challenging" instructions and two more were chosen to receive "supportive" instructions. These instructions were given orally while the remaining test was presented on audiotape. The remaining eight sections were utilized for the modes of recall analysis. Four of these sections were instructed to take notes during the lecture portion of the test and the remaining four were prevented from doing so. Two of these final four sections were also used as a control group for the involvement portion of the study.

Results

The outcome of the various types of instructions by forms of listening behavior is presented in Table 10-1. The interaction is significant and is confined to the STL and STL-R sections of the table. Apparently supportive instructions produced better performance on STL-R while motivating instructions produced poorer performance on STL.

TABLE 10-1

*Means of Various Forms of Listening Behavior
Analyzed by Types of Instructions Given*

	Instructions			
	Neutral	Challenging	Relaxing	Totals
Type of Listening				
STL	10.13	9.41	10.53	9.96
STL-R	9.50	9.83	11.53	10.05
Lecture	9.13	9.50	9.33	9.30
Total	9.58	9.58	10.46	
F's				
Instructions	5.224 , $p < .05$ ($df = 1,201$)			
Tests	2.232 , n.s.			
Interaction	2.936 , $p < .06$, ($df = 2, 201$)			

TABLE 10-2

Various Modes of Recall Analyzed by
Short-term Listening Ability and by Note-taking

		Without Notetaking	With Notetaking
High STL	Words	3.05	2.77
	Numbers	4.79	5.00
	General Concepts	3.89	4.15
Low STL	Words	3.09	3.34
	Numbers	4.77	4.96
	General Concepts	3.09	3.39

F's:

	Note taking	STL	Note taking by STL
Words	.09	4.04*	2.04
Numbers	.41	.005	.04
General	.66	8.63**	.01

$*p < .05$
$**p < .01$
$df = 1, 106$

Table 10-2 presents the means of the analysis of notetaking and STL. Higher performance on STL apparently produced poorer performance on items requiring recall of words. This effect seems to be confined to the notetaking groups, but the interaction is not significant. High scorers on STL did better than low scorers on general concepts.

STL-R produced quite a different effect. These results are presented in Table 10-3. Recall of word-related items on the lecture tasks seems to be enhanced by note taking, but only for low scorers on STL-R. Low scorers on STL-R did more poorly than high scorers in word-related recall.

TABLE 10-3

Various Modes of Recall Analyzed by
Rehearsal Listening Ability (STL-R) and by Note-taking

		Without Notetaking	With Notetaking
High STL-R	Words	3.29	2.93
	Numbers	5.00	5.29
	General Concepts	3.67	4.06
	Words	2.76	3.28
Low STL-R	Numbers	4.47	4.73
	General Concepts	3.17	3.36

F's:

	Notetaking	STL-R	Notetaking by STL-R
Words	.09	.03	5.40*
Numbers	.42	3.12	.01
General Concepts	.04	5.50*	.14

*$p < .05$
$df = 1,106$

When the listening scales were recombined to locate specific effects of words, numbers, and letters, some unusual outcomes were observed. The first of these analyses is presented in Table 10-4. High and low scorers on the number scales are compared on their performance on various modes of lecture recall. No interactions were observed, and only general concept recall was enhanced by good performance on the number scales.

In other words, skill in receiving numbers did not seem to relate more significantly to any of the other skills, and notetaking did not seem to have an effect on this phenomenon. This certainly argues strongly for an individualized view of the skills involved. While a general receiving ability may be useful in putting together various kinds of cognitive abilty, these data do not seem to bear out such a view.

TABLE 10-4

Various Modes of Recall Analyzed by Listening
Performance on Number Scales and Note-taking

		Without Note taking	With Note taking
High on Number Scales	Words	3.09	3.10
	Numbers	4.89	5.20
	General Concepts	3.76	4.20
Low on Number Scales	Words	3.05	3.15
	Numbers	4.75	4.82
	General Concepts	3.15	3.30

$F's$:

	Notetaking	Number Scale	Notetaking by Number Scale
Words	.09	.01	.06
Numbers	.41	.70	.25
General Concepts	.67	9.37*	.30

$*p < .01$
$df = 1,106$

Analysis by word scales is presented in Table 10-5. High scorers on word scales in short-term tasks did more poorly recalling word-related items. This difference seems to be confined to those subjects who took notes, although the interaction is not significant. However, on general concepts the opposite effect occurred--high performance on word scales correlated with higher scores. When the short-term scales were analyzed by letters, no significant differences were found in any of the three recall modes. Slightly different outcomes were observed on the other dependent variables, however. One should compare the means in Table 10-4 and Table 10-5 carefully.

TABLE 10-5

Various Modes of Recall Analyzed by Listening
Performance on Word Scales and by Notetaking

		Without Notetaking	With Notetaking
High on Word Scales	Words	3.09	2.83
	Numbers	4.76	5.12
	General Concepts	3.76	3.87
Low on Word Scales	Words	3.05	3.36
	Numbers	4.80	4.86
	General Concepts	3.15	3.52

$F's$

	Notetaking	Word Scale	Notetaking by Word Scale
Words	.09	2.98*	2.34
Numbers	.41	.23	.22
General Concepts	.63	2.79*	.24

$*p < .10$
$df = 1, 106$

In order to more carefully analyze the interactions between modes of recall on lecture items and various measures of short-term listening scales, a canonical correlation was performed between the two sets of data. A canonical correlation is essentially a paired factor analysis which seeks for a meaningful relationship among the factors that should logically be related in a global sense. Each of the "canonical variates" is essentially a factor in the broadest sense of the word. However, the factors are not exploratory as they are in true factor analysis. Table 10-6 presents the results of this analysis.

TABLE 10-6

Canonical Correlation among Various Listening
Scales and Differing Modes of Recall

Canonical Variable 1
$(r = .45, p < .01)$

Modes of Recall	
Word Items	-.243
Number Items	.110
General Concept Items	.955
Listening Scores	
Short-term (letters)	.178
Short-term (words)	.578
Short-term (numbers)	.789
Rehearsal (letters)	.625
Rehearsal (words)	.238
Rehearsal (numbers)	.319

Canonical Variable 2
$(r = .26, p < .04)$

Modes of Recall	
Word Items	.800
Number Items	.854
General Concept Items	.221
Listening Scores	
Short-term (letters)	-.184
Short-term (words)	-.275
Short-term (numbers)	-.322
Rehearsal (letters)	.501
Rehearsal (words)	.187
Rehearsal (numbers)	.724

Discussion

Although this study began as an exploration into the memory functions in listening behavior, we were surprised at the large number of questions raised by the results. While something is obviously happening differently between the short-term and long-term aspects of listening, that some thing (or things) is still by no means clear.

Different types of instructions did affect listening scores. Relaxing or supportive instructions related to higher mean scores for short-term listening (although only the STL-R results were statistically significant). Challenging instructions produced mixed feelings in such a way that for the lecture section the mean score was the highest, while for short-term listening the mean score was the lowest. The instructions added orally at the time of test administration, then, did appear to lead to test score differences.

These additional instructions may have worked to "set" or involve the subjects through a kind of interpersonal intervention by the experimenter. That is, the actual appearance of an experimenter who said anything at all (even if it were negative) might have provided a personal element which subjects found helpful as contrasted with the audiotaped "neutral" instructions for the remainder of the test.

A more dramatic effect might have been observed among the various instructions if those instructions had been perceived as being more distinctive. For example, perhaps the challenge, the "threat" of counting the test score toward course grades, was not sufficiently motivating to provoke drastic changes in scores. That is, a stronger stimulus may be needed to produce statistically significant results among the kinds of instructions.

Further study of the relationship between kinds of mental set and listening behavior ought to examine carefully the possible differences in personal contact and tape-recorded instructions, to rephrase any added instructions so as to make them more clearly single-purposed, and to examine personality variables which might affect the listening process. Considering listening as a complex process may mean that attempts to single out even one aspect--involvement or set or mode of recall--from the whole may yield distorted interpretations. We may have to be content with examining the whole despite the fuzziness that results.

On the other hand, the results from the aspects of the study which focused on modes of acquisition (note-taking and non-note-taking) merit considerable discussion. Differences between taking notes and not taking notes do appear. These results indicate that note taking leads to better overall lecture-listening performance, but runs shy of traditional levels of statistical significance. Scores on short-term listening predict fairly well the general-concept aspect of lecture listening (with or without taking notes), but only those high scorers on short-term listening with rehearsal (STL-R) predict better general concept lecture listening.

The lack of correspondence between number, letters, and words on short-term listening and on numbers, words, and general concepts in lecture listening seems disturbing. While we might interpret the lack of predictability as an indication that short-term listening and long term listening are different, we are somewhat hesitant to do so because of a strong common-sense belief of a relationship between numbers, words, and general concepts.

At the same time, this lack of correspondence may also be explained by depth of analysis and/or schematic approaches. That is, the individual may utilize various internal criteria of "meaningfulness" of the units (numbers, letters, words, concepts) which may affect his/her recall of certain test items. Or, it may be that what we are dealing with here actually represents different individual capacities and/or strategies which may make generalizations less appropriate or meaningful.

It is apparent, then, that additional research in this area should address a number of concerns. For example, different lecture topics and lecture structures need to be examined. Also, the notes used by students should also be analyzed in order to better understand how individuals actually "rehearse" for long-term listening. That is, merely looking at what happened if notes were written or not is insufficient. We must examine how the individual is processing the items and then see how well this fits with test items and scores.

Different kinds of recall might also provide useful information, especially in relation to kinds of "rehearsal" utilized. In this study only forced choice recognition recall was called for, whereas open-ended questions might lead to other conclusions. Also, in this study the answer choices consisted of terms actually used within the lecture. While clearly each question had only one correct answer, the fact that the correct information was buried among other terms heard in the lecture may have unnecessarily distracted subjects and/or may have represented an inappropriate test of recognition recall--despite the fact that the question-answer format was designed to determine if an individual could recall correctly.

We began this effort by attempting to determine some of the basic processes involved in listening behavior. Mental set or involvement and mode of acquisition do seem to be components of this process. Further research into these and other aspects of listening appears to be both necessary and useful.

CHAPTER ELEVEN

Listening for Deception: The Effects of Medium on Accuracy of Detection

Pamela J. Kalbfleisch

> It is always the best policy to tell the truth--
> unless, of course, you are an exceptionally good liar.
> ...Jerome K. Jerome

A significant problem in the process of listening is the assessment of the truthfulness of the speaker. In previous chapters we have seen that motivation, medium, gender, and setting all influence the nature and kinds of retention of oral messages. All of this research assumes that the information is *worth* retaining, i. e., that the source is a truthful person, and that information in the messages that are processed is accurate.

This assumption may be naive. As Knapp and Comadena (1979) put it,

> White lies, cover-ups, bluffing, euphemisms, masks, pretenses, tall-tales, put-ons, hoaxes and other forms of falsehoods, fabrications, and simulations have coexisted with truthfulness and honesty in human communication for centuries. Swindlers, con artists, and imposters are not new; neither is lying to a dying relative, exaggerating a person's ability in a letter of recommendation, "protecting" one's children or spouse from "hurtful" information, or lying to the public for reasons of "national security." (p. 270)

Obviously, then, listeners need to assess the truth-telling potential of their sources. The question of how well we can do this becomes central to any thinking about communication.

How well do we detect deception? What conditions make deception easier or more difficult? When people lie, do their facial expressions give them away? Or should listeners attend to other parts of the body? And very importantly, how do the various media affect the detection process?

Fortunately there is a large body of literature in the detection of deception that can help us assess our basic abilities in this fundamental communicative activity. This research has explored the effects of observational conditions on human accuracy, investigated the differential abilities of observers, and examined the deceptive performance of differing types of communicators to see if the falsehoods of some are more difficult for observers to detect than others.

Unfortunately, much of this research is contradictory. Some studies seem to indicate that people in general could identify truth and falsehoods significantly better than chance (Hemsley & Doob, 1979; Lavrakas & Maier, 1979; Potamkin, 1982), while others have failed to find these accuracy levels (Bauchner, Brandt, & Miller, 1977; Matarazzo, Wiens, Jackson, & Manaugh, 1970; Motley, 1974). The effects of observational conditions is also unclear. For example, Ekman and Friesen (1974) reported data indicating that listeners who viewed only the bodies of communicators made more accurate truth/lie decisions than those viewing the heads. Ekman and Friesen's data were supported by Littlepage and Pineault (1981). However, when Hocking, Bauchner, Kaminski, & Miller (1979) tried to repeat these findings, they found only partial support for Ekman and Friesen's results. Still another researcher, Wilson (1975), found that neither viewing the head nor the body alone was as good as a combination of both for producing accurate judgments of veracity.

Maier and Thurber (1968) and Sakai (1981) tested the possibility that visual cues might actually interfere with accuracy by removing the viewing condition altogether. They found that those listening to audio messages alone could discriminate lies from truths more accurately than those viewing videotapes. These results were not borne out in other studies, however. For example, Wilson (1975) noted that those who listened to audiotapes were not as accurate as those who viewed videotapes--the opposite of Maier and Thurber. Bauchner et al. (1977), Hocking et al. (1979), and Harrison, Hwalek, Raney, and Fritz (1978) found no significant differences in judgmental decisions between audio and video conditions.

Deception studies have not found any signficant differences between the sexes in the ability to detect deceptive communication. Sakai (1981) and Maier and Thurber (1968) contend that females are better lie detectors than males. However Atmiyanandana (1976), Parker (1978), and Rovira (1982) conclude there is no difference between the sexes. Parker (1978) noted that while a sex difference in observers was not found, observers did have more difficulty detecting the deceptive communication of female than of male deceivers. Sakai (1981) also noted a significant difference in success at detecting male versus female deceivers; however, Rovira (1982) and Wilson (1975) found no significant differences in detection of male versus female deceivers.

These studies illustrate some of the contradictory findings in the deception literature. This research poses a real problem to those of us who would like to apply this research to specific situations or settings. One approach, obviously, is to conclude that nothing can be learned from contradictory findings, and simply forget it. But a more constructive approach is to look at the research *in combination*, to see if a pattern might be observed from a more comprehensive analysis of these studies. Two basic approaches to combining are available, significance tallies and quantitative reviews.

Significance Tallies

One way of combining research results would be to simply tally signficant and nonsignificant results and see which occurred the most often. In the literature reviews that open most deception studies we often see this kind of tallying taking place. Typically, after reviewing the diverse findings in deception research, many writers call for more research to assess human lie detection abilities (Feldman & White, 1980; Harrison et al., 1978; Hocking et al., 1979; Hemsley & Doob, 1979; Maier & Lavrakas, 1976; Parker, 1978; Rovira, 1982; Rotkin, 1980; Sereno, 1981). This plea overlooks the possibility that additional exploration will only add to the contradictions. At other times, researchers attempt to explain contradictory findings by pointing out methodological limitations in those studies that contradict their line of reasoning (Comadena, 1982; Potamkin, 1982).

Unfortunately, the use of significance test tallies is not the best approach for better understanding the findings that deal with human lie detection. As Hedges and Olkin (1985) point out, these tallies are strongly biased toward the conclusion that the treatment has no effect, and that this bias is not reduced as the amount of evidence (number of studies) increases (pp.48-52).

Further, the significance test does not provide an estimation of the strength or importance of a relationship. It only suggests whether the obtained statistic differs significantly from chance (Glass, McGaw, & Smith, 1981). Significant results are classified as the presence of a relationship and nonsignificant results are classified as absence of a relationship (Hunter, Schmidt, & Jackson, 1982). Confidence intervals for obtained values are not considered in the tallies. Hence, significant and non significant results are classified as absolute (Glass et al., 1981). Further, since results from large sample sizes are more likely to be found significant than those from small samples, some strong effects from small samples may be overlooked (Glass et al., 1981).

Quantitative Reviews

Quantitative reviews (meta-analyses) use summary statistics other than the significance test to aggregate study findings. Thus these meta-analyses avoid the problems inherent in using the significance test for combining research results (see Hunter et al., 1982, for a review of meta-analytic techniques).

Two attempts have been made to quantitatively review the deception detection literature. Zuckerman, DePaulo, and Rosenthal (1981) and Kraut (1980) used two different meta-analytic methods in their reviews which each deserve careful attention.

The most extensive of the quantitative reviews of the deception literature was completed by Zuckerman et al. (1981). They reviewed the literature concerning accuracy in deception detection and the literature which examined verbal and nonverbal behaviors in deceptive communication. They sought to use Cohen's d statistic (Cohen, 1977) as a comparative measure of effect size. In this review they calculated d as $2 \sqrt{F} / \sqrt{df}$ where F equals the obtained value for F and df equals the degrees of freedom for the variable of interest. However, this computation is inappropriate for studies with repeated measures, *i.e. the majority of deception studies.*

The Zuckerman et al. meta-analysis contains several problems. The first is that studies are presented with their corresponding d estimate of effect size. The problem is that d is defined as a statistic based on a comparison (Cohen, 1977). However, only one set of comparisons made in the meta-analysis is defined. In this set the d is the effect size of the difference between truthful and deceptive judgments. In the other sets of comparisons it is unclear exactly what is being compared. In interpreting the d values provided, knowledge of what comparisons the effect estimates represent is critical.

A second problem in interpreting the tables in the Zuckerman meta-analysis is that the results are provided in standard deviation units only. No other summary information is made available for interpreting these findings. The standard deviations alone do not provide sufficient information from which to determine accuracy. For example, If one group detects deception at 1.2 standard deviations and another at 1.4, how accurate is either group? The standard deviations, of course, suggest that the observers in one study are more accurate than those in another, but the magnitude of this accuracy is not specified.

This meta-analysis contains a more serious error in applying the d statistic to research using the research design with repeated measures. These designs are implemented in deception detection by having each observer judge the veracity of a number of communicators who lie or tell the truth. Typically each judge will view a number of communicators who represent different manipulations of the independent variables in the design. The judge may also be asked to make the decisions in different viewing conditions. The differences in judges are typically treated as between-subjects factors and the differences in the communicators and the conditions under which they are observed are treated as within-subjects factors (repeated measures).

The major problem with the Zuckerman et al. use of the d statistic is that it fails to properly estimate the effect size of these repeated measures. There are several reasons for this failure. The first problem with estimating the effects of within-subjects factors in this way is that the variance of within-subjects factors is the variance of difference scores and not an estimate of the within-cell variance. The d as used by Zuckerman et. al. assumes an estimate of the within-cell variance and does not properly assess the variance of difference scores.

The degrees of freedom estimate for the within-subjects F values are also not comparable to the degrees of freedom value assumed by Zuckerman et al. to be $N - 1$. Within-subjects F values will differ depending on the error term associated with the degrees of freedom. This difference in the size of the degrees of freedom is another reason the Zuckerman d values estimated from within-subjects designs will not be comparable to those from between-subjects designs.

The problems with the d statistic in the within-subjects case created by an inappropriate estimate of variance will manifest themselves in over-inflated d values. Also, Zuckerman et al.'s meta-analytic estimation of effect size based on the value of F for within-subjects factors may not even be possible without access to the original data. Current statistical reporting practices in many social science journals do not include the publication of the variance estimates necessary for determining the effect sizes for these within-subjects designs.

A final criticism of the Zuckerman et al. meta-analysis is that for singular studies, estimates of effect size were not provided. Instead, Zuckerman et al. dealt with these studies by narratively describing their results in terms of statistical significance. Since the authors of these studies provided the necessary summary statistics for the computation of Zuckerman's d statistic, the results of the individual studies should have been provided in a common metric with the studies cumulated in the meta-analysis.

The Zuckerman et al. meta-analysis is the most comprehensive quantitative review of the deception literature to date. However, it has severe problems in the operationalization and application of Cohen's d effect size statistic and hence the results should be considered with caution.

The Kraut (1980) quantitative literature summary of accuracy in deception detection is less extensive. He presents a fairly simple analysis of this research in the form of an average compiled from the results of ten studies. His estimate of average human lie detection ability is 57 percent where 50 percent accuracy would be expected by chance.

Kraut used the mean as a summary statistic, which is more easily understood than the Zuckerman et al. effect size measures. However, Kraut's results may be misleading. In Kraut's review he summarizes a sizable body of complex and somewhat contradictory studies with a single average (57 %) and its standard deviation (7.8%). Overlooked is the fact that these studies have measured accuracy of judges placed in several different types of observational conditions in experiments testing the effects of a number of different independent variables in varying experimental paradigms. Many of the studies in the Kraut meta-analysis are simply not comparable (Kalbfleisch, 1986). Some of the comparisons included Kraut and Poe (1980)--a study in which customs inspectors were compared to laypersons, Helmsley (1977)--where genders were compared, Maier and Thurber (1968)--where persons playing different roles were compared, and Ekman and Friesen (1974)--where comparisons were based on video tapes without sound. Kraut's single overall average does not indicate what differences if any there may be under these different conditions and others.

By consolidating the accuracy ratings for each study into one score for averaging, Kraut may have misrepresented the findings of this body of research. For example, Maier and Thurber (1968) found that those who listened to and those who read transcripts of people lying and telling the truth were more accurate (77.0% and 77.3%) than those who watched people lying and telling the truth (58.3%). However Kraut averaged these conditions to yield 70.9 percent as the representative summary statistic for the Maier and Thurber study in his overall cumulation of the deception studies. By doing this Kraut not only overlooked differences in experimental conditions when constructing his overall average but his results may also be misleading, with an overall average of a study's accuracy levels across conditions not providing a very good picture of the outcomes of the Maier and Thurber study or others.

Further problems in the utility of Kraut's overall estimate lie in the sample of studies he selected for inclusion in the average. These problems lie in: 1) the derivation of mean accuracy ratings, 2) the chance probability associated with included estimates, and 3) the selection procedures used in obtaining the mean accuracy ratings. For example, Kraut utilized an accuracy estimate of 46 percent from the Kraut and Poe (1980) experiment. However, their published report does not contain any reference to a mean accuracy estimate. Possibly Kraut's use of an unreported mean estimate can be understood given that he was senior author of the study and had ready access to the unpublished raw data.

This was not the case in the Maier and Janzen (1967) article. In this report, counts were provided, recording the number of observers who correctly identified liars and truthtellers. To obtain a mean accuracy rating in a 0-1 metric, Kraut was required to convert this count to a percentage by dividing the number of correct judgments by the total number of judgments made. Dividing the Maier and Janzen count of 97 correct judgments by the 228 total judgments yields a mean accuracy estimate of 43 percent. However, Kraut listed an estimate of 61 percent from the Maier and Janzen study in constructing his overall mean accuracy.

The origin of the mean accuracy estimates that Kraut used to represent the Kraut and Poe (1980) and Maier and Janzen (1967) studies is unclear. A brief explanation by Kraut regarding their derivation would have added credibility to their usage as estimates of accuracy in deception detection.

A second problem lies in the chance level of one of the studies. While Kraut interprets his overall estimate as having a chance level of 50 percent in all studies, the chance level in the Geizer, Rarick, and Soldow (1977) study appears to be 33.3 percent. Instead of asking observers to decide whether people were lying or telling the truth (where chance would be 50%), they asked their observers to decide which of three people was telling the truth in a "To Tell The Truth" game show excerpt. In this case the possibility that the judges would make the correct choice by chance was 33.3 percent. Kraut notes this difference in probability, but he still includes the Geizer et al. estimate in his overall average of detection ability. In doing this he has created an overall estimate based on estimates not converted to the same metric; hence the Hemsley and Doob estimate is not comparable to the others included in the same overall estimate.

The specific sample of studies may also contribute to the problems with Kraut's review. The total number of lie detection judges is 855 people. Across 32 studies reporting mean accuracy ratings in a metric ranging from 0 to 1 (with .5 chance accuracy level), there are 3439 possible judges in the deception literature or 3,577 if one wishes to include the Kraut and Poe (1980) and Geizer et al. (1977) studies. Why Kraut choose to use less than half the available studies is not clear, nor are the selection procedures that he used to compile his sample. For example, he chose to use three of the four deception detection studies reported by Maier and his associates (Lavrakas & Maier, 1979; Maier & Janzen, 1967; Maier & Thurber, 1968), but did not indicate why the Maier and Lavrakas (1976) study was not included. Other lines of research were totally excluded. This incomplete selection of studies brings the representativeness of the Kraut estimate into question.

In summary, problems with the quantitative review by Kraut include use of a small unrepresentative sample, failure to differentiate the variables considered in studies included, and utilization of misleading accuracy estimates that resulted from study-wide means pulled into the middle range by averaging overall experimental conditions. Use of estimates that were possibly unsuitable for this review also added to the reduced utility of this quantitative summary.

In other words, problems with the Zuckerman et al. (1981) and Kraut (1980) meta-analyses indicate that these analyses may be misleading. An accurate assessment of human lie detection ability and the observational conditions and individual difference variables that may mediate it are not available.

Given our dependence on deception detection ability in legal, business, and social settings, a more general assessment of this skill is essential. A reexamination of the deception detection literature in a different context should provide a more enlightening understanding of our ability to detect deceit. Because this body of research relies heavily on mixed and repeated measures designs, a meta-analysis is needed that uses a technique allowing for cumulation of effect sizes across these designs. The meta-analytic techniques of Hunter et al. (1982), Glass et al. (1981), and Levine, Romashko, and Fleishman (1973) currently do not provide the methods necessary for this type of cumulation.

In this chapter a different approach to meta-analysis was undertaken. Since most deception detection research habitually uses within-subjects and mixed research designs, it does not easily lend itself to traditional meta-analytic procedures. The most widely used meta-analytic techniques were developed for designs that utilize between-subjects factors (Glass et al., 1981; Hunter et al., 1982; Levine et al., 1973; Rosenthal, 1978). The variance of within-subjects factors is difficult to estimate if it is not provided by the authors. Variance estimation for each factor in a design is critical in the determination of the size of effect present.

In the past, researchers encountering repeated measures in construction of meta-analyses have removed them from consideration. However, deception detection research is not an area of study where the issue of within-subjects factors can be coped with by simply excluding those studies which employ repeated measures from cumulation of data. Questions of interest in deception detection studies are often directed at factors affecting the accuracy in veracity judgments. The designs of these studies typically match these research questions by asking the same observers to make such decisions across a number of different observation conditions, over a number of different deceivers/truthtellers or with differing amounts of information. This type of design results in judgments being made by the same individuals across different conditions, e.g. a design of repeated measures.

Dichotomous Judgments as Units for Meta-analysis

Lacking complete summary statistics, estimation of effect sizes for within-subjects factors is not possible. However, a solution to cumulation of within-subject effect sizes in a specific case can be found, since these are measurements of phenomena recorded in naturally occurring dichotomous units.

Conceptually, it is easy to see why this form of measurement has been popular with deception researchers. Researchers who report their results in terms of counts, proportions, or percentages derive them by asking observers to make the the dichotomous decision of "truth," if they believe the communicator is telling the truth, and "lie," if they believe the communicator is lying to them. The observers judgments then are compared to the actual behavior of the communicator: i.e., Did the communicator actually lie or tell the truth? The correct judgments are then tallied and the results presented as proportions or percentages of correct judgments or as a simple count of the number of times the observers were correct. Measurements of accuracy in deception detection reported in these natural units easily lend themselves to a straightforward method of meta-analysis that is appropriate for cumulation of study results for both within-subjects and between-subjects variables. The repeated measures and mixed designs of deception detection research, along with the occasional between-subjects designs, can all be assessed using this method provided the accuracy scores are reported in percentages, proportions, or counts. Results reported in counts can easily be converted by the reader to proportions by noting how many times the observers are asked to make judgments and comparing the number of judgments on which the observer responded correctly.

These naturally occurring measures provide the meta-analyst with a constant unit magnitude that is scaled both within studies and across studies. This constant unit can be used for cumulative comparison, a type of comparison currently not possible with estimates from within-subjects designs that do not use this form of measurement. Comparison of means with the same scale of magnitudes allows the researcher to avoid the problems of differing variance composition that are inherent in the comparison of effect sizes computed with non comparable variances.

Proportions or percentages of correct veracity judgments measured on a dichotomous rating of truth or lie create a scale with possible values ranging from 0 to 1 with chance accuracy represented by .5 or 50 percent. One benefit of this type of scale is that it can be easily understood. A cumulative proportion of .5 simply means that people are correct in their judgments half of the time. This percentage/proportion scale is equally useful for understanding a question posed in a primary study as it is for understanding a question posed in a meta-analysis.

In summary, the reconstruction of original responses for meta-analysis can be done for studies in which respondents were asked to give truth/lie responses to communicative stimuli which were half truth and half lies. In this reconstruction, care should be taken to include only those studies where experimental manipulations do not affect the chance expectation of .5 correct responses.

Sample Selection. In searching for studies for inclusion, several criteria were used. First studies were selected if they included measurements of deception detection rated on dichotomous scales of truth or lie that were converted to proportions or percentages, or they included sufficient information to convert the counts into proportions or percentages. In addition, they also must have contained a counterbalanced manipulation of truth and lies so that each person observed an equal number of truthful messages and deceitful messages. Asking an observer to discriminate lies from truths when only lies are present does not measure deception detection ability because the measurement is confounded with the variable of suspicion. When only lies are present, highly suspicious people will make the most judgments of deception and hence will have the highest accuracy rating. These people may actually have very poor lie detection ability as defined in this meta-analysis, as they may consistently make the error of suspecting truthful messages are deceptive. Experiments that only supply truthful messages also provide a confounded measure of deception detection. In this case very trusting or gullible people would have the highest accuracy scores. Again these people may be very poor at discriminating lies from the truth, trusting not only those who are telling the truth, but also those who are deceiving.

Excluded from this meta-analysis is lie detection research that relied on Likert-type scales, such as that of Geis and Moon (1981), Hemsley and Doob (1978), and Rotkin (1980). The basic assumption of researchers that measure lie detection accuracy thus is that lie detection is a matter of degree. Therefore, high accuracy scores can be achieved by extremely certain judgments that are correct. People who are extremely certain in their correct decisions receive higher accuracy scores than people who are somewhat certain and correspondingly people who are extremely certain in their incorrect decisions are less accurate than people who are less certain of their incorrect decisions. The weakness of using this measurement scale to assess accuracy in deception detection is that the observers' accuracy judgments are confounded with an assessment of personal assuredness in their decision.

Research by Miller and Kalbfleisch (1982), Hocking (1976), and Littlepage and Pineault (1979) indicates that the relationship between accuracy in veracity judgments and confidence in these judgments is weak. Hocking (1976) reported correlations between accuracy and confidence ranging from .061 to .063. Miller and Kalbfleisch (1982) noted that high confidence scores accompanied low accuracy ratings. Miller and Kalbfleisch also found that observers were more confident in their judgments of women than in their judgments of men.

Studies which use a measure of confidence as an accuracy measure, such those of DePaulo et al. (1985), Geis and Moon (1981), Hemsley and Doob (1978), and Rotkin (1980), result in an accuracy measure that is confounded by an unrelated variable. This scale will assess cautious observers that make mostly accurate veracity decisions as less accurate than observers who are extremely certain on a few correct judgments and unable to make a judgment of truth or deceit on the remainder of the messages. On the other hand, some observers may express extreme confidence in their judgments of truth, but be cautious in their attributions of deceit. Researchers finding significant differences in observers' ability to detect deception in male as opposed to female communicators through use of Likert type scales may actually be finding sex-related differences in judgmental confidence and not differences in discerning truth from lies.

Studies that utilized a second technique to assess accuracy in deception detection were also excluded from this meta-analysis. These studies (DePaulo, Davis, & Lanier, 1980; DePaulo Lanier, & Davis, 1983; DePaulo & Rosenthal, 1979; DePaulo, Stone, & Lassiter, submitted; Olson, 1978; and Streeter, Krauss, Olson, & Apple, 1977) had observers rate their veracity decisions on scales from 1 to 6 or from -3 to +3 with the lower rating indicative of extreme certainty that the communicator was lying and the highest rating indicative of extreme certainty that the communicator was telling the truth. The ratings between these extremes represented lesser degrees of certainty in the observers' decisions. Researchers using this method then subtract observers' ratings of truthfulness when the communicators were telling the truth from observers' ratings of truthfulness when the communicators were lying. The resulting value was used to represent the accuracy score of each observer. These accuracy scores are confounded by confidence in judgments, as were the untransformed Likert measures of accuracy. Extreme confidence in a correct judgment is also assumed to be a more accurate assessment of veracity than a less confident correct judgment.

Other studies not included in this meta-analysis have idiosyncratic components that make them unsuitable for cumulation. The deception detection studies by Geizer, Rarick, and Soldow (1977) and Zuckerman, Amidon, Bishop, and Pomrantz (1982) were excluded because they used a trichotomous measure of accuracy instead of a dichotomous measure. For these studies chance accuracy would be .33 rather than .50. Percentage accuracy means from these studies cannot be accurately cumulated with the percentage accuracy means generated from dichotomous judgmental choices and ultimately tested against an overall chance accuracy of .50.

Kraut and Poe (1980) and Fugita, Hogrebe, and Wexley (1980) were also excluded from this meta-analysis because neither study reported the experimental means. Finally, Hildreth (1953) and Littlepage and Pineault (1978) were excluded. While these researchers provided observers with a dichotomous truth/lie measure, observers were also given the option to avoid making a decision if they were not sure of their judgment. The difficulty in including these studies is that the mean percentage accuracy is based on only confident judgments, unlike the other studies in the meta-analysis which did not exclude the judgments made in uncertainty. It is possible that by excluding uncertain judgments Hildreth (1953) and Littlepage and Pineault (1978) measured only those observers with confidence in their deception detection ability. Conversely it is also possible that the accuracy ratings from these studies is yielded from judgments based on only those communicators who presented themselves in an obviously deceitful or honest manner.

The studies of deception detection included in this meta-analysis are those that assessed accuracy by dichotomous truth/lie measures without a no judgment option. These studies either reported mean accuracy ratings in proportions/percentages or their results were convertible to proportions/percentages.

Procedures for Cumulation. After the identification of an appropriate body of research, the second step was the extraction of the mean accuracy score for each level of research design. These mean accuracy ratings were then placed into tables with other means taken from studies that measured these same variables. These tables are arranged according to the combinations of variables and levels that conceptually form general designs for the deception detection studies. Entries in these tables are averaged to provide cumulative estimates of the effect of each variable. Information is provided on the number of observers that each mean effect size represents. Means from deception detection studies that investigate variables not considered in other experiments are presented narratively after the cumulative estimates have been discussed.

In evaluating the effect sizes yielded from this meta-analysis, the size of each cumulative mean was considered relative to the chance criterion of .5. Since variances cannot be determined for the means represented in these cumulative estimates, significance tests of the difference between the means and .5 are not possible. Instead visual comparisons of relative size are made. In the analysis of cumulative means, these comparisons are made in light of the sizes of accuracy ratings common to this area of research. Since variance estimates are unavailable, sampling error cannot be assessed in this meta-analysis.

Results

The results of this meta-analysis indicate that humans are not very skilled at detecting deception. The cumulative accuracy ratings cluster from .45 to .70 with only a few cumulative accuracy ratings surpassing or falling behind these scores. These results also suggest that lie detection ability varies only slightly across experimental conditions. Keeping these modest differences in mind, the design tables from this meta-analysis will be evaluated for those variations present in the human ability to detect deception.

Observational Conditions

The first part of this meta-analysis examines the support for two major theories of deception detection: Ekman and Friesen (1969, 1974) and Maier and Thurber (1968).

Ekman and Friesen (1969, 1974) suggest that people are less aware of their bodies and extremities than they are their faces. They contend that since the face has a larger message sending capacity, most people learn to control their facial movements in order to accurately communicate with others. Consequently, when people are confronted with the task of concealing or distorting messages they will exercise control over their facial regions.

Accordingly since the body and extremities have less sending capacity for messages (Ekman & Friesen, 1969), people will have used them less to convey meaning and therefore be less aware of their movement when they are concealing or distorting messages. Ekman and Friesen reason that given this tendency of communicators to concentrate on control of the facial regions and to remain unaware of other body movement, observers attempting to detect deception should focus on changes in body movement and to place less emphasis on facial displays.

TABLE 11-1

Deception Detection Accuracy: Conditions Under Which Truthful and Deceptive Messages Are Observed[a]

Year	Study	Head Only	Body Only	Head and Body
'77	Bauchner, Brandt & Miller			.47
'74	Ekman & Friesen	.46	.52	
'79	Hocking, Bauchner, Brandt & Miller	.51	.51	.52
'79	Littlepage & Pineault	.53	.76	
'81	Littlepage & Pineault	.49		
'75	Wilson	.49	.61	.60
'85	Zuckerman, Koestner & Colella	.59		
	Mean	.51	.60	.53
	No. of Observers Represented by Estimate	1395	1169	984

[a] Mean accuracy ratings for Hocking et al. are the combined ratings from both factual and emotional lies/truth. Bauchner et al., Ekman & Friesen, and Littlepage and Pineault (81) did not have audio.

Table 11-1 displays the cumulative results of studies that presented experimental conditions that test this theory. One condition offering full shots of both heads and bodies was added to the design to examine the impact of full visual information in comparison to the body only and head only conditions.

While the differences between these conditions appear small, the experimental condition of body only, where persons were allowed to observe only the bodies of communicators, yields the highest mean accuracy ratings. Conversely, observers were the least accurate in their observations of the head only condition. This cumulation of mean accuracy ratings provides some support for Ekman and Friesen's theory. Specifically, observers in the viewing condition that Ekman and Friesen posit displays the most deception clues, the body, were more accurate than those observers who viewed the area Ekman and Friesen maintain is the most readily controlled, the face.

Those observers who viewed full head and body shots were more accurate than those observers that viewed heads only, but were less accurate than those observing bodies only. Deception clues supplied by the body, in the combined head and body condition, may enhance accuracy ratings when compared to ratings yielded from head only observations. On the other hand, full body and head information may inhibit accuracy ratings achievable when viewing bodies only. In this instance, the face, which is readily controlled by the communicator, may present contradictory information to the body's messages which confuses the observers, or facial cues may be attended to more readily by observers than cues from the body.

Maier and Thurber (1968) theorize that observers are overwhelmed by verbal, nonverbal, and content information when they decode messages. This overabundance of information distracts the observers from noticing clues that indicate they are being deceived. Maier and Thurber reason that deception clues will be more apparent if nonverbal information is reduced.

Table 11-2 presents the cumulative results of studies which test the experimental conditions of transcripts, audio only, and audio/visual. The results presented in Table 11-2 expand the conditions originally tested by Maier and Thurber by adding a condition of visual only, where the observers can see but not hear deceptive and truthful messages. This addition, adopted by some primary researchers, balances the audio only condition in this design.

TABLE 11-2

Deception Detection Accuracy: Conditions Under
Which Truthful and Deceptive Messages Are Observed[a]

Year	Study	Visual Only	Audio Only	Audio/ Visual	Tran- Script
'77	Bauchner, Brandt & Miller	.47	.32		.47
'74	Ekman & Friesen	.49			
'41	Fay & Middleton		.56		
'79	Hocking, Bauchner, Kaminski & Miller	.48	.54	.55	.57
'79	Littlepage & Pineault			.64	
'81	Littlepage & Pineault	.49	.63		
'68	Maier & Thurber		.77	.58	.77
'74	Motley		.67		
'81	Sakai	.51	.58	.58	
'75	Wilson	.62	.53	.57	
'84	Zuckerman, Kernis, Driver & Koestner			.51	
'85	Zuckerman, Koestner & Colella	.56	.62	.62	
Mean		.52	.58	.58	.60
Number of Observers Represented		1623	1676	1536	1018

[a] Mean accuracy ratings for Hocking et al. are the combined ratings from both factual and emotional lies/truths.

The cumulative estimates reported in Table 11-2 indicate observers were the most accurate at detecting deception when they read transcripts of deceptive/truthful messages. These results support Maier and Thurber's contention that reduction of nonverbal information will increase accuracy in detecting deception. In this condition both visual and paralinguistic cues were unavailable to the observers. The cumulative findings reported in Table 11-2 also suggests that persons with access to only audio cues and persons with access to both audio and visual cues have the same accuracy rates.

TABLE 11-3

Observational Conditions and Accuracy of Judgments of Deception

Year Study	Head Only Audio	Head Only No Audio	Body Only Audio	Body Only No Audio	Head & Body Audio	Head & Body No Audio	Audio Only	Transcript
'77 Bauchner, Brandt, & Miller					.57	.47	.32	.47
'74 Ekman & Friesen		.46		.52				
'41 Fay & Middleton							.56	
'79 Hocking, Bauchner, Kaminski & Miller	.54	.47	.53	.48	.56	.49	.54	.57
'79 Littlepage & Pineault	.53		.76					
'81 Littlepage & Pineault	.64	.49						
'68 Maier & Thurber					.58		.63	.77
'74 Motley							.77	
'81 Sakai	.58	.51					.67	
'75 Wilson		.49		.61	.57	.62	.58	
'85 Zuckerman, Koestner, & Collella	.62	.56					.53	
Mean	.58	.50	.65	.54	.57	.52	.58	.60
Number of Observers Represented by Estimate	1157	1543	751	1137	1203	984	1676	1018

This observation does not support Maier and Thurber's position that due to absence of distracting nonverbal information, observers in the audio only condition will be able to perform better than those in the full information condition. The new condition added to Maier and Thurber's original three displayed the lowest accuracy ratings. When compared to the full audio visual condition, the low rating in the visual only condition suggests that the audio channel provides helpful information for the detection of deception.

Table 11-3 incorporates both the head and body conditions on which Ekman and Friesen concentrated their theory with the audio, audio/visual, and transcript conditions focused on by Maier and Thurber. The full head and body condition and the visual only condition added to Table 11-1 and Table 11-2 are also included.

This combined design suggests that persons are the most accurate in detecting deception when observing: 1) the transcript only condition, 2) the audio only condition, 3) the body only condition with full audio information, 4) the combined head and body viewing condition with full audio information, and 5) the head only condition with full audio information. The three conditions with the lowest accuracy ratings are: 1) the body only viewing condition without sound (6th), 2) the combined head and body viewing condition without sound (7th), and finally, 3) the head only viewing condition without sound (8th).

In general this table indicates that observers were more accurate in observational conditions that contained the content of the message than observational conditions that did not. These higher accuracy scores may have resulted from additional information available in message content. This information may have allowed observers to check messages for logic, consistency, and length.

Observers viewing body only shots were more accurate than those viewing heads only. However, when observers viewed combined head and body shots, they were less accurate than when viewing bodies only and more accurate than when viewing heads only. While the body may be a source of helpful clues to deception as Ekman and Friesen contend (1969, 1974), this may only be the case when it is viewed alone without a view of the face and head.

Discussion

Comparison with Previous Meta-Analyses. The findings of this meta-analysis are both similar and different from the findings generated by Zuckerman et al. (1981) and Kraut (1980). One of the major findings of this quantitative review was that humans were the most accurate in detecting deception when they had access to message content. Transcripts were found to yield higher accuracy than audio information, and the transcript only condition facilitated the highest accuracy ratings.

Zuckerman et al. also found that people were more accurate when they had access to message content. However these researchers found that observers exposed to audio information were more accurate in detecting deception than those who were exposed to transcripts only. Expressed in standard deviation units, accuracy scores yielded by the audio only condition had a mean of 1.09, and accuracy scores for the transcript only condition had a mean of .70. Zuckerman et al. also found that all visual observational conditions when combined with audio information yielded higher accuracy scores than the transcript only condition. Observations of the body only with audio had a mean of 1.49. Observations of the body and face with audio had a mean of 1.00. And, observations of the face only with audio yielded a mean of .99. These accuracy scores, expressed in standard deviation units, suggest that the audio channel may be more useful for detecting cues to deception than the transcripts.

A second major finding of this meta-analysis was that in the context of visual observations, shots of the body yielded the highest accuracy ratings. This condition was followed by accuracy ratings from the combined body and face condition, and the head only condition. This pattern was the same for visual conditions with audio and the visual conditions without audio, with visual conditions with audio having higher accuracy ratings than visual conditions without audio.

Zuckerman et al. also found this pattern. With audio information, body shots yielded the highest accuracy (1.49), followed by combined body and head shots (1.00) and shots of the head only (.99). Without audio information, body shots yielded the highest accuracy (.43), followed by combined body and head shots (.35) and shots of the head only (.05). These accuracy ratings are expressed in standard deviation units.

Zuckerman et al. concluded their meta-analysis by indicating that observational conditions substantially moderate deception detection. These researchers further indicate that humans are more accurate than chance in detecting deception in all of the observation conditions with the exception of the head only condition without audio.

These statements seem to conflict with the results of this meta-analysis, which found human accuracy to be low and to not differ greatly from the chance rate of .50. The "substantial" differences in observational conditions are also in conflict with the slight variations found in this meta-analysis.

One explanation for these differences may be that the d statistic as operationalized by Zuckerman et al. is inflated and has provided estimates of accuracy much larger than the actual population values. This inflation might account for substantial differences and for the significant accuracy rates yielded in the Zuckerman et al. meta-analysis. Furthermore, these inflated values might also explain the differences in accuracy patterns for the transcript condition and audio conditions.

Conclusion. This meta-analysis has implications for researchers engaged in several areas of scholarly inquiry.

For the deception researcher, this meta-analysis may provide some guidelines for future deception research. The most powerful guideline should come from the observational conditions. These conditions yielded the most distinct pattern in accuracy ratings and, with their large sample sizes, they should contain the least amount of sampling error. Perhaps future deception research can further explore the viability of message content in facilitating increased deception detection accuracy. Second, the guessing bias found in judgments of truth and deceit should caution researchers to counterbalance truthful and deceptive messages. Finally, the low accuracy ratings evident in this meta-analysis may direct investigation into understanding how humans might best cope with poor lie detection skills.

For the research methodologist, this meta-analysis illustrates the need for methods of extracting effect sizes from within-subjects designs when complete summary statistics are unavailable. While the present study is an initial step in extracting effect sizes from within-subjects designs, it provides only a partial solution to the problem. Techniques need to be developed for extracting effect sizes from studies that use a variety of measurement schemes, and which may provide differing amounts of summary information. Development of appropriate estimates for sampling error should also be considered.

For the listening researcher, this meta-analysis emphasizes the importance of listening in accurate deception detection. In the studies considered in this quantitative review the audio information consistently enhanced the ability to detect deception. Furthermore, the importance of comprehending the content of deceptive messages is emphasized in the transcript only condition. In this condition, with the absence of nonverbal information, the observers relied on their assessments of inconsistencies in the message content to obtain the highest accuracy rates. Accordingly, with increased comprehension skills observers should be able to increase their accuracy scores when listening for deception. Perhaps it is listening research that holds the key to enhancing our ability to accurately detect deceptive communication.

CHAPTER TWELVE

Listening and the Mass Media

Milton J. Shatzer

> The medium may be the message--but it also may be the massage.
> ....Marshall MacLuhan

Introduction

As mentioned earlier in Chapter Three, most listening occurs in situations where audio and visual messages are transmitted at the same time. This is particularly true for television, a mass medium that has far reaching effects in contemporary society. Because of television's ubiquitous nature and its importance as a socializing factor in modern Western society, this chapter will review the important research involving the influence of listening in the process of attending to, comprehending, and retaining audiovisual messages presented via television.

What Do People Do While Viewing? The fact that people are engaged in a number of simultaneous activities while "watching" television is well documented (Allen, 1965; Bechtel, Achelpohl, & Akers, 1972; LoScuito, 1972; Lyle & Hoffman, 1972). Lyle and Hoffman (1972) found, for example, that first-graders often eat, play, talk, draw, study, and read while they view television. Among adults, LoScuito (1972) has noted (from self-report data) that work and housework were most frequently mentioned as accompanying viewing. This was followed in order by eating, talking, reading, and child care. Sewing, needlework, personal care, hobbies, and schoolwork also

---

The author wishes to acknowledge the invaluable assistance of James B. Weaver in the preparation of this manuscript.

received frequent mention. Bechtel and associates (1972) videotaped 12 families over a six-day period while they watched television. They found that consistently the most frequent type of behavior accompanying viewing (next to talking) was eating (Bechtel et al., 1972). Actual time spent watching a program while "viewing" was between 55 and 76 percent of total program time. Bechtel et al. (1972) demonstrated that what is commonly called television "viewing" is really a complex set of behaviors which occurs at varying levels of actual attention to the television screen.

These studies provide empirical evidence for what most television viewers already know. That is, television viewing is not a solitary, all encompassing activity; but rather one that is oftentimes accomplished while performing other behaviors. Interestingly enough, even though persons do not always attend to the television set, they do not necessarily miss program content content (LoScuito, 1972). As LoScuito observed, half the respondents who reported they were talking during programs were talking about the programs themselves.

Auditory and Visual Presentation of Material. Therefore, listening is a very important part of the multifaceted television "viewing" process. Monitoring television aurally enables viewers to look away from the screen for long periods of time while still comprehending and responding to key aspects of the program content. Israel and Robinson (1972) have found that viewing actually occurs in short periods of attention to the set interspersed with periods of partial or non-attention. That is, the viewer tunes in or tunes out during programs according to an evaluation of cues as to whether discrete episodes will or will not be of interest (Lyle, 1972). Based on this axiom, it is important to ask: What role does the aural processing of information (i.e., listening) play in selective exposure and visual attention to television, comprehension of content, and retention information? It is to this question we now turn.

Interaction of Auditory and Visual Presentations. Before providing specific answers to the questions above, it must be noted that there appears to be an interaction of the auditory and visual presentational modes in television productions. Television content is presented in visual pictorial or visual symbolic images and in auditory forms, both verbal and nonverbal (Huston & Wright, 1983). Huston and Wright (1983) have noted that information presented simultaneously in both visual and verbal modes is generally better understood than content presented in either form alone. They commented that this suggests an interaction between modes of presentation and/or sensory modalities, as has been reported by other researchers (Calvert, Huston, Watkins, & Wright, 1982; Friedlander, Wetstone, & Scott, 1974). Since the major content information of most television programs appears to be carried by visual analogs and verbal symbolic representations (Huston & Wright, 1983), there is therefore a confounding of the aural and visual sensory modalities. Any research investigating the effects of either presentational mode must take this interactive relationship into consideration. The lion's share of the limited research exploring the relationship and interplay of the auditory and visual modes of presentation in television has been done by researchers focusing on the developmental viewing skills of children. This has been, in part, because children demonstrate developmental differences in their dependence on each sensory modality for the processing of information from television. Younger children gain information primarily from attention to nonverbal auditory features (Calvert et al., 1982). Older children, on the other hand, select only important dialogue for attention and ignore other formal production features (e.g., camera zooms) (Calvert et al., 1982). Research from this developmental perspective has had a great deal of impact of the basic theories of audience behavior, i.e., whether the audience is active or passive in processing information from television. It is important to look at these theories in greater detail.

Theories of Audience Behavior

Passive Viewing. The popular theory of audience viewing behavior (until the present decade) has been that visual attention is primarily reactive or passive (Anderson & Lorch, 1983). Anderson and Lorch (1983) and others have argued, according to this rather implicit theory, that visual attention is generally under the control of superficial, nonmeaningful characteristics of the medium (particularly for young viewers). Television is seen to elicit and maintain attention through salient formal features (e.g., visual complexity, movement, camera cuts, pans, and zooms), and some auditory features (e.g., sound effects). Attention is also seen to be maintained by past reinforcement for attending, higher arousal, etc. (Bandura, 1977; Lesser, 1977; and Singer, 1980). In short, even though according to this perspective the child is regarded as an active, cognitive, and social being, television is seen to be such a powerful influence that the child becomes reactive to its offerings (Anderson & Lorch, 1983).

Active Viewing. More recently, a shift from the passive viewing paradigm to a more active one has occurred as the result of some ingenious experiments by Anderson and colleagues (Anderson, Lorch,

Field, & Sanders 1981). Although initially guided implicitly by the passive theory of television viewing (Anderson & Levin, 1976; Levin & Anderson, 1976), Anderson and associates have now come to recognize television viewing as an "active cognitive transaction between the young viewer, the television, and the viewing environment" (Anderson & Lorch, 1983, p. 6). The shift of their perspective occurred after a study in which the researchers were trying to rule out the possibility that formal features were somehow correlated with dialogue type (an alternative hypothesis for the finding that more comprehensible programming leads to higher attention (Anderson, Lorch, Field, & Sanders, 1981).

To do this, Anderson and his researchers produced an experiment with four conditions. In an experiment they used three different production techniques in order to keep dialog and content uncorrelated (Anderson & Lorch, 1983). In one condition, they rearranged scenes with the program *Sesame Street* making the sequence of actions logically inconsistent and difficult to comprehend. In the second, they used Greek language *Sesame Street* to preclude dialogue incomprehensible to the audience of English speaking children. In the third, they used a special editing procedure to dub the original English dialogue in backward. A normal segment was used as control in the fourth contition.

Anderson and Lorch (1983) found that the normal segments of the show received higher attention from the children than the randomly rearranged scenes, and much higher attention than the Greek dialogue or the backward-dubbed segments. Their interpretation of these findings is that children are guided by the comprehensibility of the television message. That is, children are active processors of television, and visual attention is guided by the ongoing process of comprehension (Anderson & Lorch, 1983).

Anderson and Lorch (1983) posited four premises to their active theory of visual attention to television. Premise One states that visual attention to television depends on the degree to which the viewing environment supports available alternative activities. Premise Two contends that visual attention is maintained by the viewer's ability to answer "questions" proposed by his or her comprehension schemata. Thus, if a program is overly complex or difficult, attention may be terminated. Premise Three (the premise of most interest in the present discussion) claims that during periods of visual inattention, the viewer uses informative cues (that are primarily auditory) to {guide visual attention back to the screen. The fourth premise states that visual attention and inattention are controlled not only by cognitive involvement, but by a secondary phenomenon call attentional inertia.

Attentional inertia is a phenomenon in which the longer a viewer looks continuously at television the more likely it is that he or she will continue to do so (Anderson & Lorch, 1983). The longer it has been since the viewer last looked at the television, the less probable it is that he or she will look again. Anderson and Lorch (1983) have remarked that attentional inertia is not content specific; rather, it serves ves to drive visual attention across content boundaries (i.e., attention is maintained well into the next segment). Hence, attentional inertia allows child viewers to continue processing television stimuli even when the content is not currently understandable (Anderson & Lorch, 1983). In this way, children continue to process visual stimuli even if the content is incomprehensible (regardless of what is being presented in the aural mode).

Developmental Theories of Viewing Skills. Television viewing among adults is a highly automatic behavior, oftentimes outside of conscious awareness. This poses a problem in attempting to understand the interplay of the aural and visual presentational modes in viewing among adult viewers. One way to provide more insight into the process is to look at how viewing skills develop as television viewers mature. Research in this area is sparse, however. Based on the existing empirical research, the following theoretical foundations have been presented.

It appears that age is an important factor in attention to television and the processing of information. Six-month-old infants have been found to attend to television, but only sporadically (Hollenbeck & Slaby, 1979). In general, the amount of attention to television increases dramatically from ages one through five, with purposive, systematic television viewing occurring between the ages of 2 and 3 (Levin & Anderson, 1976). Age is important not only because of general cognitive development in a Piagetian sense, but also because of the development of more sophisticated viewing skills (Collins, 1982). In discussing these viewing skills, Wright and colleagues (Wright and Vliestra, 1975; Wright, Watkins, & Huston-Stein, 1978) suggest that younger children attend to salient perceptual features regardless of whether they are essential or peripheral to the plot. Older children, on the other hand, develop a more mature viewing style in which attention to the television is elicited due to a logical search for information (Collins, 1982).

Older children are able to focus on important or useful information while ignoring most of the incidental information (Hawkins & Pingree, 1986). Older children have been found to "chunk" information in television content in larger chunks (i.e., the stream of television program events are segmented into larger discrete units) (Collins, 1982). Younger children typically chunk segments into smaller units (less than a scene in duration) (Wartella, 1978).

What this means is that mature viewers appear to use small units when necessary to comprehend fine details but ordinarily use larger chunks for grosser perceptions of action. (Newtson, 1973). Moreover, Hawkins & Pingree (1986) have found that more sophisticated viewers are able to "read" the formal features of television production. That is, older children monitor television using previously learned strategies that associate formal features with content. They learn the symbolic intent of production techniques like zooms or dissolves and apply this knowledge to interpreting television programs.

Script and Schema Processing. As children mature, they begin to understand the "syntax" or "grammar" of the television medium (Collins, 1982). Children begin to understand the formal features of television and media conventions, and develop a greater sophistication in processing only pertinent information. This sophistication involves not only a general knowledge of formal features, but a greater world knowledge as well (Hawkins & Pingree, 1983). World knowledge has been defined as general knowledge, i.e., knowledge and expectations about situations. and how events and interactions ordinarily proceed (Collins, 1982). A number of researchers have argued that this application of knowledge proceeds via scripts or schemata (Bower, Black & Turner, 1979; Schank & Abelson, 1977; Wyer & Srull, 1981). Scripts or schemata are organized prototypic expectations of individuals, objects, and event sequences that serve as a framework for new information, as mnemonic aids, and as guides to the interpolation of missing actions, motivation, and plans (Hawkins & Pingree, 1986).

Automaticity

With experience, the processing of television conventions becomes highly automatic (Hawkins & Pingree, 1983). Due to this automaticity, very little demand is made on the viewer's cognitive resources. Thus, younger children appear to invest a greater portion of cognitive energy in processing television stimuli than older children (Anderson & Lorch, 1983; Collins, 1982). This differential is due to the cognitive development of the older child, along with greater viewing experience (Anderson & Lorch, 1983). As viewers become more experienced, the viewing experience results in habituation to the presentation of salient perceptual features (Collins, 1982). Because of increased automaticity and habituation, mature viewers appear to spend less time in attending to television and monitor the screen less frequently than younger viewers. However, it is hypothesized that auditory cues continue to be monitored to maintain comprehensibility and for features that elicit visual attention.

What Role Does Listening Play? The previous overview of the development of viewing skills was provided to illustrate how the role of listening changes as viewing skills mature and become more sophisticated. It appears that initially young children attend quite readily to both visual and auditory modes of television presentation. As their viewing skills develop, the more sophisticated viewer spends less time with eyes on screen. Program content is nevertheless monitored aurally. Consider the following quote from Anderson and Lorch (1983, p. 8):

> In periods of visual attention, during which attention may be directed to an alternative activity, the viewer uses informative cues to guide visual attention back to the television screen. These cues are primarily auditory from the program itself but can also consist of other factors such as fellow viewers' attention to television. We tentatively suggest that the viewer has a tendency not to process the audio at a semantic, conceptual level during these periods of visual inattention. Rather, he or she tends to monitor the audio for cues which indicate the presence of content relevant to the current schema. It appears at this juncture that mature television viewers are able to devote less time to having their eyes on the television screen and thus can be involved in secondary or even tertiary activities. The viewer continues to monitor the audio for information relevant to the current schema being used for cognitive processing. In short, the auditory mode plays a more important role in maintaining continuity in the processing of content information and directing visual searches for additional information.

Humor, Formal Auditory Features, and Music

In the next section, three "listening" components of television programs (i.e., components often carried in the aural mode) will be examined. These are: humor, formal auditory features (e.g., questions, pauses, personalized communication style), and music. The formative empirical research investigating the effects of these components on selective exposure to television, visual attention, and information processing will be reviewed. A great deal of the literature in this area deals with research on children's educational television, and the formal television features that enhance learning.

The Effects of Humor Humor plays a very important role in children's educational television (Bryant, Hezel, & Zillmann, 1979). Research on *Sesame Street* demonstrates that the interspersion of humor within educational programs is highly effective in attracting children's attention (Lesser, 1974). Much of the early research on the effects of humor on information acquisition proposed that humor would act as an inhibitor rather than a facilitator (Lumsdaine & Gladstone, 1958; McIntyre, 1954). Schramm (1972) suggested that the cognitive preoccupation with humor interferes with the reception of educational information (i.e., if the information is received, humor hampers the rehearsal and storage of this information). He later hypothesized that viewers might find the educational fare in sharp contrast to the humor, and thus be greatly dissatisfied with the educational material resulting in reduced attention (Schramm, 1973).

McGhee (1980) has added to this suggestion that humor creates a playful state of mind that interferes with the acquisition of novel information in educational programs. This would make rehearsing the material either undesirable or unnecessary. These claims raise a number of questions. First, at what age do children recognize much of what is presented as humor (e.g., jokes, irony, exaggeration, understatement, etc.) as humorous? Moreover, what effect does humor have upon information processing? If humor does attract exposure and visual attention, does it enhance or impede information acquisition?

In the 1970s, Shultz and colleagues performed a series of studies involving the developmental skills of children and their ability to detect verbal ambiguity, and to appreciate riddles and verbal jokes (Shultz, 1974; Shultz & Horibe, 1973; Shultz & Pilon, 1973). According to these researchers, linguistic ambiguity (in general) is said to occur whenever a sentence has more than one distinct semantic meaning. An example of phonological ambiguity (a type of linguistic ambiguity) would be the following sentence: The doctor had lost all her patience (patients). An understanding of the ability to detect linguistic ambiguity is a necessary condition in understanding children's ability to appreciate jokes or humor. From their studies with children ranging in age from 6 to 15, Shultz and associates found that children as young as 6 were able to detect phonological ambiguities. The ability to detect other linguistic ambiguities developed as a function of age. On the other hand, 6-year-olds were not able to detect the hidden meanings of ambiguities needed to understand and the incongruity of riddles (this occurred around 8 years of age).

In sum, these findings suggest a developmental theory of humor which postulates an early stage characterized by the appreciation of pure incongruity, followed by a later stage characterized by the appreciation of resolvable incongruity.

Selective Exposure and Visual Attention. Recent research by Zillman and his colleagues has looked at the effects of humor as a facilitator of selective exposure, of visual attention, and of information acquisition. In a study with 60 first- and second-grade children, Wakshlag, Day and Zillmann (1981) found that humor in educational television programs can greatly enhance selective exposure to these programs. In their study, Wakshlag et al. manipulated the presence of humor and its rate of occurrence (slow, intermediate, and fast pace). Exposure was measured by the amount of time the children spent viewing a particular program when alternative programming was available. Their findings demonstrate that programs with humor were generally superior, in terms of exposure, than those without humor. In addition, fast paced segments were most effective in facilitating exposure, followed by intermediately paced humor (in a linear digression). Slow paced humor proved to be ineffective, and not significantly different than the no-humor condition. The researchers concluded that the more frequently humor is employed and the faster the pace, the better in terms of exposure.

Zillmann, Williams, Bryant, Boynton, and Wolf (1980) examined the effect of humor on both visual attention and information acquisition among 5- and 6-year-old boys and girls. Similar to the Wakshlag et al. (1981) study, humorous episodes were edited into educational programs with either fast or slow pacing. In this study, the humorous episodes bore no particular semantic relationship with the educational message. These researchers found that the differently paced humorous episodes resulted in differential effects on attention to the screen. Fast paced humor enhanced attention to the screen sooner than slow pacing. It was concluded that interspersed humor in educational programs for children increases visual attentiveness to the educational materials in which it is presented.

Information Acquisition. Contrary to the position of Schramm (1972, 1973) and others presented earlier (i.e., that humor serves a distracting unction), Zillmann et al. (1980) found that information acquisition from a humorous version of a program was far superior to a version that contained no humor. Like visual attention, fast paced humor (even "unrelated" humor) enhanced children's acquisition of information from educational programs. This finding coincides with the findings of others (e.g., Davies & Apter, 1980; Chapman & Crompton, 1978; Hauck & Thomas, 1972; and, Kaplan & Pascoe, 1977) that suggest that humor involvement in educational television facilitates information acquisition.

Bryant, Zillmann, Wolf, and Reardon (1981) carried out virtually the same experiment (as above) with 7- and 8-year-olds and found similar results. In addition, there was some indication that the learning-facilitating effect of humor becomes weaker with an increase in age. More recent research by Hezel, Bryant, Harris, and Zillmann (1981) demonstrates that "unrelated" and "somewhat related" humor has detrimental effects on the information acquisition of adult audiences. It was found that well integrated humor combined with critical educational statements (that help make important points) does not produce negative effects and may enhance the learning process (Bryant, Zillman, & Brown, 1983).

Even more germane to the effects of listening are the studies focusing on the juxtaposition of verbal and nonverbal information (e.g., irony) and its impact on learning. Zillmann, Masland, Weaver, Lacey, Jacobs, Dow, Klein, & Banker (1984) investigated the effects of humorous distortions on kindergarten/first-grade and fourth-grade children. They varied distortion-free humor, humor that compatibly distorted educational information (exaggeration), incompatibly distorted humor (irony), and incompatibly distorted humor followed by a correction of the distortion. Humorous distortions took either visual, auditory, or verbal (i.e., spoken) form. The correction of the distortion was mostly verbal (spoken) but occasionally was visual and auditory as well. These researchers found that both exaggeration and irony produced perceptual distortions of the educational information. Irony produced underestimates, and exaggeration overestimates, of novel information provided by the educational segments. The distortions remained even after attempts at correction. Contrary to their initial expectations, the perceptual distortions did not diminish with age. Furthermore, in a follow-up study with fourth- and eighth-graders, Weaver, Zillmann, and Bryant (1988) also found that the older children were unable to correct misperceptions due to the humorous distortions.

They interpreted this unexpected finding to be due primarily to the novel nature of the information provided, rather than due to reduced cognitive abilities or attention on behalf of the eight-graders.

The Effects of Formal Auditory Features

In this section we will look at the effect of formal auditory features on attention and information acquisition. By formal auditory features we refer to such conventions as the use of rhetorical questions, pauses for reflection, and personalized communication style. In addition, the influence of "audiovisual fireworks" will be discussed.

Tamborini and Zillmann (1985) tested two opposing theories concerning educational programming for children. One view holds that children can acquire information (Zillmann, Williams, Bryant, Boynton, & Wolf, 1980) and gain cognitive skills (Lesser, 1979) from rapid-paced formats (such as *Sesame Street*). The other view condemns this type of format for having several undesirable effects, i.e., the fast pace and complex form fail to leave children time to reflect or rehearse information vital to learning (e.g., Anderson, Levin, & Lorch, 1977; Halpern, 1973, 1975; Hansen, 1974; Huston-Stein & Wright, 1977). According to this second view, children learn and benefit more from television programs like *Mr. Roger's Neighborhood* when programs: (a) leave time for children to reflect on material presented, (b) ask questions of young viewers, and (c) use more personalized communication (i.e., maintaining eye contact with the camera and addressing the audience as "you," etc.) (Singer and Singer, 1979). In their study, Tamborini and Zillmann (1985) produced six versions of a televised children's story to represent all combinations of two factors. The first manipulated factor was communication style which was varied along three levels: (a) interspersed curiosity-arousing questions, (b) the same questions addressed in a personalized form, i.e., addressed to "you," or (c) no questions. Earlier research had found that rhetorical questions enhanced recall and information processing (Zillmann & Cantor, 1973; Burnkrant & Howard, 1984). The second factor was time for reflection with two levels: (a) a pause following the pertinent information, or (b) no pause. The subjects in this study were 52 kindergarten and first-grade students (28 male and 24 female) randomly assigned to one of the six experimental conditions. Each group of children saw one videotaped production combining one level of each of the two factors. The dependent measures in this study were visual attention to the television monitor, information acquisition (measured verbally through oral responses or visually through pictorial responses), and interest and appeal of the television communicator (operationalized through the use of scales). The research found no appreciable differences for gender or grade in terms of the dependent measures

It was found that children's learning from television can be enhanced by presenting material in a personalized fashion (such as *Mr. Roger's Neighborhood*), particularly with the use of curiosity-arousing rhetorical questions. Pauses were found to enhance visual learning, and when information was presented visually as well as verbally, pauses apparently led to memory processes that facilitated recall. This is consistent with the theory that greater time for rehearsal facilitates recall. Providing pauses after question-and-answer units appears to do no harm to overall comprehension, and may enhance the learning of information presented visually. Furthermore, failure to provide pauses when presenting nonpersonalized questions can make communicators appear less interesting. Finally, the repeated use of pauses seems detrimental to visual attention thus leading to an apparent contradiction. Learning was enhanced by personalized communication style, but visual attention was impaired by such a style. This apparent discrepancy is consistent with the research of Lorch, Anderson, and Levin (1979). They noted that overall attention to television is not necessarily correlated with comprehension, but that attention at critical junctures tends to be positively correlated with retention. An alternative explanation for this phenomenon is that eyes are diverted from the screen during rehearsal and contemplation of the information. Tamborini and Zillmann (1985) noted that this may have important implications in situations where interest is low and information acquisition depends on repeated vigilance to the screen. In sum, the findings support the claim by Singer and Singer (1979) that format variables in programs like *Mr. Roger's Neighborhood* can be beneficial to children's learning.

Unfortunately, the study by Tamborini and Zillmann (1985) was not able to determine the degree to which the linguistic or nonlinguistic aspects of the personalized questions led to greater enhancement of information retention. Future studies should investigate the strength of the verbal or nonverbal elements. in the learning process. The value of the verbal dimension would be of particular interest in assessing the impact of listening.

Bryant et al. (1983) report a study by Bryant and Zillmann on the use of special effects as a facilitator of information acquisition. More specifically, Bryant and Zillmann studied the effects of both humor and audiovisual "fireworks" of children's television (e.g., fast-moving colorful objects accompanied by unusual noises, exploding stars, etc.) on increased vigilance and learning. With 5- and 6-year-old subjects, it was found that the interspersion of the stimuli "with a high potential to attract attention" facilitated information acquisition from an educational program (Bryant et al, 1983, p. 235). This occurred regardless of whether the stimuli were humorous or not, or pleasant or not (although pleasant stimuli were more effective in an attention-getting capacity). With a 7- and 8-year-old sample, results were similar except that the pleasant stimuli yielded greater information acquisition, with a slightly weaker attention-getting potential. Bryant et al. (1983) cite these results in support of their vigilance hypothesis. That is, the audiovisual fireworks may work as well as humorous stimuli in recapturing the attention of an audience whose alertness is fading.

Alwitt, Anderson, Lorch, & Levin (1980), in a study of 60 3- 4-, and 5-year-old children, obtained continuous records of the visual attention of the children to television in a distracting environment. While viewing, the children had snacks and attractive toys available to them. The researchers examined the effects of visual and auditory attributes of television on look onsets and offsets. They found three auditory attributes to maintain attention: children's voices, individual singing, and sound effects. In addition, they found three auditory attributes that terminated attention: men's voices, individual singing, and slow music. Five auditory attributes were not found to have a significant effect on attention: auditory change, peculiar voices, instrumental music, group singing, and lively music.

The Effects of Music. In a review article surveying the contributions of music to media productions, Seidman (1981) concluded that musical variables such as tempo, modality, rhythm, and harmony play an important role in determining the affective response of message receivers. Berg and Infante (1976) found that audience perception of media messages can be influenced my manipulation of the modality of the background music. Liu (1976) suggested that certain music can establish a "set" to influence the perception of ambivalent visual figures. This reinforces the media convention of opening a segment with a few bars of music to set the state emotionally for the nature of the material to follow (Herman, 1965). May and Hamilton (1977) have noted that the musical score can affect perceptions of, and interpersonal judgements about, individuals seen in accompanying visuals; and can override the affective meaning imparted by the other visual and verbal elements of a drama.

Musical accompaniment may also be involved in attitude change (Seidman, 1981). Schwartz (1971) found that wartime footage with tragic and melancholy or glorifying background music could change attitudes towards greater pacifism among tenth graders. This change did not persist over time, however. Merrill (1962), on the other hand, has indicated that films specifically designed to change people's attitudes can arouse strong fears in them, thus preventing attitude change.

Wakshlag, Reitz, and Zillmann (1982) recently conducted two studies to investigate the affect of background music on selective exposure to, and acquisition of information from, educational television programs. In their first experiment, they exposed first- and second-graders to an educational program that contained either no background music, appealing music of fast tempo, or unappealing music of slow tempo. Each subject was given the opportunity to select from competing programs being offered simultaneously with the stimulus material. The amount of time spent by each subject with the manipulated program (that was unobtrusively recorded) measured exposure. It was found that fast and appealing music resulted in significantly more selective exposure to the educational program than either slow and unappealing music or no music at all.

In their second experiment, Wakshlag et al. (1982) assessed the effects of appeal and tempo of background music on attention, information acquisition, appeal, and interest. In this procedure tempo and appeal were independently manipulated. The design in this experiment contained four conditions: (a) fast and appealing, (b) fast and unappealing, (c) slow and appealing, and (d) slow and unappealing. A no-music control group comprised the final condition. Concerning attention, their results demonstrated that slow music appeared to maintain levels of attention while the inclusion of fast music (regardless of its appeal) reduced it. This finding is somewhat contrary to that of Alwitt et al. (1980) mentioned above. In that study, slow music was found to terminate visual attention. In addition, fast music impeded learning while slow music did not appear to interefere with information acquisition.

These researchers concluded that fast and appealing background music in educational television programs can facilitate exposure (Wakshlag et al., 1982). Continuous fast paced music, however, decreased attention to the program and impeded information acquisition (irrespective of appeal). These investigators propose that educational programmers use fast paced music intermittently with a great deal of frequency (or with other gratifiers such as humor) in order to both maximize exposure to educational programs, as well as to increase attention and information acquisition.

Conclusion

What is commonly called television "viewing" is in fact a complex set of behaviors which occur at varying levels of attention to the television screen. Listening is a very important part of the "viewing" process. Monitoring television aurally allows the viewer to look away from the screen, and enables the viewer to be involved in secondary and tertiary activities. In fact, viewing actually occurs in short periods of visual attention to the screen with continuity being maintained by auditory monitoring.

The auditory and visual modes of presentation in television compose an interaction effect. Information presented simultaneously in both visual and verbal modes is generally better understood than content presented in either form alone (Huston & Wright, 1983). Any research examining the effects of these two modes must be aware of this confounding of factors. In addition, the viewing process is an active, rather than passive process (as had been thought originally). That is, television is not so overwhelmingly powerful that it totally mesmerizes the viewer. As part of this active process, visual attention to the screen is guided by the ongoing process of comprehension. During periods of visual inattention, the viewer uses informative cues (that are primarily auditory) to bring attention back to the screen.

The viewing of television is a skill that develops over time with young viewers. Thus age is an important factor in attention to television, with systematic viewing occurring between the ages of two and three. Younger children, in general, spend more cognitive effort in television viewing than older children. Younger children attend to formal features whether they are related to the plot or not older children are involved in a logical search for information. As children grow older, they learn to "read" the formal features of television. That is, they learn that formal features (e.g., zooms, pans, etc.) are related to the content of the programs. As children mature, they begin to understand the "syntax" and "grammar" of television. They appear to learn "scripts" or "schemata," possibly similar to those developed in conversational competence.

A number of entertainment features of television are transmitted via the auditory channel. The primary ones discussed in this review have been humor, formal auditory features (e.g., personalized, questions, pauses), and music. These features have generally been studied in terms of the effects they produce in the viewer, i.e., in terms of selective exposure, visual attention, and information acquisition. Among young viewers, auditory attributes such as rhyming, children's voices, and sound effects have been found to maintain visual attention.

Television programs containing humor compel greater exposure than non-humorous fare, especially if the humor is fast paced. Interspersed humor that is unrelated to the content has also been found effective in increasing visual attention and information acquisition among younger viewers. However, distorting humor (such as that found in irony and exaggeration--two major sources of humor in children's programming) can have negative effects on learning. That is, because irony understates and exaggeration overstates, this tends to produce distortions among viewers in their middle teens when accompanying information. Moreover, the facilitating effects of humor may decrease with age, and well integrated humor in the educational material may be necessary with older audiences.

The research on formal auditory features appears to support the contention that children need time to reflect and rehearse information presented via television in order for them to learn. Rehearsal time, accomplished through pauses, appears ostensibly to be a double edged sword. That is, it appears to facilitate recall while at the same time reducing attention to the screen as Tamborini and Zillmann (1985) have found. The fact that visual attention is reduced does not present a problem if it can be safely assumed that aural processing is continuing (as Bryant, Zillmann, and Brown, 1983) have proposed in their vigilance hypothesis). Future research needs to investigate this assumption Furthermore, it has been found that addressing a young audience in a very personal fashion enhances learning. Music, a formal entertainment feature exclusively presented in the aural channel, has been found to produce mixed effects (cf. Wakshlag, Reitz, & Zillmann, 1981). Fast and appealing music results in more selective exposure to various programs than slow, but reduces attention and interferes with information acquisition. Bryant and colleagues (1983) suggest that the optimum situation concerning music in educational television programs from a producers standpoint might be to intersperse fast music with a great deal of frequency throughout a program while including other effective entertainment features (e.g., humor). It appears that background music can create or set a mood, and may even be effective in attitude change (Seidman, 1981).

Future Research

One realization that should be abundantly clear from this review is the need for research focusing on listening and mass media. To date, the research is sparse and sporadic. Much of the research reviewed in this chapter has treated listening as an independent variable, e.g., the effects of listening to humor, questions, music, etc. upon selective exposure, visual attention, and learning. Future research needs to examine listening as a dependent variable in the mass communication context. That is, what formal television features enhance listening separate and apart from listening's role as a facilitator of recall or learning? Conceivably, much of the research presented in this book can be utilized in this area.

Another line of research could involve the investigation of listening attention. The active processing view of television viewing assumes to a great extent that auditory processing is being carried on fairly continuously to provide the vigilance function. Experience, however, tells us that television viewers may well tune out the auditory channel at times as well. A viewing companion may ask our reaction to a particular piece of dialog, and our response might be: " I'm sorry I wasn't listening." Anderson and Lorch (1983) have noted that the formal features of television do indeed elicit an orienting reflex, and that this orienting reflex momentarily increases the viewers information processing activity. Whether the orienting reflex alone, or combined with attentional inertia explains most of the variance in listening attention remains an empirical question.

Listening interventions that improve comprehension need to be examined as well. Friedrich and Stein (1975) found that stating verbal labels for nonverbal cues improved kindergarteners' retention of visually presented information. Moreover, Watkins, Calvert, Huston-Stein, and Wright (1980) found that adult co-viewers' statements about the nature of program events and their relationship to other parts of the plot improved comprehension for young viewers. A greater understanding of how listening affects comprehension in this sphere would be of critical importance to producers of children's television.

All in all, the role of listening in the mass media (particularly television) appears to be a fruitful area of research. Hopefully, knowledge in this area will be applied to other communication contexts with the future interchange of ideas across contexts yielding a better understanding of the phenomenon of listening.

References

Aaronson, D., & Scarborough, H.S. (1977). Performance theories for sentence coding: Some quantitative models. *Journal of Verbal Learning and Verbal Behavior, 16*, 227-303.

Aiken, E., Thomas, S. & Shennum. W. (1975). Memory for a lecture: effects of notes, lecture rate, and informational density. *Journal of Educational Psychology, 67*, 439-444.

Allen, C.L. (1965). Photographing the TV audience. *Journal of Advertising Research, 5*, 2-8.

Alwitt, L.F., Anderson, D.R., Lorch, E.P., & Levin, S.R. (1980). Preschool children's visual attention to attributes of television. *Human Communication Research, 7*, 52-67.

Anderson, D.R., & Levin, S.R. (1976). Young children's attention to *Sesame Street. Child Development, 47*, 806-811.

Anderson, D.R., Levin, S.R., & Lorch, E.P. (1977). The effects of TV program pacing on the behavior of preschool children. *AV Communication Review, 25*, 159-166.

Anderson, D.R., & Lorch, E.P. (1983). Looking at television: Action or reaction? In J. Bryant & D.R. Anderson (Eds.), *Children's understanding of television.* New York: Academic Press.

Anderson, D.R., Lorch, E.P., Field, D.E., & Sanders, J. (1981). The effects of TV program comprehensibility on preschool children's visual attention to television. *Child Development, 52*, 151-157.

Applegate, J. (1980). Adaptive communication in educational contexts. *Communication Education, 29*, 158-170.

Applegate, J. (1982). The impact of contruct system development on communication and impression formation in persuasive contextets. *Communication Monographs, 49*, 277-289.

Arntson, P., Zimmerman, B., Feinsod, P., & Speer, M. (1982). Communicating with patients: The perceptions of medical students. In L. Pettegrew, P. Arntson, D. Bush, and K. Zoppi (Eds.), *Straight talk: explorations in provider and patient interaction.* Louisville, KY: Humana, Inc., in conjunction with the International Communication Association.

Atmiyandandana, V. (1976). *An experimental study of the detection of deception in cross-cultural communication.* Doctoral dissertation, Florida State University. (University Microfilms, No. 76-29416).

Backster, C. (1963). Total chart minutes concept. *Law and Order, 11*, 77-79.

Baddely, A. (1976). *The psychology of memory.* New York: Basic Books.

Baddely, A., & Dale, H. (1968). The effect of semantic similarity on retroactive interference in long- and short-term memory. *Journal of Verbal Learning and Verbal Behavior, 5*, 471-420.

Baddely, A., & Warrington, E. (1970). Amnesia and the distinction between long- and short-term memory. *Journal of Verbal Learning and Verbal Behavior, 9*, 176-189.

Bandura, A. (1977). *Social learning theory.* Englewood Cliffs, NJ: Prentice-Hall.

Bangert-Drowns, R.L. (1986). Review of developments in meta-analytic method. *Psychological Bulletin, 99*, 388-399.

Barker, L. (1971). *Listening behavior.* Englewood Cliffs, NJ: Prentice-Hall.

Barland, G., & Raskin, D.C. (1976). *Validity and reliability of polygraph examinations of criminal suspects.* (Report No. 76-1, Contract 75-Ni-99-OOO1). Washington, DC: U.S. Department of Justice.

Bartlett, F.C. (1932). *Remembering.* Cambridge, England: Cambridge University Press.

Bauchner, J.E., Brandt, D.R., & Miller, G.R. (1977). The truth/deception attribution: Effects of varying levels of information availability. In B.D. Rubin (Ed.) *Communication Yearbook I.* New Brunswick, New Jersey: Transaction Books.

Beatty, M.J. (1981). Receiver apprehension as a function of cognitive backlog. *Western Journal of Speech Communication, 45*, 277-281.

Beatty, M.J. (1985). The effects of anticipating listening (state) anxiety on the stability of receiver apprehension scores. *Central States Speech Journal, 36*, 72-76.

Beatty, M. J., Behnke, R.R., & Froelich, D. L. (1980). Effects of achievement incentive and presentation rate on listening comprehension. *Quarterly Journal of Speech, 66*, 193-200.

Beatty, M.J., Behnke, R.R., & Henderson, L.S. (1980). An empirical validation of the receiver apprehension test as a measure of trait listening anxiety. *Western Journal of Speech Communication, 44*, 132-136.

Beatty, M., Behnke, R., & McCallum, K. (1978). Situational determinants of communication apprehension. *Communication Monographs, 45*, 187-191.

Beatty, M., & Payne, S. (1981). Receiver apprehension and cognitive complexity. *Western Journal of Speech Communication, 45*, 363-369.

Beatty, M., & Payne, S. (1984). Listening comprehension as a function of cognitive complexity. *Communication Monographs, 51*, 85-89.

Beighley, K. (1952). The effect of four speech variables on listener comprehension. *Speech Monographs, 19*, 249-258.

Beighley, K. (1954). An experimental study of the effect of three speech variables on listener comprehension. *Speech Monographs, 21*, 248-253.

Ben-Shakhar, G., Lieblich, I., & Bar-Hillel, M. (1982). An evaluation of polygrapher's judgments: A review from a decision theory. *Journal of Applied Psychology, 67* (6), 701-713

Benusi, V. (1975). The response systems of lying. *Polygraph, 4*, 52-76 (Original work published 1914).

Berg, C., & Infante, D. (1976, April). *The impact of music modality in the perception of moving images.* Paper presented at the meeting of the International Communication Association, Portland, OR. (ERIC Document Reproduction Service No. ED 122 335)

Bersh, P. J. (1969). A validation study of examiner judgment. *Journal of Applied Psychology, 53*, 399-403.

Betchel, R.B., Achelpohl, C., & Akers, R. (1972). Correlates between observed behavior and questionnaire responses: on television viewing. In E.A. Rubinstein, G.A. Comstick, & J.P. Murray (Eds.), *Television and social behavior: Vol. 4. Television in day-to-day life: Patterns of use* (pp. 274-344). Washington, DC: Government Printing Office.

Bobrow, D.G., & Norman, D.A. (1975). Some principles of memory schemata. In D.G. Bobrow & A. Collings (Eds.), *Representation and understanding*. New York: Academic Press.

Bocchino, I.L. (1985). *An exploratory study of the relationship between listening comprehension, cognitive complexity, receiver apprehension, and mood state.* (Doctoral dissertation, University of Florida). *Dissertation Abstracts International, 45*, 2692-A.

Bock, D.G., & Bock, H.B. (1977). The effects of the sex of the rater on leniency, halo, and trait errors in speech rating behavior. *Communication Education, 26*, 298-306.

Bock, D.G., & Bock, H.B. (1984). The effects of positional stress and receiver apprehension on leniency errors in speech evaluation: A test of the rating error paradigm. *Communication Education, 33*, 337-341.

Borzi, M.G. (1985). *A rose by any other name is not the same: An examination into the nature of shyness and other related constructs*. (Doctoral dissertation, University of Florida), *Dissertation Abstracts International, 47*, 344-A.

Bostrom, R. (1970). Cognitive, affective, and behavioral dimensions of communicative attitudes. *Journal of Communication, 20*, 359-366.

Bostrom, R. (1980, May). *Communication attitudes and communication abilities*. Paper presented at the Annual Meeting of the International Communication Association, Minneapolis.

Bostrom, R., & Bryant, C. (1980). Factors in the retention of information presented orally: The role of short-term listening. *Western Journal of Speech Communication, 44*, 137-145.

Bostrom, R. & Waldhart, E. (1978a, November). *The role of short-term memory in listening*. Paper presented at the meeting of the Speech Communication Association, Minneapolis, MN.

Bostrom, R., & Waldhart, E. (1978b). *The Kentucky comprehensive listening skills test*. Lexington: The Kentucky Listening Research Center.

Bostrom, R. & Waldhart, E. (1980) Components in listening behavior: The role of short-term memory. *Human Communication Research, 6*, 211-227.

Bostrom, R., & Waldhart, E. (1988). Memory models and the measurement of listening. *Communication Education, 37*, 1-18.

Bostrom, R., Waldhart, E. & Brown, M. H. (1979, May). *Effects of "motivational" instructions on listening behavior*. Paper presented at the annual meeting of the International Communication Association, Philadelphia, PA.

Bower, G.H., Black, J.B., & Turner, T.J. (1979). Scripts in memory for text. *Cognitive Psychology, 11*, 177-220.

Bradley, B. (1980). An experimental study of the effectiveness of the video-recorder in teaching the basic speech course. *Communication Education, 19*, 161-167.

Brandon, J. (1956). An experimental television study: the relative effectivenes of presenting factual information by the lecture, interview, and discussion methods. *Speech Monographs, 23*, 272-283.

Brandt, D.R., Miller, G.R., & Hocking, J.E. (1980a). The truth-deception attribution: Effects of familiarity on the ability of observers to detect deception. *Human Communication Research, 6* (2), 99-110.

Brandt, D.R., Miller, G.R., & Hocking, J.E. (1980b). Effects of self-monitoring and familiarity on deception detection. *Communication Quarterly, 28* (3), 3-10.

Brandt, D.R., Miller, G.R., & Hocking, J.E. (1982). Familiarity and lie detection: A replication and extension. *The Western Journal of Speech Communication, 46*, 276-290.

Bransford, J.D., Barclay, J.J., Franks, J.J. (1972). Sentence memory: A constructive versus interpretive approach. *Cognitive Psychology, 3*, 193-209.

Bransford, J.D., & Franks, J.J. (1972). The abstraction of linguistic ideas: A review. *Cognition, 1*, 211-249.

Braslow, J. N., & Heins, M. (1981). Women in medical education: A decade of change. *New England Journal of Medicine, 304*, 1129-1135.

Brown, J. I. (1987). Listening--ubiquitous yet obscure. *Journal of the International Listening Association, 1*, 3-14.

Brown, J., & Carlsen, R. (1955). *Brown-Carlsen listening comprehension test.* New York: Harcourt, Brace, and World.

Brown, L. (1982). *Communicating facts and ideas in business.* Englewood Cliffs, NJ: Prentice Hall.

Bryant, J., Hezel, R., & Zillmann, D. (1979). Humor in children's educational television. *Communication Education, 28*, 49-59.

Bryant, J., Zillmann, D., & Brown, D. (1983). Entertainment features in children's educational television: Effects on attention and information acquisition. In J. Bryant & D.R. Anderson (Eds.), *Children's understanding of television.* New York: Academic Press.

Bryant, J., Zillmann, D., Wolf, M.A. & Reardon, K.K. (1981). *Learning from educational television as a function of differently paced humor: Further evidence.* Unpublished manuscript.

Buchli, V., & Pearce, W. (1974). Listening behavior in coorientational states. *Journal of Communication, 24*, 62-70.

Buck, R., Miller, R.E., & Gaul, W.F. (1974). Sex, personality, and physiological variables in the communication of affect via facial expression. *Journal of Personality and Social Psychology, 30* (4), 587-596.

Buckwalter, A. (1983). *Interviews and interrogatories.* Boston: Butterworth.

Bugental, D.E., Kaswan, J.W., & Love, L.R. (1970). Perception of contradictory meanings conveyed by verbal and nonverbal channels. *Journal of Personality and Social Psychology, 16* (4), 647-655.

Burgoon, J. (1976) The unwillingness-to-communicate scale: development and validation. *Communication Monographs, 43*, 60-79.

Burgoon, J. (1977). Unwillingness to communicate as a predictor of small group behavior and discussions. *Central States Speech Journal, 28*, 122-133.

Burgoon, J. & Saine, T. (1978). *The unspoken dialog: An introduction to non-verbal communication.* Boston: Houghton Mifflin.

Burgoon, J. K., Pfau, M., Parrott, R., Birk, T., Coker, R., & Burgoon, M. (1987). Relational communication, satisfaction, compliance-gaining strategies, and compliance in communication between physicians and patients. *Communication Monographs, 54,* 307-324.

Burnkrant, R., & Howard, D. (1984). Effects of the use of introductory rhetorical questions versus statements on information processing. *Journal of Personality and Social Psychology, 47,* 1218-1230.

Burns, K., & Beier, E. (1973). Significance of vocal and visual channels in the decoding of emotional meaning. *Journal of Communication, 23,* 118-130.

Bush, D. F. (1985). Gender and nonverbal expressiveness in patient recall of health information. *Journal of Applied Communication Research, 13* (2), 103-117.

Calvert, S.L., Huston, A.C., Watkins, B.A., & Wright, J.C. (1982). The relationship between selective attention to television forms and children's comprehension of content. *Child Development, 45* (187), 1-89.

Camden, C., Motley, M. & Baars, B. (1982). Cognitive encoding processes: evidence for a graphemically based short-term memory. *Human Communication Research, 8,* 327-337.

Cantor, J., & Reilly, S. (1979, August). *Jocular language style and relevant humor in educational messages.* Paper presented at the Second International Conference on Humor, Los Angeles.

Carter, J. & Van Matre, N. (1975). Note-taking vs. note-having. *Journal of Educational Psychology, 67,* 900-904.

Cegala, D. (1981). Interaction involvement: a cognitive dimension of communication competence. *Communication Education, 30,* 109-121.

Cegala, D., Savage, D., Brunner, C. & Conrad, A. (1982). An elaboration of the meaning of interaction involvement: Toward the development of a theoretical concept. *Communication Monographs, 49,* 229-248.

Chang, T. (1986). Semantic memory: facts and models. *Psychological Bulletin, 99,* 199-220.

Chapman, A.J., & Crompton, P. (1978). Humorous presentations of material and presentations of humorous material: A review of the humor literature and two experimental studies. In M.M. Gruneberg, P.E. Morris, & R.N. Sykes (Eds.), *Practical aspects of memory.* London: Academic Press.

Charlesworth, W.W., & Krevtzer, M.A. (1973). Facial expressions of infants and children. In P. Ekman (Ed.), *Darwin and facial expression: A century of research in review.* New York: Academic Press.

Clark, R., & Delia, J. (1979). Topoi and rhetorical competence. *Quarterly Journal of Speech, 65,* 187-206.

Cline, R. J., & Cluck, G. G. (1985, April). *Status double jeopardy: A review of sex role issues in health communication.* Paper presented at the annual meeting of the Central States Speech Association, Indianapolis.

Cohen, J. (1977). *Statistical power analysis for the behavioral sciences* (Revised Edition). New York: Academic Press.

Collins, A., & Quillian, M. (1972). Experiments on semantic memory and language comprehension. In L. Gregg, (Ed.) *Cognition in learning and memory* (pp. 117-137). New York: Wiley.

Collins, W.A. (1982). Cognitive processing aspects of television. In D. Pearl, L. Bouthilet, & J. Lazar (Eds.), *Television and behavior: Ten years of scientific progress and implications for the eighties* (pp. 9-23). Washington, DC: Government Printing Office.

Comadena, M.E. (1981). *Examinations of the deception attribution process of friends and intimates.* Unpublished Doctoral Dissertation, Purdue University.

Comadena, M.T. (1982). Accuracy in detecting deception: Intimate and friendship relationships. In M. Burgoon (Ed.), *Communication Yearbook Five.* Beverly Hills, CA: Sage.

Cooper, H.M. (1984). *The integrative literature review.* Beverly Hills, CA: Sage.

Croft, R., Stimpson, D., Ross, W. Bray, R. & Breglio, V. (1969). Comparison of attitude change elicited by live and video-tape classroom presentations. *AV Communication Review, 17,* 315-321.

Cronbach, L. (1951). Coefficient *alpha* and the internal structure of tests. *Psychometrika, 16,* 297-234.

Daly, J. (1978a). Communication apprehension and behavior: applying a multiple act criteria. *Human Communication Research, 4,* 208-216.

Daly, J. (1978b). The assessment of social-communicative anxiety via self-reports: a comparison of measures. *Communication Monographs, 45,* 204-218.

Daly, J., & McCroskey, J. (1984). *Avoiding communication.* Beverly Hills, CA: Sage.

Daly, J., & Stafford, L. (1984). Correlates and consequences of social-communicative anxiety. In J. Daly and J. McCroskey (Eds.) *Avoiding communication* (pp. 125-144). Beverly Hills, CA: Sage.

Daly, J.A., Vangelista, A.L., & Daughton, S.M. (1987, November). *The nature and correlates of conversational sensitivity*. Paper presented at the annual meeting of the Speech Communication Association, Boston, MA.

Daniels, T.C., & Whitman, R.F. (1979). *The effects of message structure, required recall structure, and receiver apprehension upon recall of message information*. University of Wisconsin, Green Bay. (ERIC Document Reproduction Service No. ED 178 979).

Darwin, C., Turvey, M., & Crowder, R. (1972). An auditory analogue of the Sperling partial report procedure. *Cognitive Behavior, 3*, 255-267.

Davies, A.P., & Apter, M.J. (1980). Humor and its effect on learning in children. In P.E. McGhee & A.J. Chapman (Eds.), *Children's humor*. New York: Wiley.

DeLaduranty, J.C. and Sullivan, D.R. (1980). *Criminal investigation standards*. New York: Harper & Row.

Delia, J.G., O'Keefe, B.J., & O'Keefe, D.J. (1982). The constructivist approach to communication. In F.E.X. Dance (Ed.), *Human communication theory: Comparative essays*. New York: Harper & Row.

DePaulo, B.M. (1981). Success at detecting deception: Liability or skill? *Annals New York Academy of Sciences*, 245-255.

DePaulo, B.M., Davis, T., & Lanier, K. (1980, April). *Planning lies: the effect of spontaneity and arousal on deception*. Paper presented at the Eastern Psychological Association, Hartford, CT.

DePaulo, B.M., & Jordan, A. (1982). Age changes in deceiving and detecting deceit. In R.S. Feldman (Ed.), *Development of Nonverbal Behavior in Children*, New York: Springer-Verlag.

DePaulo, B.M., Lassiter, G.D., & Stone, J.I. (1982). Attentional determinants of success at detecting deception and truth. *Personality and Social Psychology Bulletin, 8* (2), 273-279.

DePaulo, B.M., & Rosenthal, R. (1979), Telling lies. *Journal of Personality and Social Psychology, 17* (10), 1713-1722.

DePaulo, B.M., & Rosenthal, R. (1979). Ambivalence, discrepancy, and deception in nonverbal communication. In R. Rosenthal (Ed.), *Skill in nonverbal communication*, Cambridge, MA: Oelgeschlager.

DePaulo, B.M., Rosenthal, R., Green, C.R., & Rosenkrantz, J. (in press). Diagnosing deceptive and mixed messages from verbal and nonverbal cues. *Journal of Experimental Social Psychology.*

DePaulo, B.M., Rosenthal, R., Rosenkrantz, J., & Green, C.R. Actual and perceived cues to deception: A closer look at speech. (Unpublished manuscript).

DePaulo, B.M., Stone, J.I., & Lassiter, G.D. (1984) Telling ingratiating lies: Effects of target sex and target attractiveness on verbal and nonverbal deception success. Manuscript submitted for publication.

DePaulo, B.M., Stone, J.I., & Lassiter, G.D. (in press). Deceiving and detecting deceipt. In B.R. Schlenker (Ed.), *The self and social life.* New York: McGraw-Hill

Dollinger, S.J., Reader, M.J., Marnett, J.P., & Tylenda, B. (1983). Psychological-mindedness, psychological-construing, and the judgment of deception. *The Journal of General Psychology, 108* 183-191.

Dickens, M., & Williams, F. (1964). An experimental application of cloze procedure and attitude measures to listening comprehension. *Speech Monographs, 31,* 103-108.

DiSalvo, V. S. (1980). A summary of current research identifying communication skills in various organizational contexts. *Communication Education, 29,* 283-290.

DiVesta, F., & Gray, G. (1982). Listening and notetaking. *Journal of Educational Psychology, 63,* 8-14.

Donohew, L. (1981). Arousal and affective responses to writing styles. *Journal of Applied Communication Research, 9,* 109-119.

Donohew, L., Nair, M., & Finn, S. (1984). Automaticity, arousal, and information exposure. In R. Bostrom (Ed.) *Communication yearbook eight* (pp. 323 -348). Beverly Hills, CA: Sage.

Dowling, J.L. (1979). *Criminal investigation.* New York: Harcourt Brace Jovanovich.

Downs, C. W., & Conrad, C. (1982). Effective subordinancy. *The Journal of Business Communication, 19,* 27-38.

Eagly, A.H. & Carli, L.L. (1981). Sex of researchers and sex-typed communications as determinants of sex differences in influencability: A meta-analysis. *Psycholological Bulletin, 90,* 1-20.

Edelman, R.I. (1970). Some variables affecting suspicion. *Journal of Personality and Social Psychology, 15* (4), 333-377.

Educational Testing Service, (1957). *Sequential tests of educational progress.* Princeton, NJ: Educational Testing Service.

Educational Testing Service, (1984). *Guide to the NTE core battery tests.* Princeton, NJ: Educational Testing Service.

Eisner, S., & Rhode, K. (1959). Notetaking during or after the lecture. *Journal of Educational Psychology, 50,* 301-304.

Ekman, P., & Friesen, W. (1969). Non-verbal leakage and clues to deception. *Psychiatry,32,* 88-106

Ekman, P., & Friesen, W. (1974). Detecting deception from the body or face. *Journal of Personality and Social Psychology, 29* (3), 288-298.

Erickson, A. (1954). Can listening efficiency be improved? *The Journal of Communication, 4,* 128-132.

Ernest, C. (1968). Listening comprehension as a function of type of material and rate of presentation. *Speech Monographs, 35,* 154-156.

Exline, R.V., Thibaut, J., Hickey, C.B., & Gumpert, P. (1970). Visual inter-action in relation to machiavellianism and an unethical act. In R. Christie and F.L. Geis (Eds.), *Studies in machiavellianism,* New York: Academic Press.

Fay, P.J., & Middleton, W.C. (1941). The ability to judge truth-telling, or lying, from the voice as transmitted over a public address system. *The Journal of General Psychology, 24,* 211-215.

Feldman, M., & Thayer, S. (1980). A comparison of three measures of nonverbal decoding ability. *The Journal of Social Psychology, 112* 91-97.

Feldman, R.S. (1976). Nonverbal disclosure of teacher deception and interpersonal affect. *Journal of Educational Psychology, 68* (6), 807-816.

Feldman, R.S. (1979). Nonverbal disclosure of deception in urban Koreans. *Journal of Cross-Cultural Psychology, 10* (1), 73-83.

Feldman, R.S., Jenkins, L., & Popoola, O. (1979). Detection of deception in adults and children via facial expressions. *Child Development, 50,* 350-355.

Feldman, R.S., & White, J.B. (1980). Detecting deception in children. *Journal of Communication, 30* (2), 121-128.

Feldt, L., & Mahmoud, M. (1958). Power function charts for the analysis of variance. *Psychometrika, 23,* 201-209.

Fidell, L. S. (1970). Empirical verification of sex discrimination in hiring practice in psychology. *American Psychologist, 25,* 1094-1098.

Fishbein, M., & Ajzen, I. (1975). *Belief, attitude, intention, and behavior.* Reading, MA: Addison-Wesley.

Fisher, J. & Harris, M. (1973). Effect of notetaking and review. *Journal of Educational Psychology, 65,* 321-325.

Fisher, J., & Harris, M. (1974). Notetaking and recall. *Journal of Educational Research, 67,* 291-292.

Fitch-Hauser, M. (1984). Message structure, inference making, and recall. In Robert N. Bostrom (Ed.), *Communication Yearbook Eight* (pp. 378-392). Beverly Hills, CA: Sage.

Fitzpatrick, M. (1983). Predicting couples' interactions from couples' self-reports. In R. Bostrom (Ed.), *Communication Yearbook Seven* (pp. 96-118). Beverly Hills, CA: Sage.

Floyd, J. J., & Reese, R. G. (1987). Listening theory in modern rhetorical thought. *Journal of the International Listening Association, 1*, 87-102.

Foulke, E. (1968). Listening comprehension as a function of wordrate. *Journal of Communication, 18*, 198-206.

Frandsen, K. (1963). Effects of threat appeals and media of transmission. *Speech Monographs, 30*, 101-104.

Freemouw, W., & Scott, M. Cognitive restructuring: an alternative mode for treating communiction apprehension. *Communication Education, 28*, 129-133.

Friedlander, B.Z., Wetstone, H.S., & Scott, C.S. (1974). Suburban pre-school children's comprehension of an age-appropriate information television program. *Child Development, 45*, 561-565.

Friedrich, L.K., & Stein, A.H. (1975). Prosocial television and young children: The effects of verbal labeling and role playing on learning and behavior. *Child Development, 46*, 27-38.

Fugita, S.S., Hogrebe, M.C., & Wexley, K.N. (1980). Perceptions of deception: Perceived expertise in detecting deception, successfulness of deception and nonverbal cues. *Personality and Social Psychology, 41* (4), 637-643.

Gardner, H. (1983). *Frames of mind: The theory of multiple intellegence.* New York: Basic Books.

Geis, F.L., & Moon, T.H. (1981). Machiavellianism and deception. *Journal of Personality and Social Psychology, 41* (4), 766-775.

Geizer, R.S., Rarick, D.L., & Soldow, G.F. (1977). Deception and judgment accuracy: A study in person perception. *Personality and Social Psychology Bulletin, 3*, 446-449.

Gibbons, F.X. (1983). Self-attention and self-report: The verdicality hypothesis. *Journal of Personality, 51*, 517-542.

Gilkinson, H. (1943). A questionnaire study of the cause of social fears among college students. *Speech Monographs, 10*, 74-80.

Glass, G.V. (1977). Integrating findings: The meta-analysis of research. *Review of research in education, 5*, 351-379.

Glass, G.V., McGaw, B., & Smith, M.L. (1981). *Meta-analysis in social research.* Beverly Hills, CA: Sage.

Glazner, M. (1972). Storage mechanisms in recall. In G. H. Bower. (Ed.), *The psychology of learning and motivation* (pp. 129-193). New York: Academic Press.

Goldhaber, G. (1974). *Organizational communication*. Dubuque: William C. Brown.

Goleman, D. (1978). Special abilities of the sexes. *Psychology Today*, *12*, 48-49.

Goodyear, F., & Behnke, R. (1976). Improving instructional systems through confidence testing. *Communication Education*, *25*, 60-67.

Goss, B. (1982). Listening as information processing. *Communication Quarterly*, *30*, 304-306.

Goss, B., Thompson, M., & Olds, S. (1978). Behavioral support for systematic desensitization for communication apprehension. *Human Communication Research*, *4*, 158-163.

Gray, J. (1982). The effect of the doctor's sex on the doctor-patient relationship. *Journal of the Royal College of General Practioners*, *32*, 167-169.

Green, R., & Nowlis, V. (1957) A factor-analytic study of the domain of mood with independent experimental validation of the factors. Paper. *American Psychological Association*.

Greene, J. (1984). Speech preparation processes and verbal fluency. *Human Communication Research*, *11*, 61-84.

Gruber, K. J., & Gaebelein, J. (1979). Sex differences in listening comprehension, *Sex Roles*, *5*, 229-310.

Gunter, B., Berry, C. & Clifford, B., (1982). Remembering broadcast news: the implications of experimental research for production technique. *Human Learning*, *1*, 13-29.

Gunter, B., Furnham, A., & Gietson, G. (1984). Memory for news as a function of the channel of communication. *Human Learning*, *3*, 265-271.

Hall, J.A. (1978). Gender effects in decoding nonverbal cues. *Psychological Bulletin*, *85*, 845-857.

Hall, J.A. (1980). Gender differences in nonverbal communication skills. In R. Rosenthal (Ed.), *Quantitative assessment of research domains*. San Francisco, CA: Jossey-Bass.

Hall, J. A., Braunwald, K. G., & Mroz, B. (1982). Gender, affect, and influence in a teaching situation. *Journal of Personality and Social Psychology*, *43*, 270-280.

Halliday, M. (1973). *Explorations in the functions of language*. London: Arnold.

Halpern, W.I. (1973). *Are the terrible twos becoming more terrible?* Paper presented at the American Association of Psychiatric Services for Children.

Halpern, W.I. (1975). Turned-on toddlers. *Journal of Communication*, *25*, 66-70.

Hambleton, R., Roberts, D., & Traub, R. (1970) A comparison of the reliability and validity of two methods for assessing partial knowledge of a multiple choice test. *Journal of Educational Measurement, 7*, 75-82.

Hansen, L. (1974, February 27). The *Sesame Street* Hazard. *Rochester Times Union*, pp. 1C, 3C.

Harris, T. E., & Thomlinson, T. D. (1983). Career-bound communication education: A needs analysis. *Central States Speech Journal, 34*, 260-267.

Harrison, A.A., Hwalek, M., Raney, D.F., & Fritz, J.G. (1978). Cues to deception in an interview situation. *Social Psychology, 41* (2), 156-161.

Hart, R., & Burks, D. (1972). Rhetorical sensitivity. *Speech Monographs, 39*, 75-79.

Hart, R., Carlson, R., & Eadie, W. (1980). Attitudes toward communication and the assessment of rhetorical sensitivity. *Communication Monographs, 47*, 1-22.

Haselrud, G. (1972). *Transfer, memory, and creativity*. Minneapolis: University of Minnesota Press

Hauck, W.E., & Thomas, J.W. (1972). The relationship of humor to intelligence, creativity, and intentional and incidental learning. *Journal of Experimental Education, 40*, 52-55.

Hawkins, R.P., & Pingree, S. (1986). Activity in the effects of television on children. In J. Bryant & D. Zillmann (Eds.), *Perspectives on media effects* (pp. 233-250). Hillsdale, NJ: Erlbaum.

Hays, W. (1973). *Statistics for the social sciences*. New York: Holt, Rhinehart, & Winston.

Hedges, L.V., & Olkin, I. (1985). *Statistical methods for meta-analysis*. Orlando, FL: Academic Press.

Hedges, L.V. & Olkin, I. (1985). *Statistical methods in meta-analysis*. New York: Academic Press.

HeenWold, A. (1978). *Decoding oral language*. London: Academic Press.

Heilman, A. (1951). An investigation in measuring and improving the listening of college freshman. *Speech Monographs, 18*, 302-308.

Heinberg, P. (1961). Factors relating to an individuals' ability to perceive implications from dialogues. *Speech Monographs, 28*, 274-281.

Hemsley, G.D. (1977). *Experimental studies in the behavioral indicants of deception*. Unpublished Doctoral Dissertation, University of Toronto.

Hemsley, G.D., & Doob, A.N. (1979). *The detection of deception from nonverbal behaviors.* Paper presented at the meeting of the Canadian Psychological Association Quebec City, Quebec, Canada.

Hemsley, G.D., & Doob, A.N. (1978). The effect of looking behavior on perceptions of a communicator's credibility. *Journal of Applied Social Psychology, 8,* (2), 136-144.

Hendrickson, G. (1971). The effect of differential option weighting on multiple choice objective tests. *Journal of Educational Measurement,* 1971, 4, 291-297.

Herman, L. (1965). *Educational films: Writing, directing and producing for classroom, television, and industry.* New York: Crown.

Hezel, R.T., Bryant, J., Harris, L., & Zillmann, D. (1981). *The relationship between humor and educational information: Lectures and learning.* Manuscript in preparation.

Hildreth, R.A. (1953). *An experimental study of audience ability to distinguish between sincere and insincere speeches.* Unpublished doctoral dissertation, University of Southern California.

Hirsch, R. O. (1979). *Listening: A way to process information aurally.* Dubuque, IA: Gorsuch Scarisbrick.

Hocking, J.E. (1976). *Detecting deceptive communication from verbal, visual and paralinguistic cues: An exploratory experiment.* Unpublished doctoral dissertation, University of Southern California.

Hocking, J.E., Bauchner, J., Kaminski, E.P., & Miller, G.R. (1979). Detecting deceptive communication from verbal, visual, and paralinguistic cues. *Human Communication Research, 6,* (1), 33-46.

Hollenbeck, A.R., & Slaby, R.G. (1979). Infant visual responses to television. *Child Development, 50,* 41-45.

Horowitz, M., & Berkowitz, A. (1967) Listening and reading, speaking and writing: An experimental investigation and reproduction of memory. *Perceptual and Motor Skills, 24,* 207-215.

Horvath, F.S. (1977). The effects of selected variables on the interpretation of polygraph records. *Journal of Applied Psychology, 62,* 127-136.

Horvath, F.S., & Reid, J.E. (1971). The reliability of polygraph examiner diagnosis of truth and deception. *Journal of Criminal Law, Criminology and Police Science, 62,* 276-281.

Housel, T., & Acker, S. (1977). *A critical comparison of the network and feature comparison models.* Paper presented at the Speech Communication Association, Minneapolis.

Howe, M. (1970). Notetaking strategy review and long term retention of verbal information. *Journal of Educational Research, 63*, 285.

Howe, M. (1974). The utility of taking notes as an aid to learning. *Educational Research, 16*, 222-227.

Hsia, H. (1968). Output, error, equivocation, and recalled information in auditory, visual, and audiovisual information processing with constant noise. *Journal of Communication, 18*, 325-353.

Hirsch, R. (1987). *Cultural literacy*. Boston: Houghton Mifflin.

Hunt, G. T., & Cusella, L. P. (1983). A field study of listening needs in organizations. *Communication Education, 32*, 393-401.

Hunter, F., & Ash, P. (1973). The accuracy and consistency of polygraph examiners' diagnoses. *Journal of Police Science and Administration, 1*, 370-37.

Hunter, J.E. (1982, January). A new design for psychological statistics. Unpublished manuscript, Michigan State University.

Hunter, J.E., Schmidt, F.L., & Jackson, G.B. (1982). *Meta-Analysis: Cumulating research findings across studies*. Beverly Hills: Sage

Huston, A.C., & Wright, J.C. (1983). Children's processing of television: The informative functions of formal features. In J. Bryant & D.R. Anderson (Eds.), *Children's understanding of television*. New York: Academic Press.

Huston-Stein, A., & Wright, J.C. (1977, March). *Modeling the medium: Effects of formal properties of children's television programs*. Paper presented at the biennial meeting of the Society for Research in Child Development, New Orleans.

Infante, D.A. (1982). The argumentative student in the speech communication classroom: An investigation and implications. *Communication Education, 31*, 141-148.

Infante, D.A., & Rancer, A.S. (1982). A conceptualization and measurement of argumentativeness. *Journal of Personality Assessment, 46*, 72-80.

Israel, H., & Robinson, J.P. (1972). Demographic characteristics of viewers of television and news programs. In E. A. Rubinstein, G.A. Comstock, & J.P. Murray (Eds.), *Television and social behavior: Vol. 4. Television in day-to-day life: Patterns of use* (pp. 87-128). Washington, DC: Government Printing Office.

Jablin, F. (1979). Superior-subordinate communication: the state of the art. *Psychological Bulletin, 86*, 1201-1222.

Jamison, D., Suppes, P., & Wells, S. (1974). The effectiveness of alternative instructional media: a survey. *Review of Edcuational Research, 44*, 1-67.

Johnson, M.K., Bransford, J.D., & Solomon, S.K. (1973). Memory for tacit implications of sentences. *Journal of Experimental Psychology, 98*, 203-205.

Jones, H.E. (1960). The longitudinal method in the study of personality. In I. Iscoe & H. Stevenson (Eds.), *Personality development in children.* Chicago, IL : University of Chicago Press.

Kahn, R.L., & Cannell, C. F. (1957). *The dynamics of interviewing: theory, tactics and cases.* New York: Wiley.

Kaiser, A. (1979). *Questioning techniques: A practical guide to better communication.* Pomona, CA: Hunter House.

Kalbfleisch, P.J. (1986). *Accuracy in deception detection: A quantitative review* (Doctoral dissertation, Michigan State University, 1985). *Dissertation Abstracts International,* 464453B.

Kaplan, R.M., & Pascoe, G.C. (1977). Humorous lectures and humorous examples: Some effects upon comprehension and retention. *Journal of Educational Psychology, 69,* 61-65.

Kelly, C. (1965). An investigation of the construct validity of two commercially published listening tests. *Speech Monographs, 32,* 139-143.

Kelly, C. (1967). Listening: a complex of activities or a unitary skill? *Speech Monographs, 34,* 455-466.

Kepple, G. (1982). *Design and analysis: A researchers handbook* (2nd ed.). Englewood Cliffs, NJ: Prentice-Hall.

Kibler, R., Barker, L. & Cegala, D. (1970). Effects of sex on comprehension and retention. *Speech Monographs, 37,* 287-292.

Kintsch, W. (1974). *The representation of meaning in memory.* Hillsdale, NJ: Erlbaum.

Kintsch, W. (1980). Semantic memory: a tutorial. In R. S. Nickerson, (Ed.) *Attention and performance VIII* (pp. 595-620). Hillsdale, NJ: Erlbaum.

Kintsch, W. & Busche, H. (1969). Homophones and sysnonyms in short-term memory. *Journal of Experimental Psychology, 80,* 403-407.

Kintsch, W. & Monk, D. (1972). Storage of complex information in memory: Some implications of the speed with which inferences can be made. *Journal of Experimental Psychology, 94,* 25-32.

Kintsch, W., & Van Dijk, R.A. (1979). Toward a model of text comprehension and production. *Psychological Review, 85,* 363-394.

Kleinmuntz, B., & Szucko, J.J. (1984). Lie detection in ancient and modern times: A call for contemporary scientific study. *American Psychologist, 39* (7), 766-776.

Kleinmuntz, B., & Szucko, J. (1982a). Is the lie detector valid? *Criminal Defense, 9* 13-15.

Kleinmuntz, B., & Szucko, J.J. (1982b). On the fallibility of detection. *Law and Society, 17*, 84-104.

Kleinmuntz, B., & Szucko, J. (1984). A field study of the fallibility of polygraphic lie detection. *Nature, 308* 449-450.

Klemmer, E., & Snyder, F. (1972). Measurement of time spent communicating. *Journal of Communication, 22*, 142-158.

Klinzing, D. (1972). Listening comprehension of pre-school age children as a function of rate of presentation, sex, and age. *Speech Teacher, 21*, 86-92.

Knapp, M., Hart, R., & Dennis, H. (1974). An exploration of deception as a communication construct. *Human Communication Research, 1* (1), 15-29.

Knapp, M., & Comadena, M. (1979). Telling it like it isn't: a review of theory and research on deceptive communication. *Human Communication Research, 5*, 270-284.

Knower, F. (1938). A study of speech attitudes and adjustments. *Speech Monographs, 5*, 130-145.

Koehler, R. (1971). A comparison of the validities of conventional choice testing and various confidence marking procedures. *Journal of Educational Measurement, 8*, 297-303.

Korsch, B., & Negrete, J. F. (1972). Doctor-patient communication. *Scientific American, 227*, 66-74.

Kramer, C. (1974). Womens' speech: separate but unequal? *Quarterly Journal of Speech, 60*, 14-24.

Kraut, R.E. (1978). Verbal and nonverbal cues in the perception of lying. *Journal of Personality and Social Psychology, 36*, (4), 380-391.

Kraut, R. (1980). Humans as lie detectors: Some second thoughts. *Journal of Communication, 30*, 209-216.

Kraut, R., & Poe D. (1980). Behavioral roots of person perception: The deception judgments of customs inspectors and laymen. *Journal of Personality and Social Psychology, 39* (5), 784-798.

Kraut, R., & Lewis, S. (1984). Some functions of feedback in conversation. In J. Applegate and H. Sypher (Eds.), *Understanding interpersonal communication*. Beverly Hills, CA: Sage.

Kreps, G. L., & Thornton, B. C. (1984). *Health communication*. New York: Longman.

Lane, S. D. (1983). Compliance, satisfaction, and physician-patient communication. In R. N. Bostrom (Ed.), *Communication yearbook seven* (pp. 772-799). Beverly Hills, CA: Sage.

Langer, E. (1980). Rethinking the role of thought in social interaction. In H. Harvey, W. Ickes, & R. Kidd (Eds.), *New directions in attribution research*, Vol. 2. Hillsdale, NJ: Erlbaum.

Larson, J.A. (1932). *Lying and its detection.* Chicago: University of Chicago Press.

Lashbrook, V. (1976). *The effects of cueing and storage strategies on the processing of oral messages.* Unpublished doctoral dissertation, West Virginia University.

Lavarakas, P.J. (1974). *Human differences in the ability to differentiate spoken lies from spoken truths.* Unpublished doctoral dissertation, Loyola University of Chicago.

Lavrakas, P.J., & Maier, R.A. (1979). Differences in human ability to judge veracity from audio medium. *Journal of Research in Personality, 13,* 139-153.

Leathers, D. (1979). The impact of multichannel message inconsistency on verbal and nonverbal decoding behaviors. *Communication Monographs, 46,* 88-100.

Leathers, D. & Emigh, T. (1980). Decoding facial expression: a new test with decoding norms. *Quarterly Journal of Speech, 66,* 418-436.

Lesser, G.S. (1974). *Children and television: Lessons from* Sesame Street. New York: Vintage Books.

Lesser, G.S. (1979, March). Stop picking on Big Bird. *Psychology Today,* 57-60.

Lesser, H. (1977). *Television and the preschool child.* New York: Academic Press.

Levine, J.M., Romashko, T., & Fleishman, E.A. (1973). Evaluation of an abilities classification system for integration and generalizing research findings: An application to vigilance tasks. *Journal of Applied Psychology, 58,* 149-157

Levin, S., & Anderson, D. (1976). The development of attention. *Journal of Communication, 26* (2), 126-135.

Ley, P. (1983). Patient's understanding and recall in clinical communication failure. In D. Pendleton & J. Hasler (Eds.), *Doctor-patient communication* (pp. 89-97). London: Academic Press.

Ley, P. (1977). Psychological studies of doctor-patient communication. In S. Rachman (Ed.), *Contributions to medical psychology, Vol. 1* (pp. 9-42). Oxford: Pergamon Press.

Ley, P. & Morris, L. (1984). Psychological aspects of written information for patients. In S. Rachman (Ed.), *Contributions to medical psychology* (pp. 117-149). Oxford: Pergamon Press.

Light, R.L., & Pillemer, D.B. (1984). *Summing up: The science of reviewing research.* Cambridge, MA: Harvard University Press.

Lipkin, M. (1974). *The care of patients: concepts and tactics.* New York: Oxford University Press.

Littlepage, G., & Pineault, T. (1978). Verbal, facial, and paralinguistic cues to the detection of truth and lying. *Personality and Social Psychology Bulletin, 5* (3), 461-464.

Littlepage, G.E., & Pineault, M.A. (1979). Detection of deceptive factual statements from the body and the face. *Personality and Social Psychology Bulletin, 5* (3), 325-328.

Littlepage, G.E., & Pineault, M.A. (1981). Detection of truthful and deceptive interpersonal communications across information transmission modes. *The Journal of Social Psychology, 114,* 57-68.

Littlepage, G.E., & Pineault, M.A. (1982). Detection of deception of planned and spontaneous communications. Unpublished manuscript, Middle Tennessee State University.

Littlepage, G.E., McKinnie, R., & Pineault, M.A. (1983). Relationship between nonverbal sensitivities and detection of deception. *Perceptual and Motor Skills, 57,* 651-657.

Liu, A. (1976). Cross-modality set effect on the perception of ambiguous pictures. *Bulletin of the Psychonomic Society, 7,* 331-333.

Loftus, G., & Loftus, E. (1976). *Human memory: the processing of information.* New York: Wiley.

Lorch, E.P., Anderson, D., & Levin, S. R. (1979). The relationship of visual attention to children's comprehension of television. *Child Development, 50,* 722-727.

LoScuito, L.A. (1972) A national inventory of television viewing behavior. In E.A. Rubenstein, G.A. Comstock, & J.P.Murray, (Eds.), *Television and social behavior (Vol. 4). Television in day-to-day life: Patterns of use* (pp. 33-86). Washington, DC: Government Printing Office

Lumsdaine, A.A., & Gladstone, A.I. (1958). Overt practice and audio-visual embellishments. In M.A. May & A.A. Lumsdaine (Eds.), *Learning from films.* New Haven, CT: Yale University Press.

Lustig, M. (1974, November). *Verbal reticence: a reconceptualization and preliminary scale scale development.* Paper presented at the meeting of the Speech Communication Association, New York, NY.

Lykken, D.T. (1978). The psychopath and the lie detector. *Psychophysiology, 15* (2), 137-142.

Lykken, D.T. (1979). The detection of deception. *Psychological Bulletin, 86,* (1), 47-53.

Lykken, D.T. (1981). The lie detector and the law. *Criminal Defense, 8,* 19-27.

Lyle, J. (1972). Television in daily life: Patterns of use overview. In E.A. Rubinstein, G.A. Comstock, and J.P. Murray (Eds.), *Television and social behavior: Vol. 4. Television in day-to-day life: Patterns of use* (pp. 1-32). Washington, DC: Government Printing Office.

Lyle, J. & Hoffman, H. (1972). Children's use of television and other media. In E.A. Rubinstein, G.A. Comstock, and J.P. Murray (Eds.), *Television and social behavior: Vol. 4. Television in day-to-day life: Patterns of use* (pp. 257-273). Washington, DC: Government Printing Office.

Maccoby, E. , & Jacklin, C. (1974). *The psychology of sex differences.* Stanford, CA: Stanford University Press.

Maddi, S. (1968). The pursuit of consistency and variety. In R. Abelson et al. (Eds.), *Cognitive consistency: a sourcebook* (pp. 269-276). Chicago: Rand McNally.

Maier, R.A., & Lavrakas, P.J. (1976). Lying behavior and evaluation of lies. *Perceptual and Motor Skills, 42,* 575-581.

Maier, N.R.F. (1966). Sensitivity to attempts at deception in an interview situation. *Personnel Psychology, 19,* 55-66.

Maier, N.R.F., & Janzen, J.C. (1967). Reliability of reasons used in making judgments of honesty and dishonesty. *Perceptual and Motor Skills, 25,* 141-151.

Maier, N.R.F., & Thurber, J.A. (1968). Accuracy of judgments of deception when an interview is watched, heard, and read. *Personnel Psychology, 21,* 23-30.

Mandler, G. (1982). The structure of value: Accounting for taste. In M.S. Clark and T.S. Fiske (Eds.), *Affect and cognition* (pp. 3-36). Hillsdale NJ: Erlbaum.

Mandler, J. (1978). A code in the node: The use of a story schema in retrieval. *Discourse Process, 1,* 14-35.

Mandler, N. (1987). On the psychological reality of story structure. *Discourse Processes, 10,* 1-29.

Mandler, J.M., & Johnson, N.S. (1977). Remembrance of things passed: Story structure and recall. *Cognitive Psychology, 9,* 111-151.

Marston, W.M. (1917). Systolic blood pressure changes in deception. *Journal of Experimental Physics, 2,* 117-163.

Matarazzo, J.E., Wiens, A.N., Jackson, R.H., & Manaugh, T.S. (1970). Interviewee speech behavior under conditions of endogenously-present and exogenously-induced motivational states. *Journal of Clinical Psychology, 26,* 141-148.

May, J.L. & Hamilton, P.A. (1977, May). *Females' evaluation of males as a function of affect arousing musical stimuli. Paper presented at the* Paper presented at the Miswestern Psychological Association, Chicago, IL. (ERIC Document Reproduction Service No. 143954).

McClendon, P. (1958). An experimental study of the relationship between the notetaking practices and listening comprehension of college freshmen during expository lectures. *Speech Monographs, 25*, 222-228.

Maddi, S. (1968) The pursuit of consistency and variety. In R. Abelson, R. et.al. (Eds.) *Cognitive consistency: A sourcebook* (pp. 269-276). Chicago: Rand-McNally.

McCloskey, M. (1980). The stimulus familiarity problem in semantic memory research. *Journal of Verbal Learning and Verbal Behavior, 19* 485-502.

McCracken, S. (1969). Comprehension for immediate recall of time-compressed speech as a function of the sex of the speaker and level of activation of the listener. *Speech Monographs, 36*, 308-309 (Abstract of Dissertation).

McCroskey, J. (1970). Measures of communication-bound anxiety. *Speech Monographs, 37*, 269-277.

McCroskey, J. (1977). Oral communication apprehension: a summary of recent theory and research. *Human Communication Research, 4*, 88-112.

McCroskey, J. (1978). Validity of the PRCA as an index of communication anxiety. *Communication Monographs, 45*, 192-202.

McCroskey, J. (1980). On communication competence and communication apprehension: a reply to Page. *Communication Education, 29*, 108-111.

McCroskey, J. (1982). Oral communication apprehension: A reconceptualization. In M. Burgoon (Ed.), *Communication yearbook six* (pp. 136-170). Beverly Hills, CA: Sage.

McCroskey, J., & Richmond, V. (1977). Communication apprehension as a predictor of self-disclosure. *Communication Quarterly, 25*, 40-43.

McCroskey, J. & Richmond, V. (1982). Communication apprehension and shyness: Conceptual and operational distinctions. *Central States Speech Journal, 33*, 458-468.

McCroskey, J. C., Richmond, V. P., & Stewart, R. A. (1986). *One on one: The foundations of interpersonal communication.* Englewood Cliffs, NJ: Prentice-Hall.

McCroskey, J. & Shehan, M. (1978). Communication apprehension, social preference and social behavior in a college environment. *Communication Quarterly, 26*, 41-45.

McDonald, H.C. (1963). *The practical psychology of police interrogation.* Santa Anna: Townsend.

McDowell, E.E., & McDowell, C.E. (1978). An investigation of source and receiver apprehension at the junior high, senior high, and college levels. *Central States Speech Journal, 29*, 11-19.

McDowell, E.E., McDowell, C.E., Hyerdahl, J., & Steil, L.K. (1978, November). *A multivariate study of demographics, psychological sex-roles and communication apprehensions.* Paper presented at the annual meeting of the Speech Communication Association, Minneapolis. (ERIC Document Reproduction Service No. ED 166 735).

McDowell, E.E., McDowell, C.E., Pullan, G., & Lindbergs, K. (1981, May). *An investigation of source and receiver apprehension between the United States and Australian students at the high school and college levels.* Paper presented at the annual meeting of the International Communication Association, Minneapolis. (ERIC Document Reproduction Service No. Ed 206 033).

McGhee, P.E. (1979). *Humor: Its origins and development.* San Francisco: W.H. Freeman.

McGhee, P.E. (1980). Toward the integration of entertainment and educational functions of television: The role of humor. In P.H. Tannenbaum (Ed.), *The entertainment functions of television.* Hillsdale, NJ: Erlbaum.

McIntyre, C.J. (1954). *Training films evaluations: FB 254-Cold weather uniforms* (Technical Report SDC 269-7-51). Port Washington, NY: U.S. Naval Special Devices Center.

McReynolds, P. (1976). Assimilation and anxiety. In M. Zuckerman and C.D. Spielberger (Eds.), *Emotions and anxiety: New concepts, methods, and applications.* New York: Wiley.

McReynolds, R., & Acker, M. (1966). On the assessment of Anxiety: II. By a self-report inventory. *Psychological Reports, 19*, 231-237.

Mehrabian, A. (1971). Nonverbal betrayal of feeling. *Journal of Experimental Research in Personality, 5*, 64-73.

Mehrabian, A., & Wiener, M. (1967). Decoding of inconsistent communications. *Journal of Personality and Social Psychology, 6* (1), 109-114.

Menne, J., Klingensmith, J., & Nord, D. (1969) Use of taped lectures to replace class attendance. *AV Communication Review*, 1969, 17, 47-51.

Merrill, I.R. (1962). Attitude films and attitude change. *AV Communication Review, 10*, 3-13.

Meyer, J. L., & Williams, F. (1965). Teaching listening at the secondary level: Some evaluations. *Speech Teacher, 14*, 299-304.

Miller, G. A., & Johnson-Laird, P. (1976). *Language and perception.* Cambridge MA: The Belknap Press of Harvard University.

Miller, G. R., Bender, D., Florence, T., & Nicholson, H. (1974) Real versus reel: What's the verdict? *Journal of Communication, 34*, 99-111.

Miller, G.R., deTurck, M.A., & Kalbfleisch, P.J. (1983). Self-monitoring, rehersal, and deceptive communication. *Human Communication Research, 10(1)*, 97-117.

Miller, G. R., & Fontes, N. (1979) *Videotape on trial.* Beverly Hills, CA: Sage.

Miller, G.R., & Kalbfleisch, P.J. (1982, May). *Effect of self-monitoring and opportunity to rehearse on on deceptive success.* Paper presented at the convention of the International Communication Association, Boston, Mass.

Miller, G. R., & McReynolds, M. (1973). Male chauvinism and source competence: A research note. *Communication Monographs, 40*, 154-155.

Miller, G., deTurck, M., and Kalbfleisch, P. J. (1983). Self-monitoring, rehersal, and deceptive communication. *Human Communication Research, 10*, (2), 33-44.

Mongeau, P. (1984, March). *Personal Communication.*

Monsell, S. (1984). Components of working memory underlying verbal skills: a 'distributed capacities' view. In H. Bouma and D. G. Bowhuis (Eds.), *Attention and Performance, Vol. 10.* Hillsdale, NJ: Erlbaum. *Journalism Quarterly, 50(4)*,

Motley, M.T. (1974). Acoustic correlates of lies. *Western Speech*, 81-87.

Muchmore, J., & Galvin, K. (1983). A report of the task force on career competencies in oral communication skills for community college students seeking immediate entry into the workforce. *Communication Education, 32*, 207-220.

Newston, D. (1973). Attribution and the unit perception of ongoing behavior. *Journal of Personality and Social Psychology, 28*, 28-38.

Nichols, R. (1947). Listening: questions and problems. *Quarterly Journal of Speech, 33*, 83-86.

Nichols, R. (1948). Factors in listening comprehension. *Speech Monographs, 15*, 154-163.

Nichols, R. (1957). *Are you listening?* New York: McGraw-Hill.

Norman, D. A., & Rumelhart, D. A. (1975). *Explorations in cognition.* San Francisco: W. H. Freeman.

O'Keefe, B.J. (1985, November). *The functional integration of communication concepts: Evidence for individual differences in reasoning about communication.* Paper presented at the annual meeting of the Speech Communication Association, Denver. 207-220.

O'Keefe, D. (1980). The relationship of attitudes and behavior: a constructivist analysis. In D. Cushman & R. McPhee (Eds.), *The message-attitude-behavior relationship: theory, methodology, application* (pp. 117-148). New York: Academic Press.

O'Keefe, D., & Sypher, H. (1981). Cognitive complexity measures and the relationship of cognitive complexity to communication. *Human Communication Research, 8,* 72-91.

Olson, C.T. (1978). *The effect of perceived conditions of interpersonal observation on encoding and decoding processes during deceitful self-presentations.* Unpublished Doctoral Dissertation, Columbia University.

Parker, R.J. (1978). *Age, sex, and the ability to detect deception through nonvocal cues.* Unpublished Doctoral Dissertation, Fresno Campus, California School of Professional Psychology.

Palamatier, R., & McNinch, G. (1972). Source of gains in listening skill: experimental or pre-test experience. *Journal of Communication, 22,* 70-76.

Paris, S.G. (1965). Integration and inference in children's comprehension and memory. In F. Restle, R. Shiffrin, J. Castellan, J. Lindman, & D. Pisoni (Eds.), *Cognitive theory,* Vol 1. Hillsdale, NJ: Erlbaum.

Paris, S.G., & Carter, A.Y. (1973). Semantic and constructive aspects of sentence memory in children. *Developmental Psychology, 9,* 109-113.

Paris, S.G., Lindauer, B.K. and Cox, G.L. (1976). The development of inferential comprehension. *Child Development, 47,* 660-668.

Paris, S.G., & Upton, L.R. (1971). Children's memory for inferential relationships in prose. *Child Development, 47,* 660-668.

Paschall, K.A. (1984). *The effect of receiver apprehension and source apprehension on listening comprehension.* (Doctoral dissertation, University of Florida), *Dissertation Abstracts International, 45,* 1917-A.

Paschall, K.A., & Clark, A.J. (1984). *An investigation of the effects of receiver apprehension and source apprehension on listening comprehension.* Paper presented at the annual meeting of the International Listening Association, Orlando, FL.

Patterson, C., & Kister, M. (1980). The development of listener skills for referential communication. In W.P. Dickson (Ed.), *Children's oral communication skills*. New York: Academic Press.

Pearce, B. (1971). The effects of vocalic cues on credibility and attitude. *Western Speech, 35*, 176-179.

Pearson, J. C. (1985). *Gender and communication*. Dubuque, IA: Wm. C. Brown.

Pellegrino, J., Siegel, A., & Dhawan, M. (1975). Short term retention for pictures and words: evidence for dual coding systems. *Journal of Experimental Psychology, 104*, 95-101.

Pendleton, D., & Hasler, J. (1983). *Doctor-patient communication*. London: Academic Press.

Peters, D. (1972). Effects of notetaking and of presentation on short-term objective test performance. *Journal of Educational Psychology, 63*, 276-286.

Peters, T., & Austin, N. (1985). *A passion for excellence: The leadership difference*. New York: Random House.

Peterson, G. I., Kiesler, S. B., & Goldberg, P. A. (1971). Evaluation of the performance of women as a function of their sex, achievement, and personal history. *Journal of Personality and Social Psychology, 19*, 114-118.

Peterson, L. R., & Peterson, M. S. (1959). Short-term retention of individual verbal items. *Journal of Experimental Psychology, 58*, 193-198.

Petrie, C., & Carrell, S. (1976). The relationship of motivation, listening capacity, initial information, and verbal organizational ability to lecture comprehension and retention. *Communication Monographs, 43*, 187-184.

Pezdek, K., & Hartman, E.F. (1981). Children's television viewing: *Children's television viewing: Attention and memory for auditorally versus visually presented material*. Unpublished manuscript. (Available from K. Rezdek, Claremont Graduate School, Claremont, CA.)

Phillips, G. (1968). Reticence: Pathology of the normal speaker. *Speech Monographs, 35*, 39-49.

Phillips, G. (1977). Rhetoritherapy versus the medical model: Dealing with reticence. *Communication Education, 26*, 34-43.

Phillips, G. (1980). On apples and onions: a reply to Page. *Communication Education, 26*, 105-108.

Phillips, G., & Metzger, N. (1973). The reticent syndrome: some theoretical considerations about etiology and treatment. *Speech Monographs, 40*, 220-230.

Podlesny, J.A., & Raskin, D.C. (1977). Psychophysiological measures and the detection of deception. *Psychological Bulletin, 84,* 782-799.

Popham, W. (1961). Tape-recorded lectures in the college classroom. *AV Communication Review, 9,* 109-118.

Porter, D.T. (1973, November). *Self-report scales of communication apprehension and autonomic arousal: A test of construct validity.* Paper presented at the meeting of the Speech Communication Association, New York.

Porter, T. (1979). Communication apprehension: communication's latest artifact? In D. Nimmo (Ed.), *Communication yearbook three* (pp. 241-261). New Brunswick, NJ: Transaction Books.

Potamkin, G.G. (1982). *Heroin addicts and nonaddicts: The use and detection of nonverbal deception clues.* Unpublished doctoral dissertation, California School of Professional Psychology.

Preiss, R.W. (1987, February). *Cognitive consequences of receiver apprehension: Evidence of reasoning about communication and self-persuasion.* Paper presented at the meeting of the Western Speech Communication Association, Salt Lake City.

Preiss, R.W., Rindo, J., Fishfader, T., & Wickersham, T. (1985, May). *Receiver apprehension and self-persuasion following counterattitudinal advocacy.* Paper presented at the meeting of the Northwest Communication Association, Coeur D'Alene, ID. (ERIC Document Reproduction Service No. ED 263 186).

Rankin, P. (1929). Listening ability. *Proceedings of the Ohio State Educational Conference.* Columbus, OH: Ohio State University Press.

Raskin, D. (1978). Scientific assessment of the accuracy of detection of deception: A reply to Lykken. *Psychophysiology, 15* (2), 143-147

Raskin, D.C. & Hare, R.D. (1978). Psychopathy and detection of deception in a prison population. *Psychophysiology, 15* (2), 126-136.

Raskin, D.C., & Podlesny, J.A. (1979). Truth and deception: A reply to Lykken. *Psychological Bulletin, 86* (1), 54-59.

Raskin, D.C., & Podlesny, J.A. (1978). Effectiveness of techniques and physiological measures in the detection of deception. *Psychophysiology, 15* (4), 344-359.

Rehfisch, J.M. (1958). A scale for personality rigidity. *Journal of Consulting Psychology, 22,* 10-15.

Reid, J.E., & Inbau, F.E. (1977). *Truth and deception: The polygraph ("lie detection") technique* (2nd ed.). Baltimore: Williams & Wilkins.

Reilly, R. & Jackson, R. (1973). Effects of empirical option weighting on reliability and validity of an academic aptitude test. *Journal of Educational Measurement, 3,* 165-170.

Rendero, T. (1980). College recruiting practices. *Personnel, 57,* 4-10.

Rhodes, S. (1985). What the communication journals tell us about teaching listening. *Central States Speech Journal, 36,* 24-32.

Rich, J. (1968). *Interviewing children and adolescents.* London: Macmillan.

Riggio, R.E., & Friedman, H.S. (1983). Individual differences and cues to deception. *Journal of Personality and Social Psychology, 45* (4), 899-915.

Rippey, R. (1970). A comparison of different scoring functions for confidence tests. *Journal of Educational Measurement, 7,* 165-170.

Roach, D., Hauser, M., Jackson, J., & Hanna, M. (1985, March). *The effects of receiver apprehension and noise on listening comprehension.* Paper presented at the meeting of the International Listening Association, Orlando, FL.

Robbins, C.E. (1980). *How to make dramatic use of witnesses to win at trial.* Englewood Cliffs, NJ: Executive Reports.

Roberts, C. (1984). A physiological validation of the receiver apprehension test. *Communication Research Reports, 1,* 126-129.

Roberts, C. (1986). A validation of the Watson-Barker Listening Test. *Communication Research Report, 3,* 115-119.

Rokeach, M. (1960). *The open and closed mind.* New York, NY: Basic Books.

Rokeach, M. (1973). *The nature of human values.* New York, NY: Free Press.

Rosen, B. & Jerdee, T. H. (1974). Sex stereotyping in the executive suite. *Harvard Business Review, 52,* 45-58

Rosenberg, M. (1962). Self-esteem and concern for public affairs. *Public Opinion Quarterly, 26,* 201-211.

Rosenthal, R. (1978). Combining results of independent studies. *Psychological Bulletin, 85,* 185-193.

Rosenthal, R. (1978). Combining the effects of independent studies. *Psychological Bulletin, 86,* 638-641.

Rossi, P., & Wright, S. (1977). Evaluation research: An assessment of theory, practice, and politics. *Evaluation Quarterly, 1,* 5-52.

Rossiter, C. (1972). Sex of the speaker, sex of the listener, and listening comprehension. *Journal of Communication, 22,* 64-69.

Rotkin, H. (1980). Information used in detecting deception. Unpublished doctoral dissertation, New York University.

Rotter, J.B. (1966). Generalized expectancies for internal versus external control of behavior. *Psychological Monographs, 80*, 1-28.

Rovira, M.L. (1982). *Detection of deception: A signal detection theory analysis.* Unpublished doctoral dissertation, The Catholic University of America.

Rowley, L. (1974). Which examinees are most favored by the use of multiple choice tests? *Journal of Educational Measurement, 11*, 15-23.

Rumelhart, D.E. (1975). Notes on a schema for stories. In D.G. Bobrow & A. Collins (Eds.), *Representation and understanding: Studies in cognitive science.* New York: Academic Press.

Rumelhart, D.E., & Ortony, A. (1977). The representation of knowledge in memory. In R.C. Anderson, R.J. Spiro, and W.E. Montague (Eds.), *Schooling and the acquisition of knowledge.* Hillsdale, NJ: Erlbaum.

Sakai, D.J. (1981). Nonverbal communication in the detection of deception among women and men. Unpublished doctoral dissertation, University of California, Davis.

Sayles, L.R., and Strauss, G. (1981). *Managing human resources.* Englewood Cliffs, NJ: Prentice-Hall.

Schein, V. E. (1975). Relationships between sex role stereotypes and requisite management characteristics among female managers. *Journal of Applied Psychology, 60*, 340-344.

Schank, R. (1982). *Dynamic memory.* Cambridge: Cambridge University Press.

Schank, R., & Abelson, R. (1977). *Scripts, plans goals, and understanding.* Hillsdale, NJ: Erlbaum.

Schramm, W. (1972). What the research says. In W. Schramm (Ed.), *Quality in instructional television.* Honolulu: University Press of Hawaii.

Schramm, W. (1973). *Men, messages, and media: A look at human communication.* New York: Harper & Row.

Schroder, M., Driver, M., & Struefert, S. (1961). *Human information processing.* New York: Wiley.

Schulman, H. (1971). Similarity effects in short-term memory. *Psychological Bulletin, 75*, 399-415.

Schulman, H. (1972). Semantic confusion errors in short-term memory. *Journal of Verbal Learning and Verbal Behavior, 11*, 221-227.

Schwartz, S. (1971). Film music and attitude change: A study to determine the effect of manipulating a musical soundtrack upon changes in attitude toward militarism-pacifism held by tenth grade social studies students. *Dissertation Abstracts International, 31*, 5677A. (University Microfilms No. 71-10, 977).

Scott, M.D., & Wheeless, L.R. (1977). The relationship of three types of communication apprehension to classroom achievement. *The Southern Speech Communication Journal, 42*, 246-255.

Searle, B. (1984). *The effect of medium of transmission, notetaking, sex, ability, and activation level on comprehension and retention of information.* Unpublished Ph. D. Dissertation, University of Kentucky.

Searle, B. & Bostrom, R. (1985, May). *Medium, sex of receiver, and levels of affective arousal on the retention of information.* Paper presented at the International Communication Association meeting, Honolulu, Hawaii.

Seidman, S.A. (1981). On the contributions of music to media productions. *Educational Communication & Technology Journal, 19*, 49-61.

Seifert, C.M., McKoon, G., Abelson, R.P., and Ratcliff, R. (1985). Memory connections between thematically similar episodes. *Journal of Experimental Psychology: Learning, Memory, and Cognition, 12* (2), 220-231.

Sereno, T.J.P. (1981). Children's honesty revisited: An exploration of deceptive communication in preschoolers. Unpublished doctoral dissertation, Bowling Green State University.

Shamo, G., & Bitner, J. (1972). Recall as a function of message style. *Southern Speech Communication Journal, 38*, 181-187.

Shapiro, J. (1968). Responsivity to facial or lingusitic cues. *Journal of Communication, 18*, 11-17.

Sharf, B. F. (1984). *The physician's guide to better communication.* Glenview, IL: Scott, Foresman.

Sheahan, M.E. (1976). *Communication apprehension and electoral participation.* Unpublished masters thesis, West Virginia University, Morgantown, WV.

Shiffrin, R., & Schneider, W. (1977). Controlled and automatic human information processing, II: Perceptual learning, automatic attending, and a general theory. *Psychological Review, 84*, 127-190

Short, J, Williams, E., & Christie, B. (1976). *The social psychology of telecommunications.* New York: Wiley.

Shucard, D. (1982). Linking sex with learning. *Science Digest, 90*, 99.

Shultz, T.R. (1974). Development of the appreciation of riddles. *Child Development, 45*, 100-105.

Shultz, T.R., & Horibe, F. (1974). Development of the appreciation of verbal jokes. *Developmental Psychology*, *10(1)*, 13-20.

Siegel, A. W., & Allik, J. P. (1973). A developmental study of visual and auditory short-term memory. *Journal of Verbal Learning and Verbal Behavior*, *12*, 409-418.

Singer, J. L. (1980). The power and limitations of television: A cognitive-affective analysis. In P. H. Tannenbaum (Ed.), *The entertainment functions of television*. Hillsdale, NJ: Erlbaum.

Singer, J.L., & Singer, D.G. (1979, March). Come back, Mister Rogers, come back. *Psychology Today*, 59-60.

Slowik, S.M., & Buckley, J.P. (1975). Relative accuracy of polygraph examiner diagnoses from respiration, blood pressure, and GSR recordings. *Journal of Police Science and Administration*, *3*, 300-309.

Smeltzer, L. R., & Watson, K. W. (1984). Listening: An empirical comparison of discussion length and level of incentive. *Central States Speech Communication Journal*, *35*, 166-170.

Snyder, M.(1974). Self-monitoring of expressive behavior. *Journal of Personality and Social Psychology*, *30*, 526-537.

Sperling, G. (1960). Information available in brief visual presentations. *Psychological Monographs*, *74*, 1-29.

Speilberger, C.D. (1966). *Anxiety and behavior*. New York: Academic Press.

Spielberger, C.D. (1970). Theory and measurement of anxiety states. In R. B. Cattell (Ed.), *Modern personality*. Chicago, IL: Adelene Press.

Spielberger, C.D., Gorsuch, R.L., & Lushene, R.E. (1968). *The State-Trait Anxiety Inventory [STAI]: Preliminary test manual Form X*. Tallahassee, FL: Florida State University.

Spiro, R.J. (1977). Remembering information from text: The "state of schema" approach. In R.C. Anderson, R.J. Spiro, & W.E. Montague (Eds.), *Schooling and the acquisition of knowledge*. Hillsdale, NJ: Erlbaum.

Spitzberg, B., & Cupach, W. (1984). *Interpersonal communication competence*. Beverly Hills: Sage.

Squire, L. (1986). Mechanisms of memory. *Science*, *232* 1612-1619.

Squire, L. J. (1975). Short-term memory as a biological entity. In D. Deutsch & A. Deutsch (Eds.), *Short-term memory*. New York: Academic Press.

Staats, A. (1975). *Social behaviorism*. Homewood, IL: The Dorsey Press.

Steil, L. K., Barker, L. L., & Watson, K. W. (1983). *Effective listening: Key to your success*. Reading, MA: Addison-Wesley.

Stein, N.L., & Glenn, C.G. (1979). An analysis of story comprehension in elementary school children. In R. Freedle (Ed.), *New directions in discourse comprehension*. Norwood, NJ: Ablex.

Sternberg, R. (1985). Human intelligence: the model is the message. *Science, 230*, 1111-1118.

Sternberg, S. (1969). Memory scanning: mental process revealed by a reaction time experiment. *American Scientist, 57*, 421-457.

Stewart, C.J., and Cash, W.B. (1974). *Interviewing: principles and practices*. Dubuque, IA: Wm. C. Brown.

Sticht, T., & Glassnap, D. (1972). Effects of speech rate, selection difficulty, association strength, and mental aptitude on learning by listening. *Journal of Communication, 22*, 174-178.

Stiff, J.B., & Miller, G.R. (1984). *Interrogation, level of message exposure and judgments of honesty and deceit: Toward a more interactive model of communication*. Paper persented at the Annual Western Speech Communication Association meeting, Seattle.

Stohl, C. (1983). The development of a communicative competence scale. In R. Bostrom (Ed.) *Communication yearbook seven* (pp, 765-741). Beverly Hills, CA: Sage.

Street, R. L., Jr. & Wiemann, J. M. (1987). Patient satisfaction with physicians' interpersonal involvement, expressiveness, and dominance. In M. McLaughlin (Ed.)., *Communication yearbook ten* (pp. 591-612). Newwbury Park, CA: Sage.

Streeter, L.A., Krauss, R.M., Geller, V., Olson, C., & Apple, W. (1977). Pitch changes during attempted deception. *Journal of Personality and Social Psychology, 35* (5), 345-350.

Strube, M.J., & Hartman, D.P. (1983). Meta-analysis: Techniques, applications, and functions. *Journal of Consulting and Clinical Psychology, 51*, 14-27.

Summers, W.G. (1939). Science can get the confession. *Fordham Law Review, 8*, 354-355.

Susman, E.J. (1978). Visual and verbal attributes of television and selective exposure in preschool children. *Developmental Psychology, 14*, 565-566.

Sypher, B. D. (1981). A multimethod investigation of employee communication abilities, communication satsifaction and job satisfaction. Unpublished doctoral dissertation, University of Michigan.

Sypher, B. D., Bostrom, R. N., & Seibert, J. H. (1987). *Listening abilities in the organizational context: Relationships with other communication abilities and predictors of upward mobility*. Unpublished manuscript, Department of Communication, University of Kentucky, Lexington.

Sypher, B. D., & Zorn, T. E. (1986). Communication-related abilities and upward mobility: A longitudinal investigation. *Human Communication Research, 12*, 420-431.

Sypher, H. (1980, May). *A comparison of multidimensional methods.* Paper presented at the Eastern Communication Association, Boston, MA.

Sypher, H., & Applegate, J. (1984) Schema theory in communication. In R. Bostrom (Ed.) *Communication yearbook eight.* Beverly Hills, CA: Sage.

Szucko, J.J., & Kleinmuntz, B. (1981). Statistical versus clinical lie detection. *American Psychologist, 36*, 488-496.

Tallmadge, G. (1977). *The joint dissemination review panel ideabook.* Washington, DC: National Institute of Education and U.S. Office of Education.

Tamborini, R., & Zillmann, D. (1985). Effects of questions, personalized communication style, and pauses for reflection in children's educational programs. *Journal of Educational Research, 79(1)*, 19-26.

Taylor, S., & Crocker, J. (1980). Schematic bases of social information processing. In E.T. Higgins, P. Hermann, and M.P. Zanna (Eds.), *Social cognition: the Ontario symposium,* Vol. 1. Hillsdale, NJ: Erlbaum.

Taylor, W. (1953) Cloze procedure: a new test for measuring readability. *Journalism Quarterly, 33* 415-433.

Taylor, W. (1956) Recent developments in the use of cloze procedure. *Journalism Quarterly, 36* 42-48.

Taylor, D., Lipscomb, E., & Rosemier, R. (1969) Live versus videotaped student-teacher interaction. *AV Communication Review, 17* 47-51.

Thompson, E. (1967). Some effects of message structure on listener's comprehension. *Speech Monographs, 34*, 51-57.

Thompson, T. L. (1986). *Communication for health professionals.* Cambridge, MA: Harper & Row.

Thorndyke, P.A., & Hayes-Roth, B. (1979). The use of schemata in the acquisition and transfer of knowledge. *Cognitive Psychology, 2*, 82-106.

Tierney, K. (1970). *Courtroom testimony: a policeman's guide.* New York: Funk & Wagnalls.

Toussaint, I. H. (1960). A classified summary of listening-1950-1959. *The Journal of Communication, 10*, 125-134.

Trovillo, P.V. (1939a). A history of lie detection. *The Journal of Criminal Law and Criminology, 29* (6), 848-875.

Trovillo, P.V. (1939b). A history of lie detection. *The Journal of Criminal Law and Criminology, 30* (1), 104-119.

Tucker, R. & Chase, L. (1976). Canonical correlation in human communication research. *Human Communication Research, 3*, 86-96.

Tulving, E. (1985). How many memory systems are there? *American Psychologist*, Vol, 40, No. 4, 385-397.

Van Kleeck, A., & Daly, J. Instructional communication research and theory. In M Burgoon (Ed.), *Communication yearbook five* (pp. 323-338). New Brunswick, NJ: Transaction Books.

Van Meter, C.H. (1973). *Principles of police interrogation.* Springfield, ILL: Charles Thomas.

Wakslag, J., Day, K., & Zillman, D. (1981). Selective exposure to educational television programs as a function of differently paced humorous inserts. *Journal of Educational Psychology, 73*, 27-32.

Wakshlag, J., Reitz, R., & Zillmann, D. (1982). Selective exposure to and acquisition of information from educational television programs as a function of appeal and tempo of background music. *Journal of Educational Psychology, 74*, 666-677.

Waldhart, E., & Bostrom, R. (1981, March). *Note-taking and listening skills.* Paper presented at the Annual Meeting of the International Listening Association, Washington, D. C.

Warren, W.H., Nicholas, D.W., & Trabasso, T. (1979). Even chains and inferences in understanding narratives. In R. Freddle (Ed.), *New directions in discourse comprehension.* Norwood, NJ: Ablex.

Wartella, E. (1978). *Children's perceptual unitizing of a televised behavior sequence.* Paper presented to the annual meeting of the Association for Education in Journalism, Seattle.

Watkins, B.A., Calvert, S.L., Huston-Stein, A. & Wright, J.C. Children's recall of television material: Effects of presentation mode and adultlabeling. *Developmental Psychology, 16*, 672-674.

Watson, K. W., & Barker, L. L. (1984). Listening behavior: Definition and measurement. In R. N. Bostrom (Ed.), *Communication yearbook eight.* Beverly Hills, CA: Sage.

Weaver, C. (1972). *Human listening: process and behavior.* Indianapolis: Bobbs-Merrill.

Weaver, J.B., Zillmann, D., & Bryant, J. (in press). Effects of humorous distortions on children's learning from educational television: Further evidence. *Communication Education.*

Weinrauch, J. D., & Swanda, J. R. (1975). Examining the significance of listening: An exploratory study of contemporary management. *The Journal of Business Communication, 13*, 25-32.

Wells, J., & Lashbrook, W. (1970, December). *A study of the effects of systematic desensitization of the communication anxiety of individuals in small groups.* Paper presented at the Speech Communication Association, New Orleans, LA.

Wheeless, L. (1975). An investigation of receiver apprehension and social context dimensions of communication apprehension. *Communication Education, 24,* 261-268.

Wheeless, L., & Scott, M. (1976, April). *The nature, measurement and potential effects of receiver apprehension.* Paper presented at the meeting of the International Communication Association, Portland, OR.

Wicklander, D., & Hunter, F. (1975). The influence of auxiliary sources of information in polygraph diagnosis. *Journal of Police Science and Administration, 3,,* 405-409.

Wickelgren, W. A. (1973). The long and short of memory. *Psychological Bulletin, 80,* 425-438.

Wigley, III, C.J. (1989, in press). Student receiver apprehension as a correlate of trait argumentativeness: A research note. *Communication Research Reports.*

Wiksell, W. (1946). The problem of listening. *Quarterly Journal of Speech, 32,* 505-508.

Williams, B.L. (1976). *The development of a construct of information anxiety and its* relationship to receiver apprehension. Unpublished masters thesis, West Virginia University, Morgantown, WV.

Williams, F. & Rice, R. (1983). Communication research and new media technologies. In R. Bostrom (Ed.), *Communication yearbook eight* (pp. 112-136). Beverly Hills, CA: Sage.

Wilson, S.J. (1975). *Channel differences in the detection of deception.* Unpublished doctoral dissertation, Florida State University. (University Microfilms No. 76-2726)

Woelfel, J & Fink, E. (1980). *The measurement of communication processes.* New York: Academic Press.

Wolff, F. I., Marsnick, N. C., Tacey, W. S., & Nichols, R. G. (1983). *Perceptive listening.* New York: Holt, Rinehart, and Wilson.

Wolvin, A. & Coakley, C. (1988). *Listening* (3rd edition). Dubuque, IA: Brown.

Woodall, G. & Folger, J. (1981). Encoding specificity and nonverbal cue context: an expansion of episodic memory research. *Communication Monographs, 48* 39-53.

Wright, J. , & Vleitstra, A. (1975). The development of selective attention: From perceptual exploration to logical search. In H.W. Reese (Ed.), *Advances in child development and behavior* (Vol. 10). New York: Academic Press.

Wright, J., Watkins, B. , & Huston-Stein, A. (1978). *Active vs. passive television viewing: A model of the development of television information processing by children.* Paper presented at the annual meeting of the American Psychological Association, Toronto.

Wyer, R., & Srull, T. (1981). The processing of social stimulus information: A conceptual integration. In R. Hastie, T. Ostrom, E. Ebbesen, R. Wyer, D. Hamilton, & D. Carlson (Eds.), *Person memory: The cognitive basis of social perception.* Hillsdale, NJ: Erlbaum.

Yohman, J.R. (1978). The quality knowledge technique in lie detection. *Biological Psychology Bulletin, 5,* (3), 96-103.

Zillmann, D., & Cantor, J.R. (1973). Induction of curiosity via rhetorical questions and its effect on the learning of factual materials. *The British Journal of Educational Psychology, 43,* 172-180.

Zillmann, D., Masland, J.L., Weaver, J.B., Lacey, L.A., Jacobs, N.E., Dow, J.H., Klein, C.A., & Banker, S.R. (1984). Effects of humorous distortions on children's learning from educational television. *Journal of Educational Psychology, 76* (5), 802-812.

Zillmann, D., Williams, B.R., Bryant, J., Boynton, K.R., & Wolf, M.A. (1980). Acquisition of information from educational television programs as a function of differently paced humorous inserts. *Journal of Educational Psychology, 72,* 170-180.

Zuckerman, M. (1978). *Sensation seeking: beyond the optimal level of arousal.* Hillsdale, NJ: Erlbaum.

Zuckerman, M., Amidon, M.D., Bishop, S.E., & Pomrantz, S.D. (1982). Face and tone of voice in the communication of deception. *Journal of Personality and Social Psychology, 43* (2), 347-357.

Zuckerman, M., DePaulo, B., & Rosenthal., R. (1981). Verbal and nonverbal communication of deception. In L. Berkowitz, (Ed.), *Advances in Experimental Social Psychology* Vol. 14, (pp. 1-49). New York: Academic Press.

Zuckerman, M., Kernis, M., Driver, R., & Koestner, R. (1984). Segmentation of behavior: Effects of actual deception and expected deception. *Journal of Personality and Social Psychology, 46,* 1173-1182.

Zuckerman, M., Koestner, R., & Alton, A.O. (1984). Learning to detect deception. *Journal of Personality and Social Psychology, 35* (5), 345-350.

Zuckerman, M., Koestner, R., & Colella, M.J. (1885). Learning to detect deception from three communication channels. *Journal of Nonverbal Behavior, 9* (3), 188-194.

APPENDIX

The Kentucky Comprehensive Listening Test [*]

[*] (c) 1979, The Kentucky Listening Research Center

TEXT OF TEST--FORM "A"

You are about to take a test in "listening," which will measure how well you can assimilate information aurally. The questions on this test will be presented on this tape recording, and you will mark your answers on the answer sheet. Does everyone have an answer sheet? (Pause). Make sure that on the cover of the answer sheet you have written your name, section, and student number. (Pause). Can everyone in the room hear the tape? If not, we can adjust the seating. (Pause).

PART ONE

Sometimes our listening is handicapped by conflicting signals or sounds. Good listening often consists of how well we can sort out the meaningful material from the background noise. In this tape you may occasionally hear background voices. Please try to concentrate on the questions in spite of what else you may hear. Much of what we learn is obtained by listening. Listening is of several types, including short-term recall. Listen to the series of numbers, letters, or words and then answer the question. For the first example, an item might sound like this:

In the series of numbers 5, 8, 3, 2, 9, the last number is _____.

Look on your answer sheet under "example." The correct answer was "9" so the "9" in your answer sheet is filled in. The "N" in the answer sheet is for you to mark if you think the answer was not given or was not present. Do the same for all the succeeding items. *If you cannot hear the questions or the instructions, raise your hand now.*

1. In the series of letters C, D, W, I, B, P, the fourth letter is _____.

2. In the series of numbers 4, 2, 9, 7, 5, 6, the third number is _____.

3. In the series of numbers 3, 4, 1, 6, 2, 9, the next to the last number is
_____.

4. In the series of numbers 16, 12, 7, 9, 14, 2, 8, the second number is
_____.

5. In the series of numbers 18, 10, 12, 20, 26, the smallest number is
_____.

6. In the series of numbers 8, 7, 16, 5, 6, 3, 9, the first number is
_____.

7. In the series of numbers 9, 5, 1, 8, 3, the fourth number is
_____.

8. In the series of letters G, F, D, Y, C, the first letter is
_____.

9. In the series of letters P, K, G, C, D, S, the third letter is
_____.

10. In the series of letters W, C, I, G, B, V, P, the next to the last letter is
_____.

11. In the series of letters S, A, M, Y, A, L, E, the letter that appears twice
is _____.

12. In the series of letters, Z, G, D, C, T, B, E, the third letter is
_____.

PART TWO

In this next section, you will hear a series of letters, or numbers, and these will be followed by an interval of silence. During this interval you are to try to keep the series in your mind. After this interval, you will be asked questions about the letters or numbers. Please respond as best as you can. Example: Here is the series of numbers: 1, 4, 3, 7, 6. (Pause 15 seconds). The second number is _____. Since the second number was 4, you will notice that the 4 is filled in on your answer sheet.

13. Here is the series of numbers: 7, 4, 6, 3, 8. (Pause 20 seconds). The third number is_____.

14. Here is a series of numbers: 8, 7, 3, 1, 9. (Pause 40 seconds). The second number is_____.

15. Here is a series of numbers: 9, 1, 2, 6, 5, 7. (Pause 30 seconds). The next to the largest number is_____.

16. Here is a series of numbers: 2, 3, 6, 4, 1, 6. (Pause 50 seconds). The first number is_____.

17. Here is a series of numbers: 5, 3, 6, 4, 1, 6. (Pause 20 seconds). The third number is_____.

18. Here is a series of letters: E, R, C, G, B. (Pause 40 seconds). The last letter is_____.

19. Here is a series of letters: E, J, F, S, C. (Pause 30 seconds). The fourth letter is_____.

20. Here is a series of letters: W, D, A, Y, J, I. (Pause 50 seconds). The next to last letter is_____.

21. Here is a series of letters: K, X, L, J, F, S. (Pause 20 seconds). The second letter after "X" is_____.

22. Here is a series of letters: Y, T, O, V, E, G. (Pause 40 seconds). The first letter after "T" is_____.

23. Here is a series of numbers: 3, 4, 1, 12, 7, 6, 2. (Pause 50 seconds). The third number is _____.

24. Here is a series of letters: D, V, G, W, R, X. (Pause 50 seconds). The

second letter is _____.

That is the end of Part Two.

PART THREE

Announcer: Often persons mean more than they say in communicative situations. Sometimes persons say one thing and mean something else. On the other hand, sometimes they mean exactly what they say. Listen to the following dialogues and judge what you think is implied in them... if anything.

Dialogue: He: Where are my glasses?

She: I can't be responsible for them.

Announcer: Please answer questions 25 & 26. (Pause)

25. What she really means is:
    a. You are careless.
    b. I don't know.
    c. Leave me alone.
    d. I want to help.

26. What he really means is:
    a. You never help me.
    b. I want my glasses.
    c. I'm tired today.
    d. All of the above.

Dialogue: She: Let's go out to eat.
    He: Maybe later.

Announcer: Please answer question 27. (Pause)

27. What he really means is:
    a. No way.
    b. Maybe later.

        c. I'm tired.

        d. Okay.

Dialogue: He: I don't feel well.

        She: What's the matter with you this time?

Announcer: Please answer questions 28 & 29. (Pause)

28. What she really means is:
        a. I don't believe you.
        b. I'm sorry.
        c. I wish you were better.
        d. You hypochondriac!

29. What he really means is:
        a. I don't want to go out to eat.
        b. I don't feel well.
        c. I'm tired.
        d. Leave me alone.

Dialogue: She: I've already called for reservations, in case we
            go.
        He: How did you know what time to tell them?

Announcer: Please answer questions 30 & 31. (Pause)

30. What she really means is:
        a. We're going
        b. We hope we can go.
        c. Maybe we should go.
        d. I don't care if we go.

31. What he really means is:
        a. That's nice.
        b. You always run my life.
        c. I'm not going.
        d. If I go, you won't like it.

Announcer: Please answer the rest of the questions. (Pause)

32. Which statement best describes the relationship?
  a. She is the stronger person.
  b. He is the stronger person.
  c. Neither is the stronger person.
  d. From this dialogue, no one can tell who is
     the stronger.

33. Which statement best describes the relationship?
  a. These are happy people.
  b. There are unhappy people.
  c. These people might be happy sometimes, but
     now they're unhappy.
  d. Their happiness can't be discerned from this
     dialogue.

34. Which statement best describes their future behavior?
  a. They're going out to eat.
  b. They will stay home.
  c. They will go out, but it will be unpleasant.
  d. One can't tell if they will go out or not.

PART FOUR: LECTURE

Each of us has to listen to a number of different messages each day. What follows is a brief message on the subject of language education. Please listen carefully as you hear the message. You will be asked several questions about the message after it is finished. Please do not turn your paper over or write on any portion of this test booklet during the message on language education.

LANGUAGE EDUCATION IN THE UNITED STATES

Most observers agree that the United States can be considered a monolingual nation. Successive waves of immigrants shed their accents, and in many cases their original surnames, in order to realize the "American Dream" of achieving upward social mobility and the material comforts which success offered. Even today, one of every three new Americans is an immigrant who acquires English as his/her new primary language.

Of the almost 23,000 secondary schools in the United States, more than 4,000 (or about 20%) offer no instruction in a foreign language, ancient or modern. Only 16% of all high school students are enrolled in such courses at the present time. Fewer than 2% of 1977's high school graduates were fluent in a second language. Or, to state the case in a slightly different way, fully nine out of ten Americans are unable to speak fluently, read, or write a second language.

The number of colleges and universities requiring knowledge of a foreign language for admission has dropped sharply. And, once enrolled in college, less than one in ten students studies another language. Five languages -- French, German, Italian, Russian, and Spanish -- account for 88% of the total foreign language registrations. Latin and Ancient Greek account for an additional 5%, with the remaining 7% distributed among 20 other languages. Only 7% of the ten million students pursuing degrees are studying languages spoken by over three-fourths of the world's population. Few of them reach any meaningful level of competence.

This lack of foreign language skill has been attributed to a few geographical, social, and economic conditions. It has been argued that most Americans have no need to learn a foreign language because: (a) the United States is geographically self-contained and unexposed to non-English cultures; (b) the U.S. has been relatively free from economic control by other countries and thus has not been forced to learn foreign languages to survive; and (c) the foreign language needs of the U.S. are more efficiently met by a strong cadre of language experts than by a large public generally trained in language skills. Furthermore, why should Americans learn other languages, given the world-wide success of English? English is, after all, the leading language of science and technology, international mail, cables, and broadcasting.

This view of English treats foreign languages as products of the international marketplace, convenient tools - like pocket calculators - whose use rises and falls with supply and demand. But from a communications perspective, the issues here are broader and more complex. Language must be viewed within its cultural context. Meaning is communicated by and through an entire culture. Language, as one of several important carriers of meaning, also reflects the values and structure of a culture.

One of the indicators of the willingness of Americans to accept other cultures as equal to theirs is the attitude toward linguistic minorities in the U.S. According to the 1970 census, 32.2 million citizen of the U.S. (approximately 15% of the population) do not speak English as their native language. At least 5 million children are estimated to be in need of special language programs. Language minority students have had a history of high drop-out rates and academic lag, directly attributable to language problems for which monolingual education has not proven successful.

Bilingual education has formally existed in the United States only since the late 1960s; however, there has been bilingual teaching in this country since 1840, and ethnic schools using native language instruction go back to the founding of the republic. Prior to World War I there was considerable tolerance of foreign language instruction which disappeared with the xenophobia and isolationism of the post-war years. The current struggle, focused as it is on equal educational opportunity for language minority groups, is the result of the civil rights movement, which brought national attention to the educational neglect of both racial and ethnic minority children.

The federal approach to bilingual education is based on two legal foundations: one statutory (Title VI of the 1964 Civil Rights Act) and one constitutional (the equal protection clause of the Fourteenth Amendment). The burden of proof of discrimination is on the individual. However, if a "suspect class" or a "fundamental right" is involved, then the burden is transferred to the government for justification. Categories so far recognized as "suspect" are race, religion, and national origin, but language is not. The right to maintain one's own native language is in contrast to that of the United Nations, which consistently names language along with race, sex, and religion as impermissible bases for discrimination.

The Bilingual Education Act of 1968 was the first categorical federal bilingual education law. The law provided funding for special demonstration programs for non-English speaking students and offered hope to language minority groups for further protective legislation.

The 1968 act was amended in 1969 and in 1972, increasing funding authorizations and adding special provisions to include more children. The 1972 amendments included the Emergency School Aid Act, which established bilingual education as a major tool in desegregation efforts involving national origin minority students.

The 1974 Bilingual Education Act was much more explicit, having profited somewhat from the practical experiences of the 305 federally funded bilingual programs then in operation. On November 1, 1978, a new Bilingual Act was signed into law by President Carter. It provided $20 million for research in bilingual education and also included provisions for staff training, community involvement, and curriculum development. The funding was for four to five years. Native English speakers can not total more than 40 percent of total student enrollment in the bilingual programs. But even this law stresses transitional programs, that is, programs that are designed to facilitate the transition from minority languages to English. There is no declared support for minority languages as such.

Bilingual education policy has developed also through judicial decisions. The most significant of them has been the Lau decision. The suit was brought by the Chinese public school students against the San Francisco School District. The district court ruled against the plaintiffs and the circuit court affirmed the decision, ruling that uniform use of English in the classroom did not constitute discrimination. But the Supreme Court overturned this ruling, with the conclusion that "students who do not understand English are effectively foreclosed from any meaningful education." It was left to the local authorities to work out the specific remedies.

Recently, more attention is devoted to the problem of teaching foreign languages to native English speakers. In April, 1978, President Carter established the Commission on Foreign Language and International Studies and assigned them a four fold mandate:

> to recommend means for directing public attention to the importance of foreign language and international studies for the improvement of communications and understanding with other nations.

> to assess the need and the job market in the U.S. for foreign

language specialists.

to recommend what foreign language and area studies programs are appropriate at the various levels, and how they are to be supported; and

to review existing legislative authorities and recommend changes needed to carry out effectively the Commission's recommendations.

In addition to the President's Commission, the Modern Language Association and the American Council of Learned Societies have established five task forces in order to study the various aspects of foreign language teaching in the U.S. and make recommendations. The task forces have proposed a policy statement which has six main points:

First, the secondary schools of the U.S. must offer every student the opportunity to learn a widely used international language, in addition to English. Students from non-English-speaking backgrounds should be offered the opportunity to study their native language.

Second, students wishing to acquire full proficiency in languages and international studies should have access to district-wide or regional "magnet" schools that provide such instruction.

Third, institutions of higher education have a special responsibility to provide instruction in less commonly taught languages.

Fourth, institutions of higher education must ensure a supply of competent foreign language teachers for all levels.

Fifth, international exchange and study-abroad programs should be strengthened and made more accessible, and

Sixth, national data on the acquisition of competence in foreign languages must be collected and published each year.

The problems of cultural interaction and communication are not limited to foreign language teaching or to minority rights. Scholars and observers point out that Americans receive less exposure to foreign cultures than almost any other people in the world.

America has fought in the international community for the principle of "free flow of information," but then turned it to "one-way flow." In a comparative, cross-cultural analysis of foreign news coverage in newspapers of three capitalist, three socialist, and three "Third World" nations it was found that in a variety of ways "the U.S. press ranked low in comparison with the other areas on relative measures of attention to the outside world."

Of all prime time TV programming, 74.1% of the action is located in the U.S., while only 17.5% is located outside the U.S. 4.5% takes place both in the U.S. and abroad. 76% of the TV drama characters are Americans. During prime time, 84.5% occurs in the U.S. and fully 90% of the characters are Americans. The only countries which import fewer TV programs than the U.S. are Japan and the People's Republic of China. The small number of programs that are imported to the U.S. are aired, almost exclusively, by public television.

The low presence of both foreign culture and foreign language in the American media has been documented in research. The findings show the extent to which the institutions of news, television, radio, advertising, and film systematically create a media environment which portrays an image of non-American culture as unessential to the U.S. and its citizens.

So, in spite of the increased awareness to problems of foreign language teaching, bilingual education, and cultural exchange, America seems to be still far from really communicating with the world around her. However, with the rising pride of ethnic and racial minorities, the greater self-assertion of Third World nations, and the increased interdependence of the nations of the world on each other, the American people may be forced out of their linguistic isolation sooner than expected.

Announcer: "This is the end of the "Language Education in the United States" lecture. You may now complete the remainder of the questions.

TEXT OF TEST--FORM "B"

ANNOUNCER:

You are about to take a test in "listening," which will measure how well you can assimilate information aurally. The questions on this test will be presented on this tape recording, and you will mark your answers on the answer sheet. Does everyone have an answer sheet? (Pause). Make sure that on the cover of the answer sheet you have written your name, section, and student number. (Pause). Can everyone in the room hear the tape? If not, we can adjust the seating. (Pause).

PART ONE

Sometimes our listening is handicapped by conflicting signals or sounds. Good listening often consists of how well we can sort out the meaningful material from the background noise. In this tape you may occasionally hear background voices. Please try to concentrate on the questions in spite of what else you may hear. Much of what we learn is obtained by listening. Listening is of several types, including short-term recall. Listen to the series of numbers, letters, or words and then answer the question. For the first example, an item might sound like this:

In the series of numbers 5, 8, 3, 2, 9, the last number is _____.

Look on your answer sheet under "example." The correct answer was "9" so the "9" in your answer sheet is filled in. The "N" in the answer sheet is for you to mark if you think the answer was not given or was not present. Do the same for all the succeeding items. *If you cannot hear the questions or the instructions, raise your hand now.*

1. In the series of letters W, D, W, I, C, P, the fourth letter is
   _____.

2. In the series of numbers 4, 9, 2, 7, 5, 6, the third number is
   _____.

3. In the series of numbers 7, 4, 1, 6, 2, 9, the next to the last number is
   _____.

4. In the series of numbers 12, 16, 7, 9, 14, 2, 8, the second number is
   _____.

5. In the series of numbers 18, 14, 12, 10, 26, the smallest number is
   _____.

6. In the series of numbers 6, 7, 16, 5, 8, 3, 9, the first number is
   _____.

7. In the series of numbers 9, 6, 1, 8, 7, the fourth number is
   _____.

8. In the series of letters D, F, G, Y, C, the first letter is
   _____.

9. In the series of letters P, G, B, K, D, S, the third letter is
   _____.

10. In the series of letters W, C, I, G, B, E, P, the next to the last letter is
    _____.

11. In the series of letters S, A, M, Y, L, E, M, the letter that appears twice
    is _____.

12. In the series of letters, Z, G, D, C, T, B, E, the third letter is
    _____.

PART TWO

In this next section, you will hear a series of letters, or numbers, and these will be followed by an interval of silence. During this interval you are to try to keep the series in your mind. After this interval, you will be asked questions about the letters or numbers. Please respond as best as you can. Example: Here is the series of numbers: 1, 4, 3, 7, 6. (pause 15 seconds). The second number is _____. Since the second number was 4, you will notice that the 4 is filled in on your answer sheet.

13. Here is the series of numbers: 7, 4, 6, 3, 8. (Pause 20 seconds). The last number is_____.

14. Here is a series of numbers: 8, 7, 3, 1, 9. (Pause 40 seconds). The second number is_____.

15. Here is a series of numbers: 9, 1, 2, 6, 5, 10. (Pause 30 seconds). The next to the largest number is_____.

16. Here is a series of numbers: 3, 2, 6, 4, 1, 6. (Pause 50 seconds). The first number is_____.

17. Here is a series of numbers: 5, 3, 6, 4, 1, 6. (Pause 20 seconds). The fifth number is_____.

18. Here is a series of letters: B, R, C, G, E. (Pause 40 seconds). The last letter is_____.

19. Here is a series of letters: E, J, F, S, C. (Pause 30 seconds). The fourth letter is_____.

20. Here is a series of letters: W, K, A, Y, J, I. (Pause 50 seconds). The next to last letter is_____.

21. Here is a series of letters: K, X, L, J, F, S. (Pause 20 seconds). The second letter after "X" is_____.

22. Here is a series of letters: Y, T, O, R, E, G. (Pause 40 seconds). The first letter after "T" is_____.

23. Here is a series of numbers: 3, 4, 1, 12, 7, 6, 2. (Pause 50 seconds). The third number is _____.

24. Here is a series of letters: S, E, G, F, R, X. (Pause 50 seconds). The

fourth letter is _____.

That is the end of Part Two.

PART THREE

Announcer: Often persons mean more than they say in communicative situations. Sometimes persons say one thing and mean something else. On the other hand, sometimes they mean exactly what they say. Listen to the following dialogues and judge what you think is implied in them... if anything.

Dialogue: He: I can't find my glasses!

She: Where did you last use them?

He: I don't know--don't you think you could look for them?

She: Sure, but I'd like to know where to start.

He: You never help me.

Announcer: Please answer questions 25 & 26. (Pause)

25. What she really means is:
        a. You are careless.
        b. I don't know.
        c. Leave me alone.
        d. I want to help.

26. What he really means is:
        a. You never help me.
        b. I want my glasses.
        c. I'm tired today.
        d. All of the above.

Dialogue: She: Let's go out to eat.

He: How could I read the menu without glasses?

She: We'll find your glasses.

He: It will be crowded.

Announcer: Please answer question 27. (Pause)

27. What he really means is:
         a. No way.
         b. Maybe later.
         c. I'm tired.
         d. Okay.

Dialogue: He: I have a headache.

She: Is it your glasses, or something else?

Announcer: Please answer questions 28 & 29. (Pause)

28. What she really means is:
         a. I' don't believe you.
         b. I'm sorry.
         c. I wish you were better.
         d. You hypochondriac!

29. What he really means is:
         a. I don't want to go out to eat.
         b. I don't feel well.
         c. I'm tired.
         d. Leave me alone.

Dialogue: She: Maybe we should get a reservation in case
                 you get better.

He: I can't think of a place that I like.

She: Let's go to Morey's--you always like their Beef Wellington.

He: I don't feel like Beef Wellington.

She: You'll feel even worse if you stay here.

Announcer: Please answer questions 30 & 31. (Pause)

30. What she really means is:
    a. We're going.
    b. We hope we can go.
    c. Maybe we should go.
    d. I don't care if we go.

31. What he really means is:
    a. That's nice.
    b. You always run my life.
    c. I'm not going.
    d. If I go, you won't like it.

Announcer: Please answer the rest of the questions. (Pause)

32. Which statement best describes the relationship?
    a. She is the stronger person.
    b. He is the stronger person.
    c. Neither is the stronger person.
    d. From this dialogue, no one can tell who is the stronger.

33. Which statement best describes the relationship?
    a. These are happy people.
    b. There are unhappy people.
    c. These people might be happy sometimes, but now
        now they're unhappy.
    d. Their happiness can't be discerned from this dialogue.

34. Which statement best describes their future behavior?
   a. They're going out to eat.
   b. They will stay home.
   c. They will go out, but it will be unpleasant.
   d. One can't tell if they will go out or not.

PART FOUR

Each of us has to listen to a number of different messages each day. What follows is a brief message on the subject of television news. Please listen carefully as you hear the message. You will be asked several questions about the message after it is finished. Please do not turn your paper over or write on any portion of this test during the message.

TELEVISION NEWS

Almost everyone watches television news--it is the primary source of news today. In this brief message, we will do two things: take an inside look at television news, and second, to explain how television news is put together.

Let's look at five specific questions and answer each of them in turn:

First, why is television news important?

Second, what are the basic sources of television news?

Third, how is television news formulated on a daily basis?

Fourth, what is the most significant recent development in television news?

Fifth, what are some of the current trends in television news?

Let's take a look at the first question--why is television news important? 98% of the homes in the United States have at least one television set. That's approximately 75 million homes. There is more than one set in over half of the homes. The latest Roper report shows that 67% of the people in the United States depend on television news as their number one source for news. Television competes with radio, newspapers, and magazines, and yet they supplement one another.

Let's look at some of the functions of the mass media.

First of all, there is surveillance. The mass media are the eyes and ears of a concerned public. The news media provide us with information, and alert us to changes in the status quo. Let me give you an example: Back in 1963 President Kennedy was assassinated. Radio brought America the news first, then television delivered the visual impact and also showed accused assassin Lee Harvey Oswald shot and killed by Jack Ruby. Television gave us a sense of presence at the funeral. Newspapers provided a first person account of those who witnessed the event. Magazines printed special commemorative editions for people to keep and to pass on to other generations.

A second function of the mass media is correlation. Correlation is closely related to surveillance. Correlation refers to the selection and interpretation of the news events. While the surveillance function deals primarily with factual data, the correlation function deals with both fact and opinion. Correlation is observed in television news programs in the commentaries which appear on the networks and the local news.

A third function of the mass media is entertainment. Most media entertain as they inform. This is the primary function of television as a whole, and it is also seen to some degree in news programs. Local stations have tried to make their newscasts more entertaining in two particular ways. The first is by adopting a style of presentation called "happy talk," which basically is a time when the anchor man, the sports anchor, and the weather man will all interrelate with one another--talking back and forth as they make their transitions. The second way of making newscasts entertaining is by putting emphasis on live reporting and visual impact. We'll discuss this more just a bit later.

A fourth function of the mass media is cultural transmission. Mass communication teaches us about the present and the past. Much of what we know about earlier generations in our own country, and people in cultures of other countries, comes from our exposure to mass communication. TV news is a major part of this process.

There's another reason why TV news is important. It applies to all mass media, but particularly to TV, radio, newspspapers, and magazines. It is commonly called the "agenda-setting" function of the media. Neither an individual nor society can give equal attention to everything. As individuals we are continually required to determine which problems get our immediate attention and which problems are simply endured or ignored altogether. TV news plays a big part in this determination, and helps us establish an agenda, or schedule of tasks.

The second major question that I want to address today is: what is the basic source of the news?

First of all, there are the wire services. Almost all local TV stations subscribe to the Associated Press and the United Press International. These two services continue to give us news in the newsroom 24 hours a day. They send international, national, and regional news, including weather features and sports. All of this continues on a 24-hour basis, depending on which ones local stations subscribe to. Some of them subscribe to both.

Another source of news is "news releases" that come in the mail from various organizations. They tell of specific functions that are going to take place, such as press conferences, or store openings. The releases tell when the event is going to take place and where, and usually provide some background. Occasionally news releases are telephoned in, but mostly they are mailed.

A third source of news for the local station is the local station's news staff--the reporter on a beat. Each station usually has reporting specialists-- such as an education reporter, a government reporter, and so forth.

If you were in a local TV newsroom, you would be struck by all the noise coming from the police and fire department monitors that are usually in a separate corner. All police radio and fire department radios are monitored by TV newsrooms. When the police are sent to an accident scene, or the fire trucks are on their way to a large fire, the TV reporter has advance warning and can be on the way with camera crew.

A fifth basic source of news is the network news service. Every afternoon, at about three o'clock, networks send what is usually called the "five o'clock feed." It's on closed circuit cable and doesn't go out over the air. Local stations record the feed and select the items for use on their local news shows. In this feed, the networks send sports news, news from affiliates all around the country, and feature items. Then, of course, the networks send out their own nation-wide news programs that usually appear in conjunction with the local news broadcasts. These feature network news "stars" such as Tom Brokaw or Dan Rather, and represent the work of hundreds of reporters and editors. The networks spend millions of dollars on these programs. Local stations are free to copy portions of these broadcasts for later use.

The daily routine in a local television station's news room is exciting. It involves timing, good news judgment, a sense of the dramatic, and good overall organization.

When a reporter arrives in the morning, usually the assignment editor will have a list of assignments ready for that day's activity. This will include the location of the story, who to see, what photographer will be used, and so forth. The reporter usually makes some preliminary contact with story sources on the telephone, and then goes out in the field to gather the information.

Upon returning to the station, the reporter checks with the producer, who assigns each story a specific amount of time for the evening newscast. One story might be worth three minutes, another only a minute, and so forth. When the reporter knows the time allotted, then the next step is to write the story out in detail, together with the indications about what video material to use. When each of these stories is completed, the producer is ready to assemble the newscast, assigning positions and making minor adjustments.

The next step is to submit the newscast to the news director, who plans which cameras will cover which reporter, which will cover the anchors, and so on. The director also makes minor adjustments and positions persons in the studio to the best advantage.

When the show goes on the air, the director and the producer sit together in the control room, and keep track of the time elapsed, comparing it to their master plan of how much time should be taken. If they see that early segments of news are taking too much time, they will signal to the anchors and the reporters to speed up. If they see that the stories are falling short of the time allotted, then they signal for the later stories to stretch a bit. In addition, minor adjustments are made while the show is in progress.

What is the most recent significant development in TV news?

In the opinion of most local newscasters, it is the technological developments that are becoming available to local producers. It is now possible to go "live" to local news scenes, for example, where a few years ago, a telephone hookup was required for local origination. Most local television stations now have a "remote truck" which uses microwave transmission direct from the scene to the station for videotaping. This puts new pressures on the reporters, in that accuracy is much more important. If the reporter only videotapes the report on the scene and then brings it back in for editing, then mistakes can be corrected. If, on the other hand, the reporter is reporting live from the scene of the story, then the first version of the story has to be absolutely accurate.

What is the prospect for the immediate future of TV news? First of all, there is the enormous growth of the satellite system. We are directly linked with stories breaking in Lebanon, in India, and other exotic locations never before covered with such immediacy. This gives our local news an international flavor never before available.

Second, the efforts expended on the news programs are expanding. Currently, local news operations have to compete with cable systems, some of which have intense news services. Some of the cable systems offer 24-hour news, which puts a good deal of competition on network and local news operations. As a result, the networks have increased their news "updates," added late night news programs, and increased the news available in their morning shows. Local stations have had to keep pace, and most have added reporters and producers, together with increased emphasis on local stories. It is safe to say that more and more news will be available to us in the future.

Another trend is already visible in many local stations--as the networks concentrate on the headlines of major stories, maybe only spending three or four minutes to cover a complex event, the local stations are tending to follow up with detailed coverage that expands and amplifies that story. This detailed coverage seems to meet a basic need, in that people are realizing that in-depth coverage is necessary for better understanding of an event. Newscasters are becoming aware that people are beginning to demand not just basic coverage, but an in-depth coverage, which helps them to better understand current events and their backgrounds.

Now that you understand some of the ways that television news operates, you will be a better consumer and will be able to make more considered judgments on the news that you consume.

This is the end of the lecture. You may now turn over your answer sheet and answer the questions.

Index